T0328377

# The Norwegian Mission's Literacy Work in Colonial and Independent Madagascar

Offering an original historical perspective on literacy work in Africa, this book examines the role of the Norwegian Lutheran mission in Madagascar and sheds light on the motivations that drove colonizing powers' literacy work. Focusing on both colonial and independent Madagascar, Rosnes examines how literacy practices were facilitated through mission schools and the impact on the reading and writing skills to Malagasy children and youth. Analysing how literacy work influenced identity formation and power relations in the Malagasy society, the author offers new insights into the field of language and education in Africa.

**Ellen Vea Rosnes** is Associate Professor of Global Studies and Intercultural Communication at VID Specialized University, Norway. She holds a PhD in Literacy Studies from the University of Stavanger, Norway.

**Routledge Research in Literacy**
Edited by Uta Papen and Julia Gillen
*Lancaster University, UK.*

# The Norwegian Mission's Literacy Work in Colonial and Independent Madagascar

Ellen Vea Rosnes

Routledge
Taylor & Francis Group

NEW YORK AND LONDON

First published 2019
by Routledge
52 Vanderbilt Avenue, New York, NY 10017, USA

by Routledge
2 Park Square, Milton Park, Abingdon, Oxon, OX14 4RN

First issued in paperback 2020

*Routledge is an imprint of the Taylor & Francis Group, an informa business*

*Library of Congress Cataloguing-in-Publication Data*
A catalog record for this book has been requested

ISBN 13: 978-0-367-58236-4 (pbk)
ISBN 13: 978-1-138-73915-4 (hbk)

Typeset in Sabon
by Apex CoVantage, LLC

For my parents, who introduced me to Madagascar, and for Arne Morten, Anny, Serina and Morten for your support

# Contents

# Tables

# Figures

# Foreword

This book about the Norwegian Lutheran mission in Madagascar, and how it related to political power and the influence of other missions presents an important contribution to the general literature on colonial and mission education in the 20th century and makes an important addition to the field of literacy studies. In addition, it makes a substantial contribution to the history of education in Madagascar and manages the difficult task of exploring the educational agendas of the missions and their relationship to the secular French colonial state. The research has significance and quality, and represents an original contribution to colonial history. A key part of the story relates to the variations of educational policies over time, and the changes in policy and practice in relation to the multiplicity of ethnic groups and languages engaged within the process. This is a convincing story about a complex and fascinating topic that is based on innovative research drawn from archival sources as well as interview material with teachers and students.

The subject is of interest to those concerned with colonial education, cultural studies and the legacy of culture-contact from colonial times to the present. This work shows some of the complexities of engagement with indigenous peoples within a colonial state, and it throws considerable light on various debates—not just in relation to the French colonial empire, but to the relationship between the modern global economy and the local. Even though this work focuses on Madagascar, it certainly has relevance beyond the specific geographical and historical frame that it defines. The book presents essential reading to anyone interested in the complexities of colonial language policies and their implications for African (or Third World countries) in the 21st century.

The issue of language and its link to the emancipatory or dominating ethos of colonial power lies at the centre of the problems explored. Language issues represent a rather neglected area of colonial studies at present time, and the importance of the linguistic and literacy issues raised in the context have wide ramification beyond the colonial era or the geographical context of Madagascar. The choice and matter of language of instruction is still a major issue in education policy in many African or former colonial countries—and in an increasing globalised world. In that context the experience of educationalists and teachers in earlier colonial contexts can be valuable for understanding contemporary policy guidelines and practices in education. If we cannot learn direct lessons for history, we can certainly learn to understand the field and the variables of policy more clearly through studies of this sort. One of the strengths of this work is that it engages with actual local situations and with the actual teachers and students of the schools at the end of the colonial era. It is therefore able to link that to the concrete issues of post-independence policy.

The challenge of the Norwegian Lutheran language policy—which favoured indigenous languages—represented a challenge to French colonial policies—or perhaps an ambiguous challenge—which played itself out with variations in French colonial policy over an extended period. There were various policies that were defended in a variety of contexts, reflecting much wider, comparative debates relating to the issue of educational *adaptation* in Africa and elsewhere. Understanding those positions and how they influenced educational policy and practice are the aim of the book, which is also one of its strengths in providing a platform to explore these ambiguities. This book is a unique contribution to knowledge in literacy and language education.

Peter Kallaway
Emeritus Professor at the University of the Western Cape
Honorary Research Associate, School of Education,
University of Cape Town

# Preface

This book focuses on the literacy work of the Norwegian Lutheran mission in Madagascar, and how it related to political power and other missions, with an emphasis on two periods: mid-colonisation in the 1920s and the independence period (1951–1966). Literacy is a social practice embedded in social relations and structures of power. Therefore, it is important to analyse ideologies of institutions with literacy work. This research provides an analysis of literacy practices facilitated through mission schools and of the purposes of teaching reading and writing skills to Malagasy children and youth. It is based on archival materials from Norway, Madagascar and France, as well as qualitative interviews with former Norwegian educator-missionaries and former Malagasy teachers and pupils.

The main aim of the mission was to teach reading skills in order for people to read the Bible in their own language. In their work, the Norwegian mission found common interests and strength in collaboration with other Protestant missions, both in facing competition from the Catholic mission and in adapting to changing colonial policies. Secularism was part of the colonial policy, and came to have a strong impact on the mission's work. Norwegian missionaries maintained good relations with the French colonial power, while at the same time opposing secular-based rules. The Protestant missions' use of the local language challenged the assimilationist French colonial policy of promoting French as the dominant language. At independence, the administration of the first Malagasy Republic had the possibility to base educational and linguistic policies on different experiences with literacies, thus having different effects on questions of identity. Protestant converts were among those aspiring for a more Malagasy-oriented education, and promoted the Malagasy language and culture in education. However, French kept its dominant place in education.

Using a language that is understood and used by the pupils is important for the acquisition of reading and writing skills. Why then are Malagasy pupils today still learning in a foreign language? I hope that this study, in the field of literacy and mission history, will contribute to a better understanding of the motivations behind historical institutions with literacy work that might cast today's policies in a different light.

# Préface

Ce livre vise à analyser comment la Mission norvégienne à Madagascar s'est adaptée au pouvoir politique par rapport à son travail dans la domaine de la *literacy* (aptitudes à lire et à écrire), en se focalisant sur deux périodes: mi- colonisation pendant les années 1920s à l'époque coloniale et à l'indépendance (1951–1966). La *Literacy* étant une pratique sociale intégrée dans des relations sociales et des structures de pouvoir, il est donc important d'analyser les idéologies des institutions qui travaillent dans ce domaine. Ce travail de recherche livre une analyse des pratiques de *literacy* qui étaient facilitées dans les écoles de la mission, et des motivations liées à apprendre aux enfants et aux jeunes malgaches à lire et à écrire. Il est basé sur une étude de documents d'archives norvégiennes, malgaches et françaises et sur des entretiens qualitatifs avec d'anciens éducateurs-missionnaires norvégiens et d'anciens professeurs et élèves malgaches.

Le but principal de la Mission norvégienne était d'enseigner aux gens à lire la Bible dans leur propre langue. La Mission norvégienne a trouvé, face à la compétition de la mission catholique, et devant la nécessité de s'adapter à l'évolution des politiques coloniales, des intérêts communs et une force accrue à collaborer avec les autres missions protestantes. La laïcité, parti intégrante de la politique coloniale, a eu de lourdes conséquences sur le travail de la Mission. Les missionnaires norvégiens ont maintenu de bonnes relations avec le pouvoir colonial français. En même temps, ils s'opposaient aux régulations basées sur la laïcité. L'emploi de la langue Malgache par les missions protestantes a contesté la politique coloniale assimilatrice française qui promouvait la langue française comme langue dominante. À l'indépendance, l'administration de la première République a eu la possibilité de baser les politiques éducatives et linguistiques sur des expériences différentes avec literacies, ayant des conséquences différentes sur les questions d'identité. La gestion locale des écoles protestantes a aspiré à une éducation plus malgache et était parmi les institutions qui, à l'indépendance, se focalisaient sur la langue et la culture malgaches dans l'éducation. La langue française y a néanmoins gardé son rôle dominant dans l'éducation.

Il est crucial de faire usage d'une langue qui est comprise et utilisée par les enfants pour développer les aptitudes à lire et à écrire. Pourquoi les élèves malgaches apprennent-t-ils encore aujourd'hui dans une langue étrangère dès la troisième année de leur scolarité? J'espère que cette étude, dans le domaine de la literacy et de l'histoire des missions contribuera à mieux comprendre les motivations des institutions historiques dans ce domaine, et que cette compréhension pourra placer les politiques d'aujourd'hui sous un jour différent.

# Acknowledgements

I had never imagined that archival work could be this exciting. I started out looking for a letter sent to the French governor-general by the superintendent of the Norwegian mission, quoted at the start of Chapter 1. When I finally found it among the last boxes to be searched during my second fieldwork in Madagascar, I understood that archival work is a real treasure hunt. I have felt lucky in many ways. One of my advantages throughout this study has been that I could be searching the archives among letters, notes and reports written in Norwegian, French, Malagasy, and English, without assistance of a translator. Last but not least, I have received generous support from many.

First of all, I want to express my gratitude to the Faculty of Arts and Education, University of Stavanger for this opportunity, which has been a huge privilege. The research was part of a collaboration project, *Norwegian Mission and Cultural Interaction in South Africa and Madagascar, 1880–1960*, with the School of Mission and Theology in Stavanger (MHS—which has become *VID Specialized University* after a merge of four higher educational institutions in 2016). I want to give thanks to my colleagues during these years. Deepest acknowledgments to my supervisors, Gunnar Nerheim and Kjell Lars Berge, who have shown sincere interest, believed in the project and given insightful feedback. I am extremely grateful to Ketil Fred Hansen, Uta Papen, Rhonda Semple and Wendy Urban-Mead, who gave invaluable comments and corrections. I would also like to profoundly thank the interviewees who accepted to be involved in this study. I want to express my gratitude to Sandra Tiana Jeanne Ranoromalala who assisted me in the field. I am very grateful to those who helped me in the archives and libraries. Especially, I would like to thank Paul Rasoanaivo in the FLM archives and Gustav Steensland and Bjørg Bergøy Johansen in the Mission Archives, MHS (which has now changed its name to *Mission and Diakonia Archives, VID*) for their positive attitude and help with finding the way in the archives and with providing many of the figures used in this book. I also want to express my gratitude to the Faculties of Humanities at the Universities of Antananarivo and Toliara and their employees for assistance during my fieldwork and presentation of preliminary findings. Thanks to those who read parts of the book and gave advice, especially Kjetil Aano, Øyvind Dahl, Sigmund Edland, Torstein Jørgensen, Svein Ivar Langhelle, Daniel Raherisoanjato, Faranirina Rajaonah, Monique Rakotoanosy, and my father Jakob Vea. I am grateful to my parents for my background that equipped me with necessary skills to do this work. Thanks to colleagues at the Centre for Intercultural Communication for their encouragement, especially to Bente Ofstad Skeie for assisting with corrections. The networks connected to the Yale-Edinburgh Group and the 2013 workshop in Cape Town on *Colonial Education in Africa* have inspired me (Kallaway and Swartz 2016). To my husband, Arne Morten: I appreciate all your help with this manuscript and for coping with my, at times, annoying motivation. Warm thanks to my dearest children Anny, Serina and Morten for always reminding me of the most important things in life!

# Abbreviations

| | |
|---|---|
| ANOM | Archives nationales d'outre-mer, Aix-en-Province |
| ARM | Archives de la République democratique malgache, Antananarivo |
| ASP | Protestant School Office/Affair Scolaire Protestants |
| BE | Brevet Elémentaire (teacher exam) |
| CAE | Certificat d'aptitude à l'enseignement (pedagogical exam) |
| CDA | Critical discourse analysis |
| CE | Cours elémentaires |
| CEP | Protestant Education Council |
| CEPE | Certificat d'études du premier dégrée (exam first level) |
| CESD | Certificat d'études du second dégrée (exam second degree) |
| CM | Mixed Committee/Comité mixte |
| CMI | Cours moyens I |
| CMII | Cours moyens II |
| CMS | Church Missionary Society |
| CP | Cours préparatoires |
| DEFAP | Library of the Protestant Mission Service/Département Evangélique Français d'Action |
| DHA | Discourse-historical approach |
| FAEM | Federation of Student Organisations in Madagascar |
| FFL | Education Department of FLM/Fampianarana sy Fanabeazana Loterana |
| FFMA | Friends' Foreign Missions Association |
| FIDES | Fond d'Investissement pour le développement economique et social des territoires d'Outre-mer |
| FJKM | Church of Jesus Christ in Madagascar |
| FLM | Malagasy Lutheran Church |
| FLM_NA | FLM Archives of the Northern Synod, Antananarivo |
| FLM_TA | FLM Archives of the Superintendent, Antananarivo |
| IPC | Inter-missionary Protestant Committee |
| ISC | Inter-missionary School Committee |
| KLB | Lutheran Secondary School/Kolegy Loteriana Malagasy |
| LMS | London Missionary Society |

| | |
|---|---|
| LOI | Language of instruction |
| MHS | Mission Archives, the School of Mission and Theology, Stavanger |
| MPF | French Protestant Mission |
| NMS | Norwegian Mission Society |
| SPG | Society for the Propagation of the Gospel |
| UNESCO | United Nations Educational, Scientific and Cultural Organisation |

# 1 Literacy Work for Evangelisation, Colonisation and Malgachisation*

In Madagascar, in the last centuries, there were several actors involved in teaching Malagasy children reading and writing skills. Literacy is a social practice embedded in social relations and structures of power and teaching literacy often takes place in schools. It is therefore interesting to analyse the ideologies of educational institutions teaching literacy (i.e. doing literacy work). During the colonial period in Madagascar, the French colonial power was the dominant provider of education, the one setting the official standard and defining educational policies. At independence in 1960, the administration of the first Malagasy Republic took over. In addition, there were Catholic and Protestant missions, among them the Norwegian Lutheran mission, that were active in teaching Malagasy people to read and write. These different institutions most definitely had different objectives. In this book, my focus is on how the Norwegian mission negotiated their educational work with other institutions, and why it was so important for them to do literacy work their way in their own schools.

## Focus on Two Periods

Norwegian missionaries arrived in Madagascar in 1866, 25 years after the establishment of their mission organisation: the Norwegian Mission Society (NMS). From the start, the mission's work in Madagascar was very successful. During the last decades of the 19th century, missions from different countries contributed to a significant increase in reading and writing skills among Malagasy children and youth. Education took place either in church buildings/assembly houses or in separate buildings. By the end of the 19th century the Norwegian mission had become one of the main providers of education in

---

* Because it is a matter of life and death for us to have the opportunity to practice this minimum for the teaching of reading, I solicit you, governor-general, to allow us to teach reading in our Bible classes, 1 or 2 hours a week, in places where there is no public school.
Fredrik Bjertnes, 1922 (my translation)
Superintendent of the Norwegian mission, Madagascar

Madagascar. But the missions' dominant position within education experienced a serious setback after the arrival of the French colonial government in 1896.

In this book, I will mainly focus on two historical periods; what I call the *mid-colonisation* period and *independence*. The mid-colonisation period begins after World War I. In 1920, Hubert Auguste Garbit was appointed governor-general in Madagascar. The Protestant missions used the opportunity to join forces and lobby the new governor-general for a revision of the legislation restricting their evangelisation, church building, education and literacy work. In 1924, Garbit was replaced by Marcel Achille Olivier, and of equal importance was a change in the position as director of education in 1925. Charles Renel, who had held the position as director of education since 1905, was replaced by Cheffaud. Olivier and Cheffaud introduced changes in education policies that were more adapted to the local context and different from the policies of former governors. Previously, most colonial administrators found the Protestant missions' and their literacies to be rivals to their authority, while Olivier and Cheffaud found inspiration in the missions' approach and were interested in collaboration. Therefore, the new policies were easier to accept by the missions.

The independence period covers the years between 1951 and 1966. In these years educational decrees had a large impact on the literacy work of the mission and the Malagasy Lutheran Church (FLM). Independence in 1960 was naturally a significant event in the history of Madagascar. Private schools, mostly run by the Churches that had been established by different mission organisations, were regarded as important educators of Malagasy children and youth. Increasing literacy skills was expected to play a central role in the development of the new nation. Many, among them Protestant missionaries and converts, assumed education at this time would be adjusted to the needs of Malagasies in general. But this did not happen on a scale that many had expected. Even if there were some attempts to make education more Malagasy, education and literacy teaching, after independence were clearly embedded in the specific Malagasy historical context and very much dominated by French colonisation.

These periods are chosen because they illustrate very well the tensions connected with the practice of literacy teaching and political power. In these periods, there were attempts in the governmental administration to turn education from a French-assimilationist perspective to a more locally adapted form of education. That represented windows of opportunities for the Protestant missions, who aimed for religious conversion through using the local language. Even though these policies did not last, they contributed to revitalising the interest and focus on the Malagasy language as an alternative language of instruction (LOI). Moreover, these periods are also of specific interest regarding how the Norwegian mission, often in collaboration with other Protestant missions, negotiated with the political power concerning their literacy work.

## Why Do Mission Organisations Teach Literacy?

NMS is a Lutheran mission organisation with its origins in the 19th-century Norwegian revival movements. The dissemination of reading skills was, as for Protestant missions in general, the most important instrument to achieve their goals. The quotation in the footnote that starts this chapter is taken from a letter written by the Norwegian superintendent to the French governor-general. It highlights that teaching reading skills was a fundamental task of the mission. Seen from a Lutheran perspective, every Christian should be able to read the Bible in a language they understand to grow in their personal faith. To illustrate this, I will include Patrick's story. He was a former pupil at the mission school in the town of Betafo during the 1950s. Betafo was the place where the first Norwegian missionaries settled in Madagascar. I chose the mission school in Betafo as a research case in my research and Patrick was one of the former pupils at this school who I interviewed. His story illustrates how the existence of the mission school and the church enabled children and youth living in the area around Betafo to acquire reading and writing skills (Figure 1.1).

Patrick was born in 1941. He was the third child in a family of six children. He started school at the age of seven and quit after 7 years since his family could not afford his school fees. His parents could not read and write, but learned to write their names from their children. They wanted their children to have at least some education, and when Patrick had gained basic reading and writing skills, he had to let his younger brothers and sisters go to school. He remembers how they wrote with chalk during the first years at school before they were old enough to use ink. He also tells about morning and afternoon prayers at school. Being Lutherans, his parents wanted their children to go to a Christian school. At Sunday school, Patrick remembers he got a reading book, and that, in addition to learning verses from the Bible and songs, they also became familiar with letters and learning to read. The discipline practiced at Sunday school helped him when he started school. After leaving school Patrick helped his parents at the farm and he has continued farming to this day. He tells that a major challenge is that the farmers have little money to invest so that they continue doing what they always have done. Life as a farmer has become harder over the years as more people share the same amount of land.

*Figure 1.1* Patrick's story

Source: Former pupil Patrick (2012)

Patrick got to know letters and got a reading book before starting at the mission school, thanks to the Sunday school in the local church. This illustrates how the different structures of the mission and the church were connected and that the mission's literacy campaign reached children in rural areas. Most of them quit, however, after they had learned basic reading and writing skills.

How should mission organisations engage themselves in literacy campaigns? How should they relate to other, and more formal, educational institutions? These debates were part of a broader international discussion about missiological practices where literacy was a key concept for discussion. From the perspective of an ideological model of literacy, this book regards literacy not as an autonomous skill, but as a social practice embedded in ideologies (Street 1984). The emphasis is on how the missions' work to teach reading and writing skills was shaped by the missions' convictions, strategies and practices, and by the social, cultural and political contexts where they were working. In their work, the Norwegian mission found common interests and strength in collaboration with other Protestant missions, especially in facing competition from the Catholic mission and in adapting to changing policies by the administration. The Norwegian missionaries maintained good relations with the French colonial power, while they at the same time were opposing secular-based rules. Protestant missions' use of the local language particularly challenged the assimilationist French colonial policy of promoting French as the dominant language.

## What Makes Madagascar Interesting for Literacy Studies?

Madagascar provides an interesting analytic space for literacy studies. There are many reasons for that; including the impact of Arabic writing, the literacy campaigns of the missions, and the French colonial project. The Merina monarchy, representing the politically dominant ethnic group in Madagascar before colonisation, used Arabic script for administrative purposes (Bloch 1998: 139–140). This was one reason why they managed to hold the large kingdom together. But, education in reading and writing was limited to the royal family until the British missionaries arrived (Edland 2006: 108). Probably was it only the king and fewer than 10 youths who could read and write in Arabic, the Sorabe. Comprehensive literacy first arrived on the island as a result of the work of Western mission organisations and colonisation. Through these influences new ideas were introduced and permeated through society, and the use of reading and writing became more widespread. The organisation of the Malagasy society was rapidly and fundamentally transformed from a culture based on oral transmission of knowledge to one based on reading and writing. Although not every part of society was changed, and even though parts of the population still do not possess reading and writing skills, Malagasies were, to different degrees, influenced by reading and writing in their thinking and interaction. From the colonial period, the mastery of reading and writing became an important asset for social promotion, and on many occasions, it became a requisite to engage in the larger society (i.e. relating to the government, participating in economic activities and for instance selling agricultural products).

Children learn in various settings, but educational institutions are considered main providers of literacy education for children and youth. The way children learn to read and write is therefore strongly affected by educational policies. Educational policies have changed in Madagascar over time and have been influenced by historical and political events. Changes have had an impact on what children and youth were to read and write, not least the language they were required to learn to read and write in. The standard Malagasy language was used by the mission organisations in their educational work in the 19th century. The mission's education focused on religious studies as part of their evangelising work, but it also included general education. During the French colonial period the French language became the preferred language in society and in the economy. French language, history and culture became a central part of school programmes. The colonial power regarded schools, both their own educational institutions and those of the mission organisations, as important instruments in the colonial project. After independence in 1960, the linguistic policy has shifted between favouring French or Malagasy. Today, different generations and social groups in the Malagasy population have varying and different knowledge of Malagasy and French.

## A New Perspective on Mission History

This book contributes to the understanding of how the Lutheran NMS, in their strong commitment to literacy, related to politically changing conditions in Madagascar. Another important part of this context is their collaboration and competition with other missions, particularly Protestant but also Catholic. In an article from 2002, Andrew Porter argued that there is a strong need for research on overseas missions seen in a broader context (Porter 2002). Mission history has had a tendency to be too narrow, describing domestic ecclesiastical history or overseas missions, without taking into account the broader context in which missions operated. Missionary activity, motive and impact depended on local societies and politics, as well as the missions' own characteristics. The missions' own characteristics were shaped by international missionary cooperation, but also by the missions' society of origin. In addition, when local society and politics changed, so did the ways the missions related to them. Porter argued that instead of asking if the missionary enterprise was a tool of imperialism, one should ask, "in what circumstances and why did missions and imperial authorities or indigenous governments come to rely on each other?" (Porter 2002: 563).

In my research I have tried to answer the following question: *How did the Norwegian Mission negotiate their literacy work with the political powers in colonial and newly independent Madagascar?* In order to do an analysis of this question, I focus on three areas:

1. Which resources did the mission devote to literacy work, and who had access to the literacy programmes of the mission?
2. Which literacies were promoted through the mission?
3. Did the Norwegian mission's literacy work contribute to maintain, reinforce or challenge power relations in the Malagasy society?

To answer these questions I use theories within the field of literacy studies. My data material consists of archival material and qualitative interviews. In order to understand the strategies of the mission and the effects of literacy work, I focus on issues of religion, language and identity.

## The Establishment of NMS

On the 8th of August 1842, the NMS was founded with 184 delegates entitled to vote and 65 delegates representing different mission associations from different spiritual groups and social classes (Langhelle 2006: 119, Jørgensen 1992: 22–27, Nome 1943: 33–36). The NMS was an organisation primarily established with support from lay movements, but also with significant support from church representatives. Changing social relations and industrial and economic development were important underlying factors for the establishment of NMS (Jørgensen 1992: 15–22). During the first years, the number of member associations increased dramatically. Changes within the religious domain, theological thinking and revival movements all contributed to the growth of missions, in addition to the engagement of key individuals. The appearance of a new liberal middle class at the expense of the old aristocratic bourgeoisie helped the establishment of organisations that were organised around common interests, rather than sharing class identity and geographical origin. The transnational mission movement and influence from foreign countries (like Britain, Germany and America) stimulated the mission's development in Norway (Jørgensen 1992, Birkeli 1935: 73–74, Danbolt 1947, Nome 1943).

Norway was formally united with Sweden during the period when the NMS was established, after the country had been ceded from Denmark to Sweden in 1814. The Swedish union lasted until 1905, but Norway retained its constitution created during the transition throughout this period, and Norway had its own federal institutions, apart from foreign affairs. Partly due to the fact that Norway was not completely independent, a Norwegian romantic nationalism evolved, which focused on language and literature. This was a period where Norway developed as a modern independent nation, from an agricultural to an industrialised and urbanised society. Many of the factors that shaped the development of the nation, such as nationalism and opposition of the established power, also contributed to shaping the mission organisation. According to historian of religion Karina Hestad Skeie, the lay movement, the evangelical revival and the mission movement's growth "coincided with the growth of nationalism, self-consciousness, and the quest for independence" (Skeie 2013: 21). Skeie highlighted the increase in literacy skills as an important factor for transformations in the society in which the mission developed (Skeie 2013: 18–19). By 1861, 48% of Norwegian children went to schools. It was individuals with an emphasis on literacy and challenging authorities who influenced the establishment and development of NMS as a mission organisation. The missionaries took with them this strong emphasis on reading, writing and printing to the places where they started to evangelise with the aim to build Lutheran churches.

In 1843, the Mission School was opened in order to educate missionaries. The basic motive of the mission was to bring the Gospel of Christ to people all over the world (Jørgensen 1992: 27–29). They were convinced of the universality of their religious faith. Most of the men who were sent as missionaries abroad came from rural families. Historian of missions Kristin Fjelde Tjelle argued in her book *Missionary Masculinity*, which has a focus on South Africa, that these were "self-made" men (Tjelle 2014: 36). Many of the missionaries married outside their class, with women from middle- or upper-class backgrounds (Predelli 2003: 56–57). The missionary wives contributed in the work of the mission. Many of them educated and trained girls in domestic skills (Tjelle 2014: 131). From 1871, women could become missionaries not only through marriage (Predelli 2003: 54–59). Single female missionaries were generally more educated than ordinary Norwegian women, and many of them worked in the schools of the mission. Out of the 37 single women who worked in Madagascar in the period before 1900, 24 were teachers. In 1902, the Mission School for Women was established on women's initiative. It first started as a private organisation outside NMS in Christiania (Oslo). From 1903, female missionaries in Madagascar were members with the right to vote in mission conferences, the highest authority in the mission field, whereas in South Africa this right did not come through until 1924 (Tjelle 2014: 136, Birkeli 1949: 204–205).

## Norwegian Mission Work in Madagascar

In 1843, NMS sent its first missionary, Hans Paludan Schreuder, to work among the Zulus in South Africa. The second field of the mission was Madagascar, where the first missionaries arrived in 1866. Madagascar became a success story, whereas in South Africa the results of the evangelical work developed very slowly.[1] In 1882, after 40 years, there had been only 66 baptisms among the Zulus, compared to 1,111 baptisms in Madagascar in fewer than 20 years (Tjelle 2014: 53). The difference in the number of church attendants (870 in Zululand and 38,000 in Madagascar) and school pupils (500 in Zululand and 33,000 in Madagascar) was also enormous.

At arrival in Madagascar, missionaries John Engh and Martinius Borgen experienced difficulties with both the British mission (London Missionary Society), which came to the island before the Norwegians, and the Merina Government concerning the choice of area to work in. On the 4th of December 1867, Engh and Borgen arrived in Betafo (Birkeli 1949: 61). The missionaries were well received in Betafo. According to Fridtjov Birkeli, building on Engh, this was probably due to people's interest in learning to read and write:

> Many came because of curiosity and the interest in learning to read and write. Carefully choosing his words which were decided for publication, Engh puts it this way: 'Without any doubt, many have a desire to learn; we could not decide if this desire in most cases is a desire for divine enlightenment or only for human knowledge, but we are inclined to believe the latter'.
>
> (Birkeli 1949: 62, my translation)

Merina representatives in Betafo were given orders from the Central Kingdom not to hinder the missionaries who came to teach, but to make sure that affiliation to the new doctrine was voluntary. The local aristocracy allowed the missionaries to settle down at a hill nearby. The missionaries used their huts as places for meetings and teaching. In 1869, the first religious assembly house was built, and that year the first church members, from the local aristocracy, were baptised (Strand 1937). The political context in this period was very favourable to Protestant missions. In 1869, the Merina Queen Ranavalona II and her Prime Minister Rainilaiarivony were baptised and married within the Protestant church. The congregation in Betafo experienced strong growth and soon some of the missionaries' converts joined the Norwegians in establishing mission stations in other villages (Birkeli 1942). In the following decades, Lutheran congregations and schools were established in the Betafo district.

The Protestant mission organisations divided Madagascar between them, and Norwegian missionaries developed their work in the southern parts of Madagascar (Figure 1.2). During the first 80 years, 41 Norwegian mission stations were founded (Snekkenes 1950). Educational work was crucial from the start. In 1869, the mission began medical and health work; in 1877 they established a publishing house; and in 1887 they started work among persons struck by leprosy, in 1924 among the blind and in 1950 with the deaf. The Norwegian mission concentrated its efforts in three synods: the Highlands Synod (around Antsirabe and Fianarantsoa), the West Synod (the south-west coast around Toliara and Morondava), and the East Synod (the south-east coast around Manakara and Vangaindrano) (Figures 1.3–1.5).

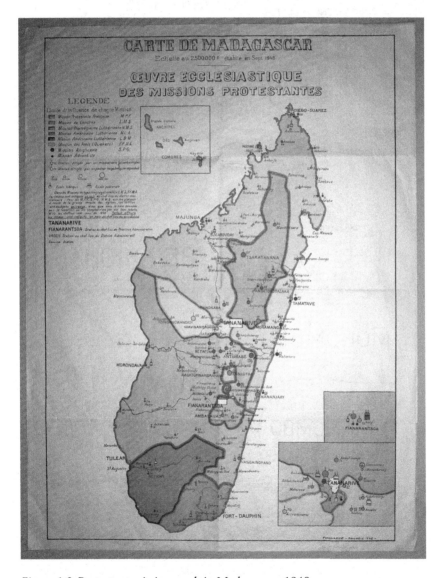

*Figure 1.2* Protestant mission work in Madagascar, 1948

Source: Mission and Diakonia Archives, VID

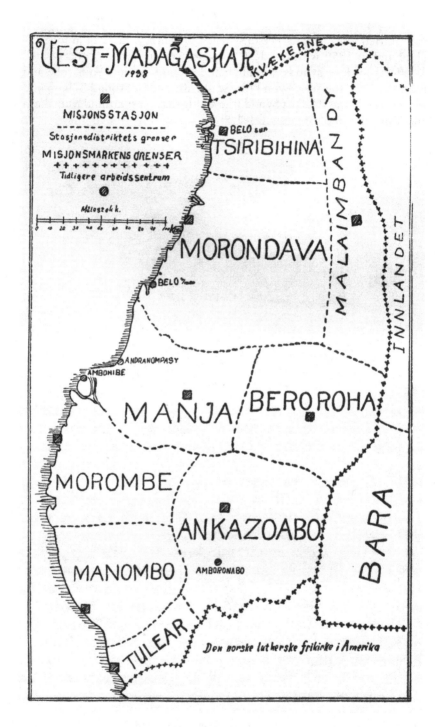

*Figure 1.3* NMS mission fields in the West Coast
Source: Birkeli (1954: 96)

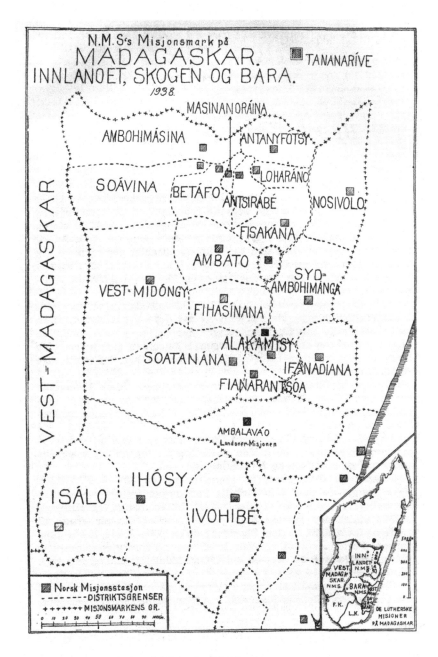

*Figure 1.4* NMS mission fields in the Highlands

Source: Birkeli (1954: 89)

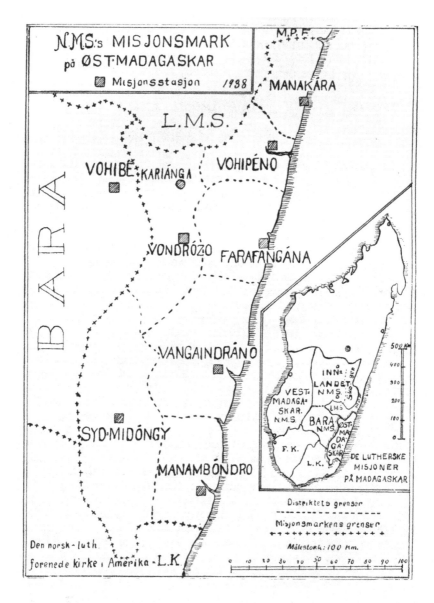

*Figure 1.5* NMS mission fields in the East Coast
Source: Birkeli (1954: 103)

In 1950, the General Synod of the FLM was constituted in the presence of 24 missionaries and 44 Malagasy delegates (Edland and Aano 1992: 369, 372, 401). But it was not until after independence that the first Malagasy president of the Lutheran church, Rakoto Andrianarijaona, was elected. Today FLM has about 3 million members and is the third-largest church in Madagascar after the Roman Catholic Church and the Church of Jesus Christ in Madagascar (FJKM) (Isabelle 2012 and e-mail 2014). In 2014, the Educational Department of FLM (Fampianarana sy Fanabeazana Loterana—FFL) had registered 300 primary schools, 60 secondary schools and 17 upper-secondary schools (Isabelle 2012 and e-mail 2014). Effects from the involvement of Norwegian missionaries in the Malagasy society are indeed observable, also within literacy and education. I will now go back to the start, when foreign powers brought literacy to Madagascar.

## Literacy Brought by the Missions to Madagascar

During the 1820s, the Protestant non-denominational London Missionary Society (LMS) arrived in Madagascar. The goal of British missionaries was to translate the Bible and establish ordinary schools for reading and writing (Ravelomanana 1968: 19). During this period, King Radama I (reigned 1810–1828) was the king of the Merina monarchy. With the king's approval, the Protestant missionaries contributed to the creation of the standard Malagasy language. King Radama I welcomed the literacy skills that the missions brought (Raison-Jourde 1991: 117, Gow 1979: 2). King Radama I was soon convinced of the value of education by the British missionaries, probably because he had "discovered that the art of reading and writing created great new possibilities for the administration of his country and his control over the army" (Edland 2006: 109).

The Merina regime's attitude towards the missions changed over time. Under Ranavalona I (reigned 1828–1861), who followed Radama I, European missionaries were expelled and Christians were persecuted. The minority of converted Christians continued to meet in secrecy and they grew in numbers. The Merina King Radama II (reigned 1861–1863) signed in 1862 a treaty with France and England, where he ensured religious freedom, and the country became open to missionaries again (Rajoelison and Hübsch 1993: 266). In addition to LMS, other British Protestant mission societies also entered Madagascar: the Anglican Church Missionary Society (CMS), the Society for the Propagation of the Gospel (SPG), and the Quaker's Friends' Foreign Missions Association (FFMA). As already noted, it was during this period that the NMS began their work on the island. The Catholic mission started their mission work in the capital (Hübsch 2008: 14–15, 1993).

The missions had both a spiritual and a social engagement, and they obtained an important position within literacy due to the educational policy of the Merina monarchy. In 1881, the Monarchy created an Educational Ministry (Gow 1979: 130). They proclaimed compulsory education for children between 8 and 16 years of age. As a consequence of this policy, mission schools received many pupils. The educational work of the missions created a new elite that was based more "on ability and education rather than on birth" (Gow 1979: 136). The elite was recruited to governmental posts. Educational statistics from the missions in this period consist of registered and attending students. Due to the fact that school became compulsory, many pupils were registered without attending school. Parents were afraid to be punished if they did not register their children in school. In 1884, LMS claimed to have nearly 60,000 pupils, out of which approximately half were active (Raison-Jourde 1991: 489). In 1895, they claimed to have nearly 75,000 pupils whereas the Quakers claimed to have about 14,000 and the Catholic mission 27,000 (Gow 1979: 131). In 1899, NMS claimed to have 56,084 registered pupils and 49,028 pupils showing up in 1,039 schools (NMS 1970: 172). This dominant position within literacy work was gradually taken over by the French colonial power after their arrival to the country in 1896. The colonial power opened their own secular schools and introduced stricter legislation. The graph of the number of pupils in Norwegian mission schools in Madagascar gives a good illustration of this (Figure 1.6). The number of students soon started to decline, especially from 1904.

### The Impact of French Colonial Policy on Mission Literacy Work

French colonial authorities in Madagascar put a strong emphasis on education. It was promoted as an important instrument in *la mission civilisatrice* that "sought to bring all dependents together under one roof and unify them through the French language and culture" (White 1996: 21). Educating indigenous peoples was promoted as a duty of the Republican colonial power to *civilise* other less *civilised* areas, while at the same time indigenous education would increase the economic productivity and facilitate the recruitment of collaborators. Mumford described two distinct schools of thought within colonial educational policy in relation to indigenous people. The first would, in line with *assimilation*, "encourage European schools on European lines with a European language as the main or sole medium of instruction" whereas the other in line with *adaptation* "would look towards nationalistic indigenous schools following native lines and looking towards native ideals, giving equal place to new and old tongues" (Mumford 1935: 820). British educational policy was known as more willing to adapt to local contexts, whereas French educational policy was based on assimilation (White 1996, Clignet 1970: 438, Mumford 1935: 840, Rosnes 2016). French colonial schools have also been described as *political* and *antireligious*, whereas most of the schools in British colonies were operated by missions and supervised by educational departments (Malinowski 1943: 654).

In Madagascar, the French colonial policy was characterised by assimilation and secularism. The colonisation of Madagascar therefore had significant impact on the missions' literacy work. In 1897, Joseph Simon

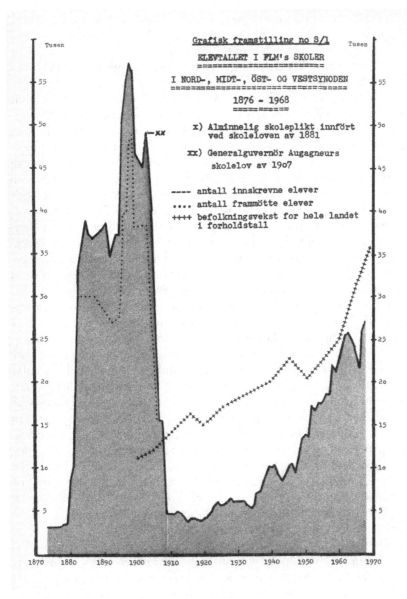

*Figure 1.6* Number of students in NMS/FLM schools, 1876–1968

Translation:

x) Decree proclaiming compulsory education (1881)

XX) The 1907 Decree of Governor-General Augagneur

---- Number of registered students

. . . . Number of active students

++++ Population growth

Source: NMS (1970)

Galliéni, the French governor-general to Madagascar from 1896 to 1905, acknowledged the success of the missions' work to increase reading and writing skills, and at the start of the colonial period, there was a friendly tone between the French colonial power and the missions (Snekkenes 1950). The colonial government even encouraged French Protestant missions to begin mission work in the country. This encouragement was rooted in a need for the colonial power to overcome the link made between Protestantism and their rival Britain. British missionaries had after all converted the most influential elite in the country to Protestantism. In the beginning of the colonial period, Malagasy was regarded as an additional LOI in primary schools, but the assimilationist aim of French colonial policy was clear: the French language should become the basis for teaching in all schools of the island (Chapus 1930: 265–281).

A few years into the colonial reign, the colonial administration seriously started to strengthen their control over literacy by introducing regulations, which the missions found more and more difficult to adhere to. From 1899, the French administration demanded that in order to open a school, an authorisation had to be issued. From 1901, teachers needed an official diploma from the French system. Further, the formal separation of the state and the church in France in 1905 impacted seriously on colonial policies. In Madagascar, Jean-Victor Augagneur was inaugurated as the governor-general and Renel became chief of education. They were both Republicans and anticlerical, and implemented the secular aims of the colonial policy. In a decree in 1906, the possibility to participate in regular teaching in church buildings and assembly houses was banned. This ban had a severe impact on the missions' literacy work. In the countryside and in small villages where they used the same building for praying and services on Sundays and school during the week, the literacy work had to stop. The new regulations led to a large decline in the number of pupils, as shown in Figure 1.6. Between 4,000 and 5,000 of the Norwegian mission's primary schools were closed, and NMS was in 1912 left with only 4,300 pupils in 106 schools in comparison to 56,084 registered pupils just 13 years earlier (NMS 1970: 172).

In 1913, the administration discovered a nationalistic movement, *Vy, Vato, Sakelika* (VVS), meaning *iron, stone, and ramification*. Their goals were to renew Malagasy culture and fight for more liberty at a political level. The colonial administration blamed the appearance of this nationalistic movement on education (Esoavelomandroso 1977: 247). The intentions of educating the Malagasy population to be loyal had not been fulfilled, and education had instead led to these unintended consequences. In administrative reports, those affiliated with the movement were described as "poorly literate, filled with social theories that their spirits wrongly digested" (Esoavelomandroso 1977: 247). A decree issued in 1916 on restructuring education was created to repair this failure. The civilising role of the French colonial power was reinforced to fight Malagasy nationalism through moral and civic education (Esoavelomandroso 1976: 105–106). It became compulsory to use local dialects in the beginning, but change to the French language as soon as possible. Focusing on dialects and avoiding the use of the standard Malagasy language, based on the Merina dialect and preferred by the Protestant missions, was part of a divide-and-rule policy used to fight nationalism. The Malagasy language was believed to fuel nationalistic feelings.

The educational work of the mission did not increase until the 1920s, in the period I have called *mid-colonisation*. The main reason for the growth in the missions' educational work was a more mission-friendly administration leading to a better atmosphere between the colonial power and the missions. This administration put in place a decree that turned Malagasy into the LOI in primary school. Later, in another policy, this decree was changed. The colonial power could, however, not ignore the existence of the standard Malagasy language. Disagreements concerning its use in the school programme occurred throughout the entire colonial period (Esoavelomandroso 1976). Figure 1.6 also demonstrates trends of growth towards the end of the colonial period in 1960, when mission schools were more recognised (Habberstad 1965: 57). The educational work of NMS experienced a considerable growth, and some of the schools were even funded by the French colonial government (The archives of the superintendent of the mission. 1962–1971). In 1960, the number of pupils attending Norwegian mission schools at lower level was 20,004 (NMS 1961). It was in this period the mission schools changed ownership and became Malagasy Lutheran schools.

## Mission Literacy Work After Independence

At independence in 1960, Protestants were satisfied that standard Malagasy, in addition to French, was declared an official language. But the relations between the Malagasy Republic and the former colonial power continued. French remained as an LOI, and mastering French was a necessity for people wanting access to power (Dahl 2011). Goguel argued that there was no real national educational system at independence in Madagascar because it was still highly dependent on "former and present decisions in different departments in Paris" (Goguel 2006: 21–22, my translation). According to Goguel, cooperation agreements, negotiated before independence, had an important impact on the policy. There were some attempts at adaptation, but these attempts were limited by the requirement of the primary and secondary diplomas. Education should be in line with diplomas valid in France. Sometimes, the objective of malgachisation was promoted, but the government had to relate not only to the former colonial power, but also to the different social and economic layers and fractions of the Malagasy society with their different aims and ambitions. In a context where the country still had strong links with the former colonial power, and where construction of identity and language still was based on a colonial ideology, it was challenging to promote a Malagasy nationalist ideology, among others through literacy programmes.

In addition to receiving development aid, especially from the former colonial power, the Malagasy government counted on private and religious schools to meet the challenge of offering education to all children (Bøe 1969b: 58, NMS 1970: 175). While the government focused most of its attention on giving Malagasy children at least 4 years of elementary education, the church began to focus more on higher education. During the 1960s, the mission received funds from the Norwegian Development Agency and the Lutheran World Federation (LWF) to strengthen their educational work. In 1969, the total number of pupils belonging to the Lutheran primary schools in Madagascar was 21,651 (NMS 1970: 140).

## Outline of the Book

In Chapter 2, I will present the theoretical perspectives that this study is based on and, in Chapter 3, I will explain my methodology and how I collected the data material constituting the base for this research.

In Chapters 4 and 5, I will analyse the literacy work of the mission during the mid-colonisation period and at independence. The focus is on structures and resources, including management of educational work, physical spaces for teaching reading and writing, and literacies and literacy practices that were promoted and experienced in mission schools. In Chapter 6, I will present the case of Betafo, where I conducted fieldwork in order to get a more detailed picture of the mission's literacy work in one area. In Chapters 7 and 8, I will analyse the ideological embeddedness of the literacy work of the Norwegian mission and of the institutions that the mission collaborated and competed with: the French colonial administration, the Malagasy state after independence, and Protestant and Catholic mission organisations.

## Notes

1. About the NMS in the Zulu kingdom see Jørgensen (1990).

# 2    Literacy as Ideologically Embedded

In this chapter, I will present the theoretical position on literacy adopted in this book. I do not understand literacy as a skill that people are in possession of, but as "something people do" (Papen 2005: 25). This research is inspired by approaches within literacy studies focusing on the necessity of studying literacy in practice, and particularly from Brian Street's focus on the ideological embeddedness of literacy (Barton and Hamilton 1998, Street 1984). Towards the end of the chapter, I will present the relation between religion and literacy.

In his book, *Literacy in Theory and Practice*, Street, aiming to describe different literacies rather than assuming one single literacy, illustrated the ideological embeddedness of literacies (Street 1984). Used in my case, this means that Norwegian missionaries to Madagascar were not only teaching Malagasy learners reading and writing skills through their literacy work. The content of what they let Malagasy pupils read and write, and the way they taught them to read, were part of not only one, but several ideologies. My understanding of *ideology* is based on Martin Reisigl and Ruth Wodak, who define ideology as "an (often) one-sided perspective or world view composed of related mental representations, convictions, opinions, attitudes and evaluations, which is shared by members of a specific social group" (Reisigl and Wodak 2009: 88). The Norwegian missionaries had a purpose based on their religion, and they operated within a specific political context, impacted by French republicanism and secularism. That context shaped the literacies they promoted in their educational work.

## An Ideological Model of Literacy

It has been at the core of literacy research whether or not there is a causal link between the capacity of reading and writing and higher cognitive levels (Berge 2006). Street refers to an *autonomous* model, in which it is argued that literacy in itself has implications for social and cognitive development (Street 1984). The famous article "The Consequences of Literacy", published in 1963 by Jack Goody and Ian Watt, has been regarded as an important contribution to the *autonomous model* (Goody and Watt 1963). Street's *ideological model* challenged the autonomous model, arguing that "this model of literacy disguises the cultural and ideological assumptions and presents literacy's values as neutral and universal" (Heath and Street 2008: 103). An ideological model emphasises that literacy may vary from one context to another. *The Psychology of Literacy*, published by Sylvia Scribner and Michael Cole in 1981, is a seminal work challenging the idea that literacy can be studied and taught regardless of socio-cultural contexts (Cole and Scribner 1981). Using a Vygotskian activity-oriented approach, they emphasised that literacy in itself does not imply cognitive development, but is related to the specific uses of literacy in formal schooling. The main argument of Scribner and Cole was that literacy only led to cognitive development under certain circumstances.

To challenge the link made within the autonomous model between literacy and individual cognitive, as well as societal, development, Harvey J. Graff used the concept of *literacy myth* (Graff 1987, 1979). It referred to

the belief, articulated in educational, civic, religious, and other settings, contemporary and historical, that the acquisition of literacy is a necessary precursor to and invariably results in economic development, democratic practice, cognitive enhancement and upward social mobility.

(Graff and Duffy 2008: 41)

Graff showed that in the 19th century oppressed groups in Canada were even more oppressed through literacy due to its links with the construction of the middle class and its specific ideology. The ruling class found it convenient to control literacy because literacy possessed the potential to strengthen lower-class groups. This also had an impact on how literacy was taught in school. Literacy became "means of social control rather than offering any real prospects of 'improvement'" (Street 1984: 107). It became more important to read acceptably in the right way than to understand the text. This teaching method did not create critical thinkers. It made them adopt "the moral norms and disciplines of the ruling class" (Street 1984: 108). According to Graff and John Duffy, colonial powers' identification of literacy with *civilisation* worked in similar ways:

In the nineteenth century, the myth of the alphabet was an element of the broader narrative of Western history and worked to ratify the educational, moral, and political experiences of colonial Western powers with the cultures of the colonized, especially those that did not practice literacy. To the extent that the alphabet was identified with civilization, its dissemination to nonliterate, nonindustrial, supposedly "primitive" cultures was intrinsic to the larger project and rhetoric of colonial expansion.

(Graff and Duffy 2008: 46–47)

These insights are very relevant for the history of literacy in Madagascar. Throughout its colonial past, the country has experienced a political order in which literacy was an instrument for oppression disguised behind discourses on *civilisation*. In today's Malagasy society, that has been independent for more than half a century, it is still highly relevant and important to question how this dominant political order from the past, and with its policy, ideology, interests and perspectives, influences what and how Malagasy children are taught in school.

Shirley Brice Heath and Street argued that formal education systems, promoting certain ways to use the written language, were created as an instrument for and tightly bound to a state or a religion, or both (Heath and Street 2008: 17–18). The norms and ideology of groups in power are in charge of planning and organising formal education for all individuals. Even though some individuals may not be reached by formal schooling, everybody is affected by its existence. Inge Birgita Kral has described how the Ngaanyatjarra people in Australia were introduced to different literacies during the 'mission time', during the 'Native Welfare times' under the state from the 1950s, and during the new federal policy of Aboriginal self-determination after 1972 (Kral 2007). During the 'mission time', "Literacy became synonymous with English and schooling, and also with adult Christian practice in the vernacular" (Kral 2007: 63). During the 'Native Welfare times', state schooling increased with a focus on literacy development based on a policy of assimilation. Under the self-determination policy from 1972, the Ngaanyatjarra were suddenly to cope with a different ideology of schooling and literacy with a lot of optimism, but also a lot of unrealistic expectations (Kral 2007: 114–116). Kral suggested that, "if literacy is to be maintained, elaborated and transmitted in this newly literate context it must be meaningfully integrated into everyday social practice in a manner that extends beyond pedagogical settings" (Kral 2007: IV). History shows that education and literacy development have primarily not been directed towards personal growth and development, argued James Paul Gee. It has rather stressed

different sorts of behaviours and attitudes for different classes of individuals: docility, discipline, time-management, honesty, and respect for the lower classes, suiting them for industrial or service jobs; verbal and analytical skills, "critical thinking", discursive thought and writing for the higher classes, suiting them for management jobs.

(Gee 2008: 56)

The anthropologist Maurice Bloch has made many seminal contributions to the ideological model of literacy with extensive studies covering Madagascar. He argued that literacy does not necessarily have liberating effects, but is often used as an instrument of power (Bloch 1998: 152). Bloch describes a day at school in a very remote Malagasy village, where education is based mostly on French models of education (Bloch 1998). Both the pupils and the teacher knew that they would not get through the exam. In spite of this, people in the village were convinced of the value of schooling and literacy. There were no known educational success stories from this village and parents did not necessarily aspire to such success for their children, since they then probably would leave the village. Bloch found the reason why education was valued in more context-oriented explanations of what people in the village thought about knowledge than in the practical advantages. Knowledge taught in school was somehow understood in the same manner as the wisdom of elders. Wisdom was, however, linked to the person who possessed it, which ensured that the wisdom of elders in the end was higher valued than school knowledge. This meant that increasing literacy would not necessarily lead to a change in the traditional hierarchy and challenge power structures and decision-making processes. According to Bloch, it would be dangerous to use this conclusion to cover all parts of Madagascar, and even for the descendants of slaves it was different in the village Bloch studied. This illustrates, nevertheless, that the effects of literacy depend on social and cultural contexts. In the case of the Norwegian mission's literacy work in Madagascar, these aspects are important to bear in mind. The ideological embeddedness of literacies conveyed through the mission must be considered, as well as the specific contexts where children were learning.

In a study of Swiss Protestant missionaries in South-East Africa, Patrick Harries described how they, from a Swiss perspective, looked on literacy as a revolutionary tool for the transformation of society. But according to Harries, the missionaries did not take into account the context in which they were working (Harries 2001: 413). The African context was dominated by an oral tradition. People read in a different way from what they were used to home in Switzerland. The missionaries were annoyed by the "parrot-like learning of words and sounds" with no emphasis on a deep understanding (Harries 2001: 416, 418). Harries argued, in the same manner as Bloch, that literacy often served to reinforce local beliefs, rather than challenge or transform them. Literacy skills were seen more as a ritual than a skill. Knowledge of reading and writing was used to enhance status, not knowledge. According to Scribner and Cole's description of literacy and cognitive development, one could say that the circumstances in which literacy was taught and learned were not favourable for the cognitive development the missionaries intended (Cole and Scribner 1981).

Throughout history, literacies have been essential for individual and cultural development. Literacies have also been instruments of oppression. Consequently, it is important to study the specific contexts of literacies, namely those that give it meaning. In the following pages, I will introduce important concepts for studying literacy in context.

## Literacies, Literacy Practices and School Literacy

Taking the social view of literacy, "we have to look at literacy not merely as a skill, as something people have learned and therefore know, but as something people do", according to Uta Papen (Papen 2005: 25). Seen from this perspective, it becomes important to acknowledge that there are different forms of literacy, different *literacies*, while also taking into consideration meanings and purposes of different literacy activities. Different literacies can be associated with different cultures, languages and domains in life (Barton and Hamilton 2000: 7). In this book the concepts *religious literacies*, *French-assimilationist literacies* and *contextualised literacies* construct a theoretical framework used in the description of the different literacies the Norwegian mission promoted in Madagascar (see also Rosnes 2016). I will describe them more in depth in Chapter 4.

In order to describe different literacies, the concept of literacy practices is useful. According to David Barton and Mary Hamilton, *literacy practices* offers, "a powerful way of conceptualising the link between the activities of reading and writing and the social structures in which they are embedded and which they help shape" (Barton and Hamilton 2000: 7). They offered the following definition of literacy as a social practice:

- Literacy is best understood as a set of social practices; these can be inferred from events which are mediated by written texts.
- There are different literacies associated with different domains of life.
- Literacy practices are patterned by social institutions and power relationships, and some literacies become more dominant, visible and influential than others.
- Literacy practices are purposeful and embedded in broader social goals and cultural practices.
- Literacy is historically situated.
- Literacy practices change and new ones are frequently acquired through processes of informal learning and sense making.

(Barton and Hamilton 2000: 8, 1998: 7)

Literacy practices are understood as being constituted by events and mediated by written text (Barton 2007: 35). Literacy events, where many are regular and repeated activities, are occasions or activities where the written word plays a role. Some researchers in literacy use both the concept of literacy practices and events. Papen has argued that the two concepts are not easy to discern and she uses only the concept of literacy practices, an approach I also use in this book (Papen 2016). It is, for instance, interesting to compare literacy practices at home, in school and in church (Barton 2007: 35). Barton and Hamilton argued that social institutions and power relations influence different literacy practices and make some literacy practices more dominant than others. Religious institutions assert a major influence through their schools, as well as through informal religious training such as Sunday schools (Barton and Hamilton 1998: 45). Education is an example of socially powerful institutions that "tend to support dominant literacy practices" (Barton and Hamilton 2000: 12). Kral argued that "School literacy practices, in particular, are bounded by culturally normative expectations of correctness, neatness, organisation and time management" (Kral 2007: 6). Dictations are typical dominant school literacy practices, writes Papen, where pupils are measured on how far they comply with certain norms, which are not neutral but based on a certain form of literacy (Papen 2005: 45). Governments "set standards for what count as appropriate reading and writing practices", and "measure literacy levels among the population, they set school examinations and define entry levels for access to professional training and higher education" (Papen 2005: 45).

In a chapter entitled "The schooling of literacy", Brian Street and Joanna Street described *school literacy* as the dominant literacy in contrast to other alternative versions of literacy (Street and Street 1991). When Street and Street talk in an abstract way about school literacy, what they mean is the diverse literacy practices that are used in school. Through different means and processes, a pedagogisation of literacy takes place, according to Street and Street, that helps construct an "autonomous" model of literacy. In the autonomous model, school literacy is presented as the only form of literacy, and taken as a matter of course. Street and Street refer to some of the means used in the process of pedagogisation, among others "the distancing of language from subjects [teacher and learner]" (Street and Street 1991: 150–151). This means that the language used in school is different from the language used by the pupils. In addition, it is a language imposed on them as passive recipients. The processes that contribute to the pedagogisation of literacy, such as a specific language used in school, are presented as though they were neutral, building on generic competencies, thereby hiding the ideological embeddedness of all literacies. Street and Street also emphasised the institutionalisation of literacy in physical and institutional spaces that are separated from other spaces children are part of in everyday life. Separating spaces for teaching and learning in school from "everyday" spaces plays a role in the pedagogisation of literacy, contributing to turning school literacy into something different from other literacies. The specific ways that teachers and parents give instructions on how to deal with a text, the use of literacy materials, and how time and work practices are organised are relevant here.

Street and Street reflected upon why school literacy has become so important in contemporary societies and find that the pedagogised literacy becomes "an organizing concept around which ideas of social identity and values are defined; what kinds of collective identity we subscribe to, what kind of nation we want to belong to" (Street and Street 1991: 161). School contributes, in other words, to the construction of identity. Focusing on how schools contribute to identity construction will help recognise which ideas of identity lie behind the pedagogised literacy that is taken for *neutral*. I find the concept of pedagogisation of literacy and its impact on identity construction relevant to understand the literacy work of the Norwegian mission in Madagascar. They preferred standard Malagasy as the LOI. Physical spaces for literacy teaching were often in church buildings or educational buildings constructed nearby the church building. The institutional space, which can be said to be formed by the institutional frames of the mission organisation and the FLM, also impacted on the pedagogisation of literacy in mission and Lutheran schools. The literacies of the mission were different from literacies in schools run by the secular colonial administration and by the Malagasy government at independence, which were secular and dominated by the French language. According to Street and Street, the pedagogisation of literacy is "a *social* process: They contribute to the construction of a particular kind of citizen, a particular kind of identity, and a particular concept of the nation [original italics]" (Street and Street 1991: 163). The different literacies promoted by different institutions in the Malagasy colonial context promoted different understandings of identity: among others a Malagasy Lutheran Christian identity, a Malagasy national identity and an identity very much influenced by French assimilation. Street is concerned with the consequences of safeguarding one hegemonic, and supposedly *neutral*, literacy. The results from failing to take into account culturally sensitive literacies are low attendance rates and high dropout rates. These challenges are highly relevant in the Malagasy educational context, where Malagasy pupils, since the beginning of formal education in the country, have been subjected to literacies and language policies, not only defined by the dominant class, but by institutions with roots in totally different foreign cultures.

## Literacy and Religion

In his project to present general tendencies of the influence of early literacy on social organisations Goody used "religion" as one of four institutional categories of "the great organizations", along with "economy", "polity" and "law" (Goody 1986: 184). Since "the word of God" was written, this helped explain the diffusion of world religions like Islam, Christianity and Judaism: "Indeed one could say that these alphabetic religions spread literacy and equally that literacy spread these religions" (Goody 1986: 3–4).

Descriptions of literacy campaigns of the Reformation and Lutheran Protestantism deliver examples to this traditional relationship between literacy and religion. One example is Egil Johansson's study of levels of literacy in Sweden during the 17th and 18th centuries where he used parish catechetical examination records as sources (Johansson 2007). The ability to read was acquired earlier than the ability to write and, according to Johansson, there were both political and religious pressure to attain literacy skills: "in the reign of Charles XI the Church Law of 1686, for example, contained a ruling concerning general literacy" and, "Everybody in the household and in the village gathered once a year to take part in examinations in reading and knowledge of the Bible. The adult who failed these examinations was excluded from both communion and marriage" (Johansson 2007: 239). Teaching children to read was basically the task of parents, and not schools. According to Graff, this literacy campaign in Sweden is considered one of the most successful in the Western world (Graff 1987: 149–150). The goal was religious conversion and the campaign transmitted religious, social and political ideologies. Graff noted that according to the campaign everyone should: " 'learn to read and see with their own eyes what God bids and commands in His Holy Word'. Here was the Protestant influence. The goal was to promote individual consciousness of Christian faith and life; the method was exposure by individual literacy—reading by and for oneself" (Graff 1987: 150). Harries described how the Protestant Swiss Calvinist approach to personal belief had an important impact on the spread of literacy in Switzerland:

> The origins of the remarkable degree of literacy in Switzerland may be traced to the Calvinist insistence on reading as a practice that encouraged introspection and mediation upon sin, and the consequent need for personal salvation and individual conversion. From birth, these Christians were taught to read in a way that allowed them to form their own judgement and opinions on the word of God and His disciples. Instead of having texts explained by a caste of priests, they saw reading as a personal, interpretive act, and as a means of entering into direct contact with God. For the Free Church Calvinists, reading was the foundation of their faith; the rock upon which they built a Church that was at once independent of government, democratic in its composition, and unencumbered by cramping, confining dogma.
>
> (Harries 2001: 407)

Harries argued that with the revival, evangelists reinforced the link between the ability to read and their belief in God. Missionaries brought this view of literacy as "a cheap and effective means of spreading the gospel" with them to South-East Africa, and "through their control of literacy, they could exert a strong influence on the forces of social change" (Harries 2001: 409). The missionaries believed in literacy leading to cognitive development, that it "would revolutionise the natives' intellectual habits and mental equipment" (Harries 2001: 409). To these Swiss missionaries, literacy was tied to economic, social and moral progress:

> literacy was associated with the cognitive conversion needed to save both the spirit and the flesh. The printed word carried not only the redemptive message of the gospel; it also promised a physical and moral rebirth by propagating the idea of a virtuous, hard-working society freed of sin, drunkenness and debauchery.
>
> (Harries 2001: 413)

With the mastering of literacy, rules and morality of society would become more fixed than it was in an oral society under the influence of kinship groups and chiefdoms. The censorship of literature made available by these Calvinist missionaries was very strong. It was important for them that the Church was in full control of literacy and they would not let education become secular as it had become back in Switzerland.

As described in Chapter 1, the NMS, based on Lutheranism and with support from revival movements, focused as well on personal reading of the Bible and a personal relationship with God. At the same time, these religious traditions were inclined towards a strong control of what people read. Action was taken to make sure they got access to "good and 'right' Christian literature" (Apelseth 2004: 93, my translation). This was also evident in the context of the Norwegian mission in Madagascar. It was an important duty of the mission to make the right Christian literature available. The mission propagated a belief system in which individuals should refine their faith through their ability to read God's word as revealed through the Bible. They desired to convert Malagasies and enable them to do the same. In turn, the Malagasy would evangelise and build their church. The missionaries had little interest in keeping the church in their hands forever, but they had an interest in how a local Lutheran Church in Madagascar would develop.

Due to the focus on a personal Christian faith and life, the mission and its people strongly believed the Bible should be read in a familiar language. Norman Etherington has shown that many languages were developed into written formats as a result of missionaries' educational programmes:

> Ferocious arguments raged over the language of instruction. While nineteenth-century governments recommended English, most missions favoured elementary education in local languages as the fastest way to spread their religion. Although the initial work of translation

was slow, once texts and concepts had been expressed in the vernacular, they could spread by word of mouth far beyond the reach of mission stations. It is safe to say that the translation of hundreds of languages into written formats would never have happened but for the missionaries' educational programme.

(Etherington 2005a: 266)

Kwesi Kwaa Prah has discussed the consequences of various missions' involvement with local languages. He emphasised that the work of Christian mission organisations was important in the development of written forms of African languages because they developed writing systems for previously oral languages (Prah 2009: 1, 4–5). One important element was that mission organisations aimed to teach literacy to the masses, and not only to a religious elite. In addition, Christianity did not choose any specific language to spread "the good news", but found that every native tongue could be used. However, "Literacy was not an end in itself", Prah emphasised: "It was primarily there to serve the purposes of evangelisation" (Prah 2009: 11). This resulted in fragmentation, according to Prah, because many languages were written down out of dialects that could have been understood as belonging to the same language (Prah 2009: 14–19). The missions' search for new languages created great confusion. Moreover, it contributed to group identity construction with a potential to be used for political purposes.

Protestant mission organisations influenced the standard Malagasy language through the translation of the Bible. It was strongly influenced by the Merina power and based on the Merina dialect. Other groups did not have the same social and cultural background to understand the translation. The embeddedness of this written language in a specific Malagasy culture and group created difficulties for mission work in coastal areas. The missions in Madagascar, in contrast to what happened in other African contexts, restrained, however, from creating several Malagasy languages. This will be described in depth in Chapter 8. The French language that came with colonisation was introduced as a *neutral* language, meaning a language that came from the outside. It was, however, primarily the elite who mastered the colonial language, which made this language an important instrument of power. The colonial power was well aware that by avoiding to use the official language based on the Merina dialect, and promoting dialects instead of the standard Malagasy language, elites could more easily be recruited from all ethnic groups on the island. This fitted well with the ideology of the colonial power promoting regionalism in fighting nationalism. The aim of *la politique des race* (the policy of the races) was endorsed by the colonial power to minimise the former hegemony of the Merina group in favour of creating elites in the coastal areas. Education played an important role in this. Since independence, the French language has continued to play its role in Madagascar as a mechanism for division between the elites and the population as a whole. The question of language remains a politically sensitive and important issue in political elections and in relation to social changes and reforms. If we were to study present literacy policies in Madagascar, it would be fundamental to take into account the historical embeddedness of literacies in the country.

## Concluding Remarks

When viewing literacy as a social practice embedded, it becomes important to analyse the purposes and motivations of institutions promoting it. Literacy might have liberating effects, but it is also an instrument of power. The effects of literacy in societies are not given, but are dependent upon the specific purposes of literacies, which are related to the social and political context.

Mission organisations developed literacy programmes in Madagascar with the main aim of religious conversion. In the Malagasy context, they also had to relate to the policies of the colonial power. Through a contextualised analysis of literacy teaching focusing on two periods in the history of education in Madagascar, I will show that these policies contributed to processes of continuation, transformation and change in the Malagasy society. Important issues are language, content and structure of the educational system. The way institutions which taught literacy introduced and created written languages had an important impact on the way Malagasy children and youth were to learn to read and write. The effects of these policies are still real in the Malagasy society today. In many contexts, missions contributed through their focus on spreading the gospel in a language that people understood, to develop written versions of oral languages. The development of a Malagasy writing system provided the Malagasy society with a writing system before the arrival of French colonists and the introduction of French-assimilationist colonial policies. This written version of the Malagasy language was, however, very much influenced by the motivations of the Protestant missions' and the Merina regime in power. The existence of two languages, Malagasy and French, that could be used as mediums of instruction and for reading and writing, has been an issue of debate in Malagasy politics up until today. This research, based on archival material and qualitative interviews, shows that literacy is indeed contested, and it is crucial to understand this in order to grasp shifting relations between different groups; that is, the educated elite (through the French language) and the wider population.

# 3 Literacy Study With a Historical Perspective

In this chapter, I will present how I approached the data material collected for this book. I define my study as a literacy study with a historical perspective. I use archival material and qualitative interviews in order to analyse the literacies promoted through the mission's educational work and in order to reconstruct literacy practices at Norwegian mission schools in Madagascar in the past. Consequently, this study does not follow the anthropological and ethnographical methodology that is an important part of Street's ideological model and is common for researchers in literacy studies. This is mainly due to the fact that my study is a historical and not a contemporary study.

The archival material that I scrutinised came from Malagasy, Norwegian and French archives, and they were in Malagasy, Norwegian and French. To get a better overview on the mission's strategic decisions and relations between the missions and other institutions that conducted literacy work, I found it important to collect information from all the synods where the Norwegian mission worked in Madagascar.

I conducted qualitative interviews with former Malagasy pupils, teachers and Norwegian teaching missionaries. These helped me to describe the literacy work of the mission in more detail. Interviews offered a more personal perspective from those who participated in this work. The interviews with former Malagasy teachers and pupils were limited to the specific case study dealing with Lutheran literacy work in the district of Betafo.

## The Choice of Methodology for Historical Research

Ethnography is a relevant and suitable method in the study of literacy (Heath and Street 2008). In this book, I aim to describe and analyse literacies that were promoted through, and reconstruct literacy practices that took place in Sunday, bush and primary schools of the Norwegian mission in Madagascar. Since I have chosen a historical approach to literacy studies, I did not have the opportunity to study pupils' actual engagements in literacy practices in church, in school or at home here and now.

On the other hand, I had access to rich archival and published materials, indicating different literacy practices. I also had the opportunity to talk with former pupils and teachers about their memories from engaging with literacy practices initiated by the mission.

Mike Baynham emphasised that historians of literacy use sources such as written records, contemporary accounts, letters and autobiographies to study literacy with historical perspectives (Baynham 2008: 173–174). He argued that "it is less easy to reconstruct the social practices that give rise to texts that are temporally remote from us", and he himself used fictional perspectives and literary texts to analyse historically distant literacy practices (Baynham 2008: 173). Kate T. Anderson emphasised that, "In Situated Literacies, the point of departure is the contextual features that produce particular instances of possibility for specific people, understood as mediated by sociocultural, political, historical, and ideological factors" (Anderson 2013: 19–20). Contextual features, such as curricular and policy documents marked by these factors, are highly relevant in this study. I mainly approach literacy practices from two perspectives: How were they supposed to be *facilitated*, and how were they *experienced*? In the archival material I found documents, for instance political documents, schedules and curricula documents, with guidelines for how teachers should facilitate literacy practices. Of importance here was also the kind of schoolbooks the mission made available to their pupils. In describing how literacy practices were experienced, I partly base the analysis on articles in the mission's magazines, especially those written by teaching missionaries about their work. But, most importantly, I rely on statements of former pupils and teachers at the mission school in Betafo, and on former Norwegian teaching missionaries to Madagascar.

## Archival Material

In this research, I have used extensively the former Mission Archives of the School of Mission and Theology, Stavanger (now part of Mission and Diakonia Archives—VID) and the archives of FLM in Antananarivo (now situated at Lovasoa, Antsirabe), Madagascar. I found my primary sources about Madagascar in the NMS archives in Stavanger in conference reports, yearbooks and mission magazines. The bulk of this material was printed and easily accessible. Information about missionaries, their background, education and where they worked are, when other sources are not mentioned, accessed from the electronic archive of VID: "NMS: People and places" (MHS).[1] As the archival work progressed, I found that the conference reports were a very important source of information for throwing light on the mission's educational work. During the whole period, the missionaries in Madagascar met at annual meetings in the Highlands and on the West Coast. From 1934, missionaries on the East Coast had their own separate conference. From 1949, a yearly joint conference was arranged, where all Norwegian missionaries on the island met to discuss common matters of interest. The annual conferences constituted the highest authority, and these conferences made decisions that were sent for acceptance to the central mission board in Norway. The conferences were a very important and exciting event for the missionaries. Here, they could meet and discuss with their Norwegian missionary colleagues working in other parts of the island. The written conference reports started with an annual report from all the mission stations followed by minutes of the discussions during the meetings. The discussions were reported in great detail, and before World War II they included citations with reference to the views specific people, by name, had expressed during the meeting.

In my analysis of the conference reports, I focused especially on issues regarding the mission's educational and literacy work, and also the mission's relations with other institutions. These discussions often dealt with practical matters related to expenses, experiences and challenges that the missionaries met in their work, but they also discussed strategies and content of their educational and literacy work. When I refer to the conference reports in the text, it is not always obvious which conference report I refer to, reports dealing with the Highlands (*Innlandet*), the West Coast (*Vestmadagaskar*), the East Coast (*Østmadagaskar*) or the joint conference (*Felleskonferansen*). This information is, however, given in the title in the references. The conference reports were printed, considered to be confidential, and addressed to the central mission board in Norway. The central board in Norway sent replies to major questions raised in these reports. I have not gone through the answers from the central board in Norway systematically, but only consulted their answers on specific issues. This study is first and foremost focused on the mission and its relation with other institutions in Madagascar, and it does not focus to any large extent on the internal relations between the missionaries in Madagascar and their board in Norway.

In his study of Norwegian missionaries and the Dii people in Cameroun, Tomas Sundnes Drønen referred to the conference reports as *back stage* publications in comparison with the official printed sources of NMS, which he referred to as *front stage* publications. The most important among the front stage publications was the magazine *Norsk Misjonstidende* (*NMt—Norwegian Mission tiding*). This magazine was:

> the missionaries' show window to the mission-interested audience in Norway. When analysing the NMt articles we have to keep in mind that the missionaries stepped into a century-long tradition of mission-communication. The message had to be presented a certain way in order to trigger the readers' interest to make them invest their currencies, money and prayer, into the mission project.
>
> (Drønen 2009: 19)

Skeie has argued that literature aimed at actual and potential mission supporters in Norway belonged to a certain "literary genre" (Skeie 2013: 11–12). Marianne Gullestad has a chapter on "Propaganda for Christ" in her study on missionary photography in Cameroon pointing to the mission's need to portray a certain picture of Africans in order to raise money in their homelands (Gullestad 2007).

NMt was published twice a month from 1878, and its content was mostly based on missionary reports. From 1925, it was published weekly, and the editors encouraged the missionaries to write short stories and thematic articles (Tjelle 2014: 16–17). According to Tjelle, short articles had already been published in the mission magazine for women's associations, *Missionslæsning for Kvindeforeninger* (MKF—*Mission readings for women associations*), published between 1884 and 1925, and the youth magazine *Kamp og Seier* (*Battle and Victory*), published between 1900 and 1925. Short articles were also used in the mission's magazine for children, *Missionsselskapets Barneblad* (*The Children Magazine of the Mission*) established in 1896 and published throughout the period covered by this study. The name of this magazine was changed to *Kom og Se* (*Come and See*) in 1946. This magazine is of special relevance to this study due to its audience of children and youth. The magazines NMt and the magazine for children has been analysed systematically for the period of my study. I search systematically for relevant articles in MKF for the period 1920–1925, looking especially for articles written by female teaching missionaries. Articles about Madagascar dealing with the mission's literacy and educational work were of special interest as well as articles commenting on the missions' relations with the local population, the government and other mission societies.

Another front stage publication was the NMS yearbooks, which included reports and statistics from both the mission work back in Norway and in the countries where they worked. Yearbooks were distributed to subscribers of the NMt (Tjelle 2011: 36). I have consulted chapters dealing with the Highlands, the West Coast and the East Coast (from 1934). During the period analysed, the superintendents were in charge of editing the different chapters. In the early years, reports from every station were included, but after World War II they tended to become more general, and from 1964 there was only one chapter about the mission's work in Madagascar. In the use of front stage publications, I was aware of the specific genre they were meant to fit into: to present the work of the mission in a favourable light to mission supporters and their children in Norway.

I mainly found archive material concerning the educational and literacy work of NMS in Madagascar and its relations to other institutions in the archives of the Lutheran Church (FLM archives). The archives of the superintendent of the mission, *Tillitsmannens arkiv* (FLM_TA) contain quite a lot of information on the educational and literacy work of the mission. The main sources are minutes from meetings, correspondence with the government, inter-missionary committees, and missionary colleagues. With regard to the case of Betafo, I consulted some archival material from the mission station in Betafo in the archives of the North Synod, *Nordsynodens arkiv* (FLM_NA). I have also used the archives of FJKM in Antananarivo (*Centre des archives et musée Protestantes—* FJKM), and the library of Protestant missions in Paris (*Département Evangélique Français d'Action—*DEFAP). These archives contained printed sources on inter-missionary cooperation and mission education in Madagascar.

I mainly found Archival materials on the French colonial administration between 1920 and 1960, and the Malagasy government during the 1960s, in the Archives of the Malagasy Democratic Republic (*Archives de la République Démocratique Malgache*, Antananarivo—ARM). I consulted decrees, reports and letters dealing with official educational policy and mission/private education during the colonial period. In the archives of the presidency (*La Presidence*), I found much information on the first Republic generally, but much less on educational policy. In the monographs of the archive, I found information about the region of Betafo. There were also some printed sources on educational policy at ARM. Printed sources on educational policy, mission education and Betafo were also collected from the library of the Malagasy Academy and the National Library in the capital. Most of the documents relating to the administration of the colonies were left in the former colonised countries at independence. Some printed and unprinted sources of interest for this project are, however, located at the Archive of French Oversees Territories in Aix-en-Province (*Archives nationales d'outre-mer—*ANOM). In *Fond Madagascar* (MAD)—*Governor General* (MGG), I uncovered documents with relevance for educational policy—reports of inspections, annual educational reports, and reports on the mission organisations and their involvement with education. In order to describe the colonial educational policy and the policy at independence in general, I have also relied heavily on former research published on this issue. The archival material on public administration that I consulted mainly covered the ruling power's relation with and evaluation of the missions.

The main work in the NMS archives in Norway was done during the autumn of 2011. The Faculty of Arts and Education at the University of Stavanger financed a 3-month fellowship to work in archives in Madagascar from November 2011 to February 2012. A second, but shorter, stay was financed in March 2013. I conducted the archival work in relevant French archives in July 2012. In many cases, I have translated quotations from archival materials and secondary literature into English. The languages used in the original texts are often coloured by the period when they were written. That is not reflected in my translations.

## Interviews with Former Teachers and Pupils

I interviewed nine former Norwegian missionaries, of whom eight had worked at different schools in the Highlands and on the East Coast. One of them, a man, had worked at a teacher training college during the 1960s. He had also been involved in collaboration on educational work between the different mission societies. I conducted the interviews mostly in the homes of the interviewees in different parts of Norway. On one occasion, I interviewed three of them separately during the same visit in the home of one of them. The interviews took place in the period from May 2010 to November 2012. I found my interviewees by recommendations. I only knew about a few women who had been working in schoolwork for NMS in Madagascar. When I had completed my interviews with them, they in turn gave me other names. Three of the women were working in Madagascar during the 1950s and 1960s, and five of them during the 1960s. The interviews allowed me to go beyond what I could read in the documents in the archives and get a better understanding. The former missionaries helped me get a better understanding of the context the Norwegian missionaries were working in, and they gave me advice about how to find other relevant sources of information. I did the interviews based on an interview guide. I recorded the interviews and transcribed them. The interviewees were given the opportunity to read through the transcription and give me their feedback. These former missionaries felt no need to be referred to anonymously.

In Madagascar I interviewed Malagasy teachers and pupils who had participated in the mission's literacy work. A research assistant who was working as a teacher at the Lutheran school in Betafo, helped identify former teachers and pupils for interviews. The main aim was to find 10 former pupils on the basis of a class list, found in the archives, willing to tell me their life stories. The list was identified after I met someone on this list in Betafo willing to participate in the study and help me find former classmates. In the beginning, I planned to systematically search for every third or fourth pupil on the list so it would be a random choice. It was, however, a challenge to find people due to the fact that some had moved to other places, people did not know them, and some had died. I therefore ended up interviewing those people on the list who I was able to find, and in order to have 10, three new names were added from other lists where at least one of the first interviewees appeared. One consequence of this was that I did not talk with former pupils who lived far out in the countryside, but with those who local people knew about, and who lived nearby. I planned to interview five women and five men, but only three of the interviewees were women. I did not want to make the choice of anonymity before I had asked the pupils what they preferred. Only one wanted to be presented in the analysis with another name, but in the end

I chose to present everyone with fictitious names. This is because a life story can consist of sensitive information and they themselves did not have strong opinions about it.

Eight of the interviews took place in the home of the interviewees or in their yard, whereas I interviewed one at his working place, and one in the apartment I rented. Two of the interviewees still lived in the town of Betafo, five in villages nearby, two in the nearby town of Antsirabe, and one in the capital. The interviewees were asked to tell me about their life freely without any suggestion from me. Afterward, I asked them several questions concerning some of the issues that they had raised and especially concerning their experiences with literacy practices. Seven of the interviews lasted for about an hour, two for 1 and a half hours, and one for 40 minutes. They were done in Malagasy, recorded and transcribed. According to Amia Lieblich et al., personal stories are discovered as well as the context and social world of the interviewees through a life story approach (Lieblich, Zilber, and Tuval-Mashiach 1998: 8). In the process of constructing a life story, narrators grapple with two tasks: "telling a story of their being and development, and providing explanations as to how and why they have reached their present situation or identity" (Lieblich, Zilber, and Tuval-Mashiach 2008: 613). The life stories I collected provided me with information about the society in one of the places where the mission taught literacy. With a life story approach, in contrast to asking questions only about the period when the former pupils went to the mission school in Betafo, I gained insights into the importance the informants themselves put on the period when they attended the mission school, and its impact on them later in their lives. I said as little as possible about my research before the interview, to avoid leading the interviewees to focus too much on the period they went to the mission school.

The life stories were particularly valuable in reconstructing literacy practices. Barton and Hamilton have argued that a life history approach can provide a frame of analysis for people's experiences with literacy practices:

> A person's practices can be located also in their own history of literacy. In order to understand this we need to take a life history approach, observing the history within a person's life. There are several dimensions to this: people use literacy to make changes in their lives; literacy changes people and people find themselves in the contemporary world of changing literacy practices. The literacy practices an individual engages with change across their lifetime, as a result of changing demands, available resources and people's interests.
>
> (Barton and Hamilton 1998: 12)

The Norwegian mission collaborated and was challenged to different degrees by other missions and the colonial power. A main concern of this project is to compare the different literacies promoted by these institutions, along with their ideological embeddedness; in other words the world-views that influenced them. Some of the life stories show how former pupils in mission schools were taught different literacies and switched between them throughout their lives. The story of Olga, a former pupil in the mission school in Betafo, is a good illustration of this (Figure 3.1). Different institutions with different literacies had an impact on Olga's life. She attended Sunday school, and she also attended the mission's primary school in the village, even though her father was a teacher at a public school. She received a higher education within the educational structures of different churches before she got a job within educational institutions run by the government. In other words, her education through the missions gave her an opportunity to work as a teacher in public institutions. Consequently, even though literacies in these institutions were embedded in different ideologies, there were links between them that made it possible to use acquired literacies across institutions with different purposes.

I revisited the interviewees in March 2013 because I wanted to check my understanding of what they had said with them, but also for ethical reasons, that they should better understand the research they had

---

Olga was born in 1944, and was the oldest of eight siblings. Her father was in charge of a section at a public vocational training school. As a bureaucrat, he had access to newspapers at work and could bring schoolbooks back home. Her mother had attended the mission school in Betafo for 5 years as a child and subscribed to Lutheran magazines. Olga remembers that she brought her sisters and brothers to Sunday school. All of Olga's sisters and brothers went to school from the age of six due to their father's position as a bureaucrat. Moreover, the French administration did not accept that bureaucrats kept their children above the age of 6 away from school. The mission school was close to their home, and since their parents were Lutherans they wanted their children to go to this school. Olga went to the Norwegian mission's girls school in Antsirabe for her last years of primary school. She went to a private secondary school in Antananarivo and continued at a Protestant domestic training school for 3 years, and also studied at the Lutheran teacher training college in Antsirabe for two and a half years. For a long time, she searched for a position as a teacher and she also sent applications to Lutheran schools. Finally, she found a position at a private school where she worked for 4 years. She continued working as a teacher in public schools where she stayed until her retirement. She married at the age of 41, and had one child.

---

*Figure 3.1* Olga's story

Source: Former pupil Olga (2011)

been participating in. I showed them the part of the analysis where they were referred. This gave them an opportunity to see how their life stories were used in the research project, give me feedback and an opportunity to correct misunderstandings. I appreciated these second meetings, as I could discuss the results with them, share more of my own interest in the subject and have a conversation. I also felt the interviewees appreciated being informed about the study and not least see more concretely how I used the information they had given me. Meeting the interviewees who had told me their life stories for a second time created trust between us and made me, as a researcher, more convinced that I had understood well what they had told me.

In addition to the life story interviews with former pupils, I also interviewed five former teachers and eight former pupils at the mission school in Betafo. These interviews were done in Malagasy based on an interview guide, recorded, and at some later date notes were extracted from these recordings. I did not find it necessary to transcribe these interviews, and the number of 13 seemed to be sufficient since they were to be used as background informants and as additional informants to the life story interviews. These informants were also treated anonymously in the analysis. In addition, I conducted three interviews concerning the work of the Sunday school with a former Sunday school teacher in the Lutheran Church, concerning the Catholic school with the Catholic priest and concerning the history of the city of Betafo with an elder in the city of Betafo.

I sometimes received the phone number of potential participants in this study and could contact them by phone for a meeting. In other instances, I searched for them in their homes, or at the Lutheran school, and then made an appointment for the interview. If I was able to meet them in advance, I gave them information about the project. If I did not have the opportunity to meet with them first, they got the opportunity to read the description of the topics to be covered before the interview. Communication and getting in touch with people can be a challenge in Madagascar since not everybody has a phone, and if they do have one, their numbers are not necessarily listed on the internet or in a phone book. Due to the relatively short time I spent in Madagascar to collect both archival material and interviews, I sometimes had to take the opportunity to interview people when I had the chance without giving them time to refresh their memory first, which can be important when asking people about things that happened a long time ago.

According to Dunaway, "Ageing affects remembrance in subtle ways: some subjects can't recall certain events; some do not wish to; some do not even pretend to try" (Dunaway 1992: 42). Due to the age of my informants, with the oldest one being over 90 years old, some considerations had to be taken during the preparation and carrying out of interviews. The former missionaries were given an informed consent that described the research project and a semi-structured guide for the interview in suitable time before the interview took place. They got time to prepare themselves to remember as far back as to the 1950s and 1960s. Several gave me written answers to these questions, which on some occasions functioned well as a frame for the interview. From time to time, my interviewees introduced their answers with "I wonder if . . .", "I am not sure . . .", "Perhaps . . ." and "I cannot remember . . .". We talked about how accurate they themselves thought their memory was of the relevant period.

Graham Gardner argued that informants might have forgotten things that took place; they might also be lying or be unaware of important information; take information for granted; be unwilling to share information; and not be aware of the consequences of their previous actions (Gardner 2001). Informants also have specific motivations and capacities that need to be considered. Memory is, according to Gardner, a "living field" continually in process and affected by both internal thoughts and reflections, and the social world. This social world is partly affected by institutions and power mechanisms, which have to be kept in mind when analysing biographical material. This means that it is important to be aware that the data from the interviews are impacted by current reflections of the interviewees and experiences they have had after what we talked about took place. Texts based on interviews are therefore very different from letters, circulars and reports that were written when the events actually took place. The present motivations and capacities of former teachers, pupils and missionaries had to be taken into account during the analysis. One evident example is how the educational work of the mission was promoted, as mainly an instrument for evangelisation or as an instrument for development. During the 1920s, 1950s and 1960s, it was more acceptable to present the educational work of the mission, at least for mission supporters, as an instrument for evangelisation. After several decades of critics towards missionaries of how they were mixing evangelisation with development work, the way they, in reacting to this criticism, talked about their educational work changed. One of the former teachers told me for instance that when she was accused of being a cultural imperialist, she emphasised that missionaries had contributed to the promotion of the national language as the true instrument for reading and writing. With these considerations in mind, the conclusion is that the interviews contributed with important information about what took place in the mission schools, and about the current opinion of these informants on the mission's educational and literacy work.

## Analysing the Data Material

Before we read a text, we already have a pre-understanding, shaped by our traditions, culture and history. *Pre-understanding* and *pre-judgment* are important concepts taken from hermeneutics. We do not see an historical event objectively, but we see it from our own historical point of view (Gadamer 1989). Pre-understanding is essential to understanding; it is by the historical and linguistic situation that understanding first becomes possible. In other words, pre-understanding is necessary to understand. Pre-understanding might also lead to misunderstanding, if we do not question how our interpretations are coloured by our pre-understanding. My pre-understanding for doing this work is coloured by many factors. One important factor being my earlier and present relations with Madagascar and the mission. My parents worked for the NMS, and I was born and partly grew up in Madagascar. In addition, as an adult I did my master's thesis within human geography on the use of ethnicity in Malagasy politics, and I worked for 2 years as an educational officer in UNICEF, Antananarivo. Due to my background, I had a certain amount of knowledge about the Norwegian mission, Madagascar and education before I started working on this project. My background has been of considerable positive value to getting in contact with and access to relevant persons, both in Norway and Madagascar. My background knowledge of Malagasy history, culture and geography made it easier for me to find my way through the archival materials than if I had not such background. In addition, I have basic knowledge of the Malagasy language, which made it possible for me to read documents and do interviews in that language. I had, however, also to be aware of how my background impacted on the way I analysed the archival material and interviews, and how my background impacted on the interviewees and the information they gave me.

Being the daughter of missionaries, I had to be aware of the fact that former missionaries might look on me as an *insider* and tell me things that they would not tell other researchers. I believe that giving them written information on the research project and letting them read through the transcriptions after the interviews helped in dealing with this situation. Concerning the Malagasy pupils and teachers, I did not present myself as a daughter of missionaries, but due to the fact that I am Norwegian and speak Malagasy, this fact often was obvious to them. One consequence of this could be that some of the Malagasy interviewees avoided telling bad things about the mission's work. As my strategy was to say as little as possible before the interviews started, I did not tell the interviewees to be critical and not only share issues that put the mission in a positive light. The life-story approach was helpful in this regard as it was their stories that were in focus, and not the story of the mission. Even though they were mostly positive towards the mission school, some also revealed stories about physical violence, like beatings, that had happened in this school.

The emphasis in this research project is not to describe the literacy work of the mission based along a timeline, but to use a thematic analysis to describe different issues related to that work during specific periods. A consequence of this approach is that, in some paragraphs and chapters, I move between different periods of time while concentrating on a single issue. In my work with the archival material as well as transcriptions and notes from interviews, specific themes were put under subcategories such as language, content in school, relations with government, etc. with the help of a computer programme designed to assist in analysing qualitative data (NVivo). This helped me get an overview of the material and to quickly move between the texts searching for utterances on specific themes and issues.

In approaching the data material and in the analysis, I loosely draw on a discourse-historical approach (DHA) (Reisigl and Wodak 2009). I found parts of this discourse analytical approach relevant in order to answer my research question about how the mission negotiated their literacy work with the political power. This approach helped me to understand the mission's literacy work within its historical and political context and it also helped me analyse the ideological embeddedness of the literacies promoted through the mission schools. In the following, I will present some of the concepts that I found useful in this approach, and how I use them in my research.

According to Fairclough and Wodak, some principles of critical discourse analysis (CDA) have evolved that refer to language use seen as a form of social practice which implies "a dialectical relationship between a particular discursive event and the situation(s), institution(s) and social structure(s) that frame it: the discursive event is shaped by them, but it also shapes them" (1997:258 in Martin and Wodak 2003: 5). Discourses might therefore reproduce or transform social reality, including power relations between different social groups, and consequently they have major ideological effects. I use the concept discourse especially in Chapter 7, where I aim to examine my data material closely, mainly the text I found in the archival material. I try to analyse whether the texts were within or challenged the main ideology behind different institutions of literacy work, with a special attention to the Norwegian mission's literacy work. Ideologies (see Chapter 2, p. 19) are means of establishing, maintaining, but also transforming power relations through discourses by the use of language. *Power* is by DHA defined following Weber as "the possibility of having one's own will within a social relationship against the will or interests of others" (Weber 1980: 28 in Reisigl and Wodak 2009: 88). Discourses help to legitimise and de-legitimise power, and texts often illustrate the fight for power. *Discourses* are considered by DHA according to Reisigl and Wodak to be:

- a cluster of context-dependent semiotic practices that are situated within specific fields of social action;
- socially constituted and socially constitutive;
- related to a macro-topic; and
- linked to the argumentation about validity claims such as truth and normative validity involving several social actors who have different points of view.

(Reisigl and Wodak 2009: 89)

Since discourses are not fixed, but change over time, and when it is possible to identify dominant and alternative discourses, discourse is a helpful concept in an analysis of the history of literacy with a focus on the institutions providing literacy work, the relations between them, competition and cooperation. Texts, such as archival material, are related to a specific *genre*, and are part of discourses. Genre is defined by Fairclough as "a socially ratified way of using language in connection with a particular type of social activity" (Fairclough 1995: 14 in Reisigl and Wodak: 90). Exploring "how discourses, genres and texts change in relation to sociopolitical change" is an important task of DHA and it is also relevant for my study (Reisigl and Wodak 2009: 90). *Fields of action* is another concept used within DHA, which "indicates a segment of social reality which constitutes a (partial) 'frame' of a discourse" (Reisigl and Wodak 2009: 90). Used in my research, I identified the following fields of action related to the Norwegian mission's literacy work: administration, communication with mission supporters in Norway, relation with the government, relation with other mission organisations and relations with the local population (see Figure 3.3, p. 44). Regarding the French colonial power and the Malagasy government, I only focused on the field of action related to the official educational policy. In order to analyse how the Norwegian mission related to the colonial power in Madagascar, the institution which set the rules and policy on literacy work, it is necessary to understand the discourses that the literacy work of the mission and the French colonial power were built on. This research project does not perform a linguistic analysis, as is often done in DHA, but it analyses how utterances of different actors related to dominant and alternative discourses. The focus is on political events within different institutions in times of great socio-political changes relevant for literacy policies, such as the successions of different governors-general of the colonial government, the coming of independence, and decrees related to educational policy (Figure 3.2).

Madagascar is an interesting case to study the French colonial rule. The dominant and traditional educational policy built on French republican traditions was especially challenged in this context due to three important circumstances that impacted strongly on the way the colonial educational policy developed and was implemented. One circumstance was the predominance of Protestant mission schools in the pre-colonial era. A second important element was the existence and status of the written standard Malagasy language. In accordance with the French hegemonic assimilation discourse, the French language became the dominant LOI. Hegemonic here means the main discourse that ensured power to direct other institutions' educational and literacy work even though it at times was against these organisations' own objectives. A third circumstance was the dominant position of the ethnic group Merina. One argument against the use of the Malagasy language was that by using this written local language, built upon the dialect of the Merina, this ethnic

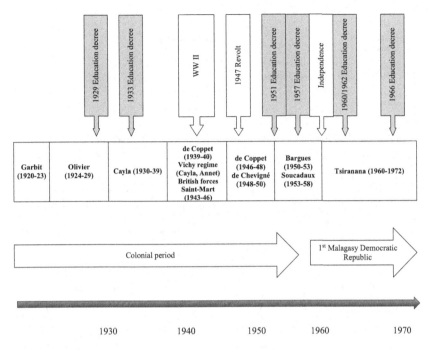

*Figure 3.2* Elements of the political context in Madagascar, 1920–1970

group would be favoured too much. The French colonial administration always had to have in mind how to deal with the dominant position of the Merina, especially regarding construction of elites. *La politique de races* (the race policy) was a policy by the colonists that built on the idea of splitting the population based on ethnic identity rather than unifying the population. Due to these contextual circumstances, I have identified *secularism/religion*, *language* and *identity* as important discourse topics in my analysis of mission and literacy in Madagascar (Figure 3.3).

Using some perspectives from the DHA helped me look at literacy as being shaped by different purposes, shifting to meet the social, political and religious context within which it had meaning. This approach was helpful in my intention to analyse the ideological embeddedness of the literacy work of the mission.

## Concluding Remarks

In this chapter, I have explained how my literacy research has a historical perspective. The intention is to make an analysis of literacies transmitted to children and youth through the Norwegian Mission's work in Madagascar, how the mission negotiated their literacy work with other

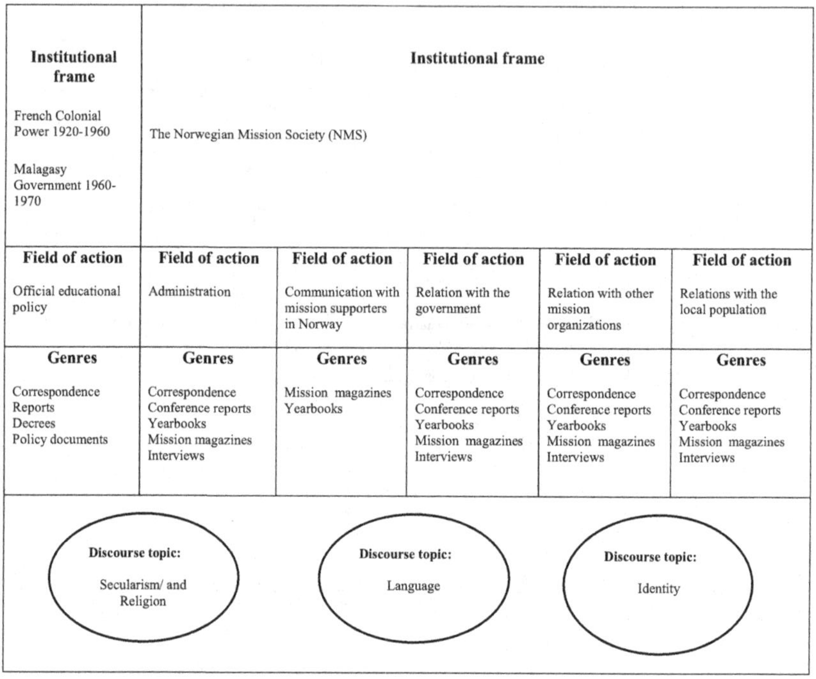

| Institutional frame | Institutional frame | | | | |
|---|---|---|---|---|---|
| French Colonial Power 1920-1960<br><br>Malagasy Government 1960-1970 | The Norwegian Mission Society (NMS) | | | | |
| **Field of action** | **Field of action** | **Field of action** | **Field of action** | **Field of action** | **Field of action** |
| Official educational policy | Administration | Communication with mission supporters in Norway | Relation with the government | Relation with other mission organizations | Relations with the local population |
| **Genres** | **Genres** | **Genres** | **Genres** | **Genres** | **Genres** |
| Correspondence<br>Reports<br>Decrees<br>Policy documents | Correspondence<br>Conference reports<br>Yearbooks<br>Mission magazines<br>Interviews | Mission magazines<br>Yearbooks | Correspondence<br>Conference reports<br>Yearbooks<br>Mission magazines<br>Interviews | Correspondence<br>Conference reports<br>Yearbooks<br>Mission magazines<br>Interviews | Correspondence<br>Conference reports<br>Yearbooks<br>Mission magazines<br>Interviews |

Discourse topic:

Secularism/ and Religion

Discourse topic:

Language

Discourse topic:

Identity

*Figure 3.3* Discourse analytical framework

Source: based on a figure in Reisigl and Wodak (2009: 91)

institutions and the effect this work had on the Malagasy society. For this purpose, I collected archival material and qualitative interviews as described in this chapter. In the following three chapters, I will, based on archival material and the case of Betafo, describe the physical and institutional literacy spaces and literacy practices promoted and experienced in mission schools during the periods under study, the mid-colonisation period (the 1920s) and independence (1951–1966). In Chapters 7 and 8, the emphasis will be on the ideological embeddedness of the literacies transmitted through the Norwegian mission in Madagascar. In this part, I will use concepts taken from the DHA, such as discourse and ideology, and focus on issues of secularism/religion, language and identity.

## Note

1. Based on Meling and Kjøllesdal (1977) and Danbolt (1948).

# 4 School Literacies During the Mid-Colonisation Period

The aim of this research is, as previously stated, to find out how the Norwegian mission negotiated their literacy work with the political powers in colonial and newly independent Madagascar. In this chapter, I focus on the period from 1920 to 1929 that I have called the mid-colonisation period. I will describe the political educational context in which the Norwegian mission operated their physical and institutional literacy spaces. Inspired by Street and Street, I understand physical and institutional literacy spaces as the physical building where teaching of literacy takes place as well as the social relations involved in literacy teaching, such as the rules for engagement between teachers and pupils within this physical building (Street and Street 1991). Consequently, I understand 'space' both in a physical and a metaphorical sense; that is, space understood as a frame for shaping social relations and expected forms of behaviour. I will try to answer whether the political context favoured or restricted the mission's engagement in literacy work.

I will also discuss the resources that were used in the mission's literacy work and which children and youth that had access to the mission's literacy programmes. Based on an ideological view of literacy, it is important to identify who initiated and owned the schools registered as Norwegian mission schools, and how they were managed. In the colonies of the British Empire, administrators often looked very favourably on the activities of mission schools (Etherington 2005b: 11). In South Africa, for instance, different missions controlled around 90% of indigenous education and they received financial support from the colonial government until the government took over mission schools in 1955 (Hodne 1997: 100, 166). In contrast, French colonial administrators were trained in a strong anti-clerical tradition. Therefore, the Norwegian mission's educational work in Madagascar depended heavily on motivation and economic support from the local Malagasy Lutheran congregations. In addition, the school had to demand school fees from their pupils. Not only did the French administration avoid financial support to educational mission work, they also put in place strict restrictions for literacy work. Let me use an example. Protestant missions found it practical to use church buildings as classrooms for teaching reading. This skill was necessary for Protestants to practice their religion. But, the secular colonial administration, which supported a separation of church and state, found this solution problematic and insisted teaching of reading and writing should take place in separate educational buildings. Later in this chapter, I will describe the missions' lobbying work for more flexible and predictable regulations of their institutions for literacy work.

Finally, in this chapter I will describe the literacies that the mission promoted through different educational institutions during the 1920s. The reason for the existence of mission schools was their eagerness to promote *religious literacies*. In addition, the mission schools promoted *French-assimilationist literacies* in order for their pupils to be accepted in the educational system, pass exams and receive public diplomas. An addition to this was the mission's focus on teaching the Malagasy language through which I have called *contextualised literacies*. This will be elaborated on page 64.

## Educational Institutions of the Mission

The mission had *primary* and *secondary schools*[1] leading to diplomas recognised by the colonial administration (Table 4.1). These institutions followed much of the same curriculum as schools governed by the colonial administration. The mission's *primary schools* led to the same primary school exam as that from colonial secular schools. They consisted of three sections lasting all together 5–6 years (NMS 1922: 157). Pupils had to pass an exam at every level to continue to the next level. Children in primary schools should preferably be offered teaching 5 hours 5 days a week (NMS 1924a: 94, Bjertnes 1923: 23). In some primary schools, there was one class in the morning (4 hours) and one in the afternoon (3 hours).

In addition, the mission had *bush* and *Sunday schools* (Table 4.1). *Bush schools* is my translation of *Garderies* in French, literally meaning a place where children are taken care of. The colonial administration accepted bush schools as a temporary solution until the missions became better acquainted with the educational regulations of the 1906 decree (see Chapter 1, p. 16). In contrast to primary schools, these schools used Malagasy as the LOI, and the teacher did not need a diploma obtained through the French system. The teacher's salary was lower than in primary schools, and it was often the catechist who was teaching as part of his job for the church. The aim of *bush schools* was to teach children to read and write in Malagasy, solve simple math problems, and give basic knowledge in Christianity (NMS 1922: 157–158). The colonial power considered the mission's bush schools to be temporary institutions since they did not contribute to educating the Malagasy population on French terms. They survived, however, throughout the entire colonial period.

Table 4.1 Educational institutions of the Norwegian mission in Madagascar

| Type of School | Physical Building | Teacher | Language | Certificate Provided |
|---|---|---|---|---|
| **Sunday school** | Church | Catechist | Malagasy | None |
| **Bush school** (elementary level) | School building | Proof that the teacher knows how to read and write | Malagasy | None |
| **Primary school** *Cours préparatoires* (CP) – 1 year *Cours élémentaires* (CE) – 2 years *Cours moyens* (CM) – 2 years | School building | Teacher exam required; Assistant teacher: CEPE or CESD Main teacher: CAE or BE | French and Malagasy | *Certificate de fin d'etudes primaires élémentaires* (CEPE) |
| **Secondary school** 6ième 5ième | School building | Teacher exam required: CAE or BE | French and Malagasy | Inter-missionary pedagogy exam *Certificat d'etudes Second degree* (CESD) |
| **Teacher training** 4ieme 3ième | School building | Teacher exam required | French and Malagasy | *Certificat d'Aptitude à enseigner* (CAE) *Brevet Elémentaire* (BE) |

According to the 1908 NMS conference report, every church should have a Sunday school led by a catechist (NMS 1908: 92–95). Further, teaching should be at least 2 hours weekly, primarily on Sundays, but also during the week, if possible. There should be examinations four times a year, and the churches, especially the women's organisations in the churches, should supply the material needed. All Christians with the right to have communion were obliged to send their children to Sunday school. Subjects were Bible stories, catechism, singing and reading the New Testament. The main goal of Sunday schools was to teach children Lutheran religion and faith, but also to teach those who did not go to primary or bush schools to read.

The Protestant missions tried to obtain support for alternative physical and institutional spaces (bush and Sunday schools) when they lost their opportunity to teach in churches, and did not have enough resources to meet the requirements of the educational policy to construct primary schools. Discussions around these issues illustrate very well how the literacies that the mission promoted were part of and thus shaped by their religion. But these were also influenced by the policies set by the colonial government and these policies were embedded in ideologies of republicanism and secularism. I will describe these cases later in this chapter. First, I will explain the colonial educational context.

## The Colonial Educational Context

The most important characteristic of the public educational structures in Madagascar during the colonial period was the division between what the colonial administration called *European* (for Europeans as well as well-assimilated Malagasy pupils) and *indigenous* education. The division between the two was not according to racial terms, as indigenous and Europeans went to the same schools (Colonie de Madagascar et Dépendances 1928). European children were allowed to go to indigenous schools in remote areas where there was no European school, and indigenous "youth who distinguished themselves with their intelligence" could go to European schools and "receive all the culture that corresponds with their skills" (Colonie de Madagascar et Dépendances 1928: 66, my translation). Nevertheless, in practice it was very difficult for indigenous children to enter European schools. European education consisted of three levels: elementary, primary and secondary. European elementary schools existed in 14 towns and primary schools in four towns. There were only two institutions at the secondary level, and these were located in the capital, *Lycée Condorcet* for boys and *Lycée Jules-Ferry* for girls. Where the European schools followed the same curriculum as the schools in the *metropole*,[2] the curriculum in indigenous schools was somehow adapted. Pupils in indigenous schools were for instance given slightly more time to learn French before it became the LOI. I will describe indigenous education in more detail, based on a description given by the director of education in 1922 (Renel 1922: 3–16).

Indigenous education was provided for free by the colonial state, and consisted of three levels. In 1922, there were 788 schools with about 83,500 pupils providing education at the first level (primary school) (Renel 1922: 19, 33). There were five different grades. Secondary level (2 years) was provided by 21 schools in different parts of the island with about 1,450 pupils. The third level was only provided by one school in the capital with 172 male pupils. These numbers show that primary education was not available to most of the population, and it was very few of those who passed primary school who could continue onto higher levels. Those who past to the second level within the indigenous educational system did not have access to more general education, such as the baccalaureate. They received a vocational education aiming mainly to provide teachers, doctors and bureaucrats for the colonial administration. French colonial educational policy in general has been described as assimilationist by many authors (e.g. White 1996, Clignet 1970: 438, Mumford 1935: 840). The existence of a separate educational system and the content of education indicates, however, that the French colonial educational policy was not purely assimilationist, especially when it came to structure and educational opportunities.

That education already from the first level in the indigenous system was an instrument in colonisation is clear from the following quotation taken from Renel. He explained that the teacher used all the occasions he had to: "make them understand the grandeur of France, the duties of recognition and the fidelity towards France and the French" (Renel 1922: 20, my translation). Primary education within the indigenous system was "adapted to the indigenous' intellectual development and according to their needs" (Renel 1922: 20, my translation). From the first years in school, French was the dominant LOI. Every day, pupils spent 90 minutes on practical work, and every school, except for those in the big cities, had an agricultural area. In some schools, pupils were even breeding animals. *Vocational education* was a preoccupation of the educational administration in order to "give the indigenous a taste of manual work and prepare for the colonisation, professional- and methodologically trained labour" (Renel 1922: 24, my translation). In some primary schools, there were also possibilities to learn carpentry work, and girls were trained in embroidery and sewing in addition to domestic work. As a result, education was gendered. It was different for men and women, girls and boys. At the end of primary level there was an exam in order to receive the *Certificat d'études du premier dégrée* (CEPE).

At secondary level in the indigenous system there were 15 regional schools with dormitories for boys (Renel 1922: 20–21, 33). A regional school for boys could have three sections: general, industrial (woodwork, iron, industrial drawing) and agricultural. The period of study was

3 years and the aim was to educate bureaucrats who were "necessary in the colonial enterprises" (Renel 1922: 20, my translation). The pupils, at a maximum age of 14, were recruited through competitions. The number of pupils was limited and "according to the needs of the administration and the colonisation" in order to "avoid the training of the declassed" (Renel 1922: 23, my translation). The purpose was avoiding educating more people than needed for the administration. When it came to the language "an important place is reserved to the study of the French language, which is the only language of instruction" (Renel 1922: 20, my translation). In addition to the principal, who was European, there were local Malagasy teacher assistants and one in charge (*contremaître*) of the industrial and agricultural sections.

For the girls, there were six regional domestic training schools (Renel 1922: 33). They learned embroidery in addition to other small-scale professions. The girls should also become familiar with the French language: "The French conversation occupied a large place of the general educational programme" (Renel 1922: 21, my translation). The female principal was European, and she had Malagasy teachers working at the school. At the end of secondary level, both boys and girls could take an exam to receive the *Certificat d'études du second dégrée* (CESD).

*Le Myre-de-Vilers* in the capital was the only third-level indigenous school. Students at *Le Myre* were recruited from the general education section in regional schools to one of four sections: *normal* for the education of teachers, *administrative* for the education of writers/ translators, secretaries and other administrative personnel, *topographic* in order to work with geometry and the *preparatory section for medical school* (Renel 1922: 21). Third level lasted only 1 year and, at the end of the year, pupils had to pass an exam in their respective sections in order to obtain an administrative position. *Le certificat d'aptitude à l'enseignement* (CAE) was given to future teachers. The test was to "ensure that the candidates have received sufficient pedagogical training and developed their knowledge of the French language" (Renel 1922: 22–23, my translation). There was a medical school that could be seen as a specialisation after the third level. Medical education, which produced *doctors* for the state service, was a priority for all colonial powers although not with full complete medical degrees (Kiwanuka 1970: 305–309).

The colonial administration ensured that pupils at Le Myre, who were to become the new elites of the country, came from all ethnic groups in the island. This was an important instrument in *La politique des race*.[3] This policy was based on an ideology promoting regionalism and fighting nationalism mainly through promoting the coastal population as a counterbalance to the Merina dominance. Before 1916, the third level lasted 2 years. This was reduced to 1 year to limit the time that youths from other regions would have to spend studying with intellectuals from the capital, who represented the majority of participants in the nationalistic rebellion VVS, discovered in 1913 (see Chapter 1, p. 16) (Esoaveloman-droso 1977: 247). These actions could not change the fact that, in the end, Le Myre educated both bureaucrats who tended to adopt the moral norms and disciplines of the colonial power, and critical thinkers who played a leading role in nationalistic movements.

One could argue, according to the vocational characteristics of indigenous education in Madagascar described previously, that the indigenous education was adapted from the European education. The assimilationist character of the system still remained strong through teaching French moral and civilisation and using French as the LOI. The use of the French language in favour of the standard Malagasy language was also based on an ideology of promoting regionalism to fight nationalism. The standard Malagasy is based on the spoken dialect of the Merina. Even though different dialects are spoken across the country, the official language has been considered as unifying for the Malagasy people. Sinfree Makoni and Alastair Pennycook have argued that languages are socially constructed, not real entities in the world to be explored and described, and many were invented as part of Christian, colonial and nationalistic projects (Makoni and Pennycook 2006: 1–3). This construction of languages is closely linked to identity and geographical location, and the way we define language and language policies create real effects in the world. The potential of the Malagasy language to feed a national identity was threatening for the colonial powers. Many administrators in the colonial administration therefore promoted the French language as the only option of schooling. This in spite of the opportunities for children to, for pedagogical reasons, use Malagasy.

The number of public schools expanded considerably under Renel as director of education from 1905 to 1925 (Renel 1922: 19, 33–34). In contrast, the number of mission schools decreased (458 in 1922). Table 4.2 shows statistical data of the educational work of the missions in 1925. Protestant schools counted a total of around 41,000 pupils, whereas Catholic schools had approximately 29,000 (Guitou 1925).

*Table 4.2* The educational work of the missions, 1925

|  | *Schools* | *Bush Schools* | *Pupils* |
| --- | --- | --- | --- |
| LMS | 78 | 47 | 10,988 |
| FFMA | 25 | 18 | 4,026 |
| MPF | 95 | 25 | 11,913 |
| NMS | 59 | 46 | 8,598 |
| Anglican | 39 | 38 | 5,771 |
| Protestants | 296 | 174 | 41,296 |
| Catholic | 216 | 69 | 29,113 |

Source: Guitou (1925)

If you compare this with the dominant position of Protestant mission schools in pre-colonial times, when LMS, the Quakers and the NMS had about 145,000 registered pupils whereas the Catholic mission had 27,000 (as was described in Chapter 1), this speaks strongly about the impact the colonial regime had on Protestant mission educational work. This could explain why Renel, director of education from 1905 to 1925, was described in NMS yearbooks as the worst and permanent enemy of the Norwegian mission in Madagascar (Bjertnes 1921: 77, 1923: 12, 1923b: 64).

## The Norwegian Mission's Literacy Spaces

As described in the introduction of this chapter, literacy spaces are understood as the physical buildings where teaching of literacy takes place as well as the social relations involved in literacy teaching. The physical and institutional spaces of the Norwegian mission where children and youth acquired reading and writing skills were Sunday schools, bush schools and primary schools.

How were these physical and institutional spaces for the mission's literacy work initiated and managed? Since 1908, the Norwegian mission organised the indigenous Lutheran church on three levels: the congregation, the parish and the district (Birkeli 1949: 220–221). District committees consisted of all pastors from the different parishes, the missionary in the area and two elected laymen from each parish. Schools should be located near the congregations and it was the responsibility of the district or the congregation to construct the school and provide a salary for the teacher. The district committee sent an application, approved by the Norwegian missionary in the area, to the Norwegian superintendent (NMS 1924a: 75, 94). The Norwegian Mission Conference made the final decision about sending the application to the government. According to the colonial policy, the application should be in the name of the future principal/teacher at the school, not in the name of the mission organisation. Teachers authorised by the government to run schools should not be legally bound to the mission (NMS 1933b: 160). This meant that the school was very much dependent on the teacher in whose name the school was erected. In this way, the mission could not fire the teacher without having to close down the school and send a new application to the government in the name of another teacher. In this way, the governmental regulations gave less power to the missions and more power to the teachers.

Norwegian teaching missionaries acted as principals in the schools on the main mission stations, like Betafo. They were usually single women with a teacher degree from Norway and an exam in French from France, which was required for principals in the French colonies (Bjertnes 1920: 52). Teaching missionaries, like the other missionaries, also learned and passed an exam in Malagasy. For the missionaries, the local language was, according to Otto Christian Dahl, their only channel of communication and the one and only way to enter into people's way of thinking (Dahl 1984: 2).

The aim of the Norwegian mission was to develop a Lutheran educational structure that was financed by the congregations, parishes and districts themselves (NMS 1924a: 94). School fees helped with paying the expenses. On the one hand, in order to recruit pupils in areas where people had low purchasing power, school fees had to be kept at a low level. On the other hand, low school fees meant that teachers received a low salary that could not compete with the salaries of public schools. In 1929, the salaries in public schools were about three times more than in the mission schools (NMS 1929: 33). In a context where educated teachers were few and wanted, due to the colonial teacher training system that only allowed a few to pass, this was a challenge and a great worry for the mission. The number of Norwegian mission schools and new teachers in the Highlands and the East Coast in the period from 1922 to 1929 are listed in Table 4.3:

In 1930, the number of new teachers was almost the same as the number of teachers who resigned from their positions (NMS 1930a: 149). Due to the difficulties of constructing school buildings and educating teachers, the mission stuck to Sunday schools in order to at least provide their congregation members with reading skills. If they managed to construct an educational building, but lacked educated teachers, bush schools were a better alternative. They had to fight, however, for these opportunities, as the colonial power aimed to slow down the mission's literacy work through governmental regulations. To illustrate this, I will in the following pages present the controversy about regulations in bush schools and the ban to teach reading in Sunday school.

*Table 4.3* Number of primary schools and new teachers in the Highlands and the East Coast, 1922–1929

| Year | Primary Schools | New Teachers |
| --- | --- | --- |
| 1922 | 44 | 12 |
| 1923 | 50 | 7 |
| 1924 | 50 | 10 |
| 1925 | 49 | 9 |
| 1926 | 47 | 7 |
| 1927 | 53 | 12 |
| 1928 | 55 | 3 |
| 1929 | 50 | 15 |

Source: NMS (1930a: 149)

## The Controversy About Bush Schools

As described in Chapter 1, the secular colonial administration put in place a decree with regulations for schoolwork in 1906. This decree also included regulations of bush schools. Bush schools were allowed for children under the age of 12 in areas where there was no private or public school or a bush school of another denomination within a radius of 6 km (Le Gouverneur Général de Madagascar et Dépendances 1906). An application to open a bush school had to be addressed to the provincial commissionaire, and the governor-general had to approve the decision. The following had to be attached to the application: a confirmation that the applicant (the teacher) was at least 20 years old, had a certificate of good conduct for the last 5 years, proof that the applicant knew how to read and write in Malagasy and a description of the school building. No pedagogical teacher qualification was required. One rule was clear: "Under no circumstances could private schools or bush schools be established in a temple or another place intended for worship" (Le Gouverneur Général de Madagascar et Dépendances 1906, my translation).

In 1920, the Protestant missions asked the government to loosen the regulations of bush schools (Devaux 1920). They proposed that the required distance between a bush school and a public school could be 3 instead of 6 km. The missions also wanted to be able to move their non-educated teachers around. As per the 1906 decree, bush schools were allowed to keep their non-qualified teachers as needed, but they were not allowed to move to another school. The intention was that they could run the bush schools until the missions had built up a larger pool of educated teachers within the French system. But, according to the educational administration, the missions did not aim to transform their bush schools into ordinary schools. Instead, they asked to multiply those institutions (Devaux 1920: 2). Different administrators put forth arguments to the governor-general in order not to accept the missions' request. Bush schools led by the catechist would only increase "religious propaganda without contributing to the educational work" (Machard 1920, my translation). Mission schools had a tendency to try to make their "religious propaganda work into a veritable educational work" (Renel 1921, my translation). What did "veritable", or put differently, *real* education work mean? From a perspective on literacy as embedded in ideologies, *real* education was rooted in French secular and republican ideology. The dominant literacy, presented as the one and only obvious education, was not neutral, but shaped by the colonial administration. This colonial administration was French. It had brought French secular educational traditions to Madagascar and formed this education into a colonial setting where it became an important instrument in the colonial project.

In a decree from February 1921, the distance between a new bush school and already-existing schools and bush schools was adjusted to 5 km (Garbit 1921). Changes of greater importance to the missions' bush schools did not come until 1923, and as a result of communication between the French Superintendent Gustave Stéphane Mondain and Governor-General Garbit. Mondain sent letters concerning the regulation of bush schools to the governor-general in March, April and May 1923 (Mondain 1923a, b, c). Mondain argued that due to the lack of governmental schools and the limitations placed on mission schools, the rate of illiteracy had gone up. The percentage of illiterates in the countryside in the Highlands had increased from 20% under the Merina regime to 50% under the French colonial administration. The existing regulations were unpredictable, as bush schools would be closed if a school was constructed in the area. He suggested that the government should guarantee that a bush school could exist for a minimum of 10 years even if a primary school was opened nearby. One mission's primary or bush school should not hinder the opening of a bush school of another denomination. In addition, the teacher's age limit should be the same as in primary schools (18 years).

In a letter to the governor-general, Director of Education Renel advised that none of these requests should be granted (Renel 1923a). Bush schools did not contribute to the fulfilment of the aims of French colonial educational policy. Reading the Bible in the dialect of the dominant ethnic group Merina and teaching pupils to read only in Malagasy were not educational aims within this policy and did not count as 'literacy' in the director's view. Renel also pointed to the secular nature of the colonial policy, which prevented them from adopting regulations to the needs of the missions. Renel did, however, agree to reduce the number of kilometres there should be between a primary or another bush school and a bush school (Renel 1923b). He proposed a 6-month time limit for a bush school to transform to a primary school after a primary school had been opened within a radius of 3 km. In the letter in the archive, there is also an additional comment in writing that teachers in bush schools should be able to read and write in French. This was not enforced, but if it had been enforced, it would have deprived the missions of most of their bush schools. As Renel looked on bush schools as only having the purpose of religious propaganda, he rejected most of Mondain's propositions, instead wanting stricter restrictions for the mission's bush schools.

In a note to the governor-general signed by Béréni in the office of Civil Affaires, Béréni seemed more willing to listen to the arguments presented by Mondain. After 15 years of experience, regulation of bush schools was not reasonable in a context with low levels of literacy, according to him (Béréni 1923). He was in favour of providing opportunities for people in remote areas to at least learn to read the Malagasy language and to get a taste of education, which indicates that he accepted reading and writing in Malagasy as a form of literacy. This is interesting, as here a French colonial administrator is acknowledging the missions' literacy work as an alternative to the dominant school literacy that should be in French. The result from this discussion was that it became possible to open bush schools at a distance of 5 km from a government-run school and 3 km from a mission school (Brunet 1923). If a government school was opened within a radius of 5 km, the bush school should disappear or transform itself into a primary school within 6 months. If a mission school was opened, the bush schools could continue, but no new bush school could be built within a radius of 3 km. Bush schools should be closed or transformed into primary schools within 10 years. In rare cases, it would be possible to prolong this period if closing the bush school would deprive the population of the opportunity to be educated. The regulations to open a bush school were more or less kept as before. It was now noted, however, that the applicant (the teacher) had to know how to read and write, but without specifying if it was in Malagasy or French. In addition, the new regulations stated that students above the age of 18, who had finished 1 year of teacher training, could be teachers in bush schools, even if they had not yet reached the age of 20.

These modifications represented some relief for the Norwegian mission (Bjertnes 1923b: 64). The fact that they did not need to close bush schools after the establishment of a mission school of another denomination was a relief. This had been a problem related to competition between different missions. Previously, if for instance the Catholic mission constructed a primary school nearby a Lutheran bush school, the bush school would have to close down. As a consequence, the missions could strategically, due to the competition between Catholic and Protestant missions that will be explained in Chapter 7, construct primary schools where others already had a bush school in order to attract pupils and possibly church members to their congregations. This made it difficult to plan and invest in educational work. Whereas the bush schools represented 46% of the total number of the Norwegian mission schools and 20% of students in 1920, they represented 61% of the schools and 39% of the students in 1950 (NMS 1970: 140, 1952c, b, a, 1921, :statistical attachment). Looking at these statistics, it is clear that creating bush schools became an important strategy for the Norwegian mission when facing governmental regulations for primary schools, as explained in Chapter 1. Educating teachers was a challenge throughout the entire period, and since teachers who did not master French-assimilationist literacies (see p. 46) could teach in bush schools using their own language, bush schools were seen as successful transmitters of religious literacies (see p. 59). Also other Protestant missions and the Catholic mission had bush schools and constructed new ones during this period. The government presented the modifications described previously as a replacement of the ban from 1906 to teach reading in Sunday schools (Bjertnes 1923a).

That was another dispute between the missions and the colonial administration at the beginning of the 1920s.

## The Ban on Teaching Reading in Sunday School

As explained in Chapter 1, the mission lost many of its schools due to the 1906 decree. This led to a renewed interest in Sunday schools where they could reach children and youth (NMS 1970: 172, Bjertnes 1923: 12). The 1906 decree forbid, however, teaching of reading in church buildings where Sunday schools took place. At the start of the 1920s, it became evident that in certain regions illiteracy was growing. The Norwegian mission observed that other missions started to use, despite the decree, their church buildings for educational purposes (Bjertnes 1923: 12). They chose to do the same. In 1922, the French NMS missionary Abel Parrot received a letter from the local administrator insisting on the ban to teach reading in churches (Parrot 1922). He asked the NMS superintendent, Bjertnes, what to do. As explained earlier, enhancing reading skills was necessary for the mission. Since there were no schools in many of the places where the mission worked, this ban became a question of "life or death". Parrot wrote, "if evangelical Christians cannot read and do not read the Bible, it is finished" (Parrot 1922, my translation).

In cooperation with the other Protestant missions, Bjertnes fought to change the regulations. It was a long process. He started by seeking advice from the superintendent of the French mission, Mondain, but he was not willing to challenge the government on the issue (Bjertnes 1923: 12–17). He then, on his own initiative, sent a letter to the governor-general asking for permission to teach reading in religious schools for 2 hours a week in areas were no other school existed (Bjertnes 1922). Through the mission's yearbook, he explained to missionary friends in Norway how he had pointed out for the governor-general that Protestants built their religion on reading the Bible and that "Reading skills are, in other words, a question of life in the practice of our religion" (Bjertnes 1923: 14, my translation).

Governor-General Garbit showed some understanding, but he could not give in to Bjertnes's demand. Bjertnes then brought the issue to the local Inter-missionary Protestant Committee (IPC). With the exception of the French superintendent, its members agreed to promote the case. The missions were nervous due to rumours that Director of Education Renel put pressure on the governor-general to send a circular asking all local administrators to reinforce the ban to teach reading in church buildings. The IPC managed to hinder this through meetings with the governor-general (Bjertnes 1923: 16). They also sent a letter to the governor-general asking for permission to teach reading through religious education for children under the age of 14 outside school hours in places where there were no schools (IPC 1922a). The governor-general's answer included a number of conditions, such as the age (excluding school-aged children), the distance to the nearest public school and the time for teaching (days with official education and between 7 a.m. and 5 p.m. should be avoided): They were also obliged to inform the government about these kinds of activities (Bjertnes 1923, Garbit 1922: 16). Garbit underlined in his response that reading the Bible was considered a cultural activity that was not forbidden. There was, however, a difference in reading the Bible and teaching to read the Bible. Teaching literacy skills should be done in regular schools, and not in church buildings. This is a clear indication that the government searched to define and control what was to count as literacy education or, as Street and Street call it, what was to count as school literacy. Teaching reading skills was to take place only in specific physical and institutional settings according to specific regulations issued by the government. This conflict illustrates well the ideological embeddedness of literacy. The purposes for literacy teaching are not neutral, but in the case of the mission's literacy work the purposes were part of on the one hand the mission's goals and on the other the colonial administration's aims for education. The institutions who offer literacy teaching have in mind goals for that teaching. The example with the ban to teach reading in Sunday schools illustrates clearly the conflicting goals for literacy education of the mission and the colonial administration.

The Protestant missions could not agree to the governor's conditions, and they decided to reply. They stated that it should be accepted to educate people above school age whenever and wherever they wanted, as people above school age were not under the colonial school law (Bjertnes 1923: 17, IPC 1922b). They also insisted on the fact that in places more than 5 km away from an official school, they should be able to teach children below this age during the whole day. Reading was a part of religious practice, they argued, and they only taught these skills where the government had not yet been able to provide schools. In their reply, the missions tried to define literacy as a religious practice to avoid conflict with educational authorities and their regulations. The answer from the governor was negative again (Garbit 1923). To reintroduce education in churches, a practice that was common before the French colonial power came to the island, would be in opposition to secular educational regulations.

It was not until 1924, when Bjertnes again brought the case to the new governor-general, Olivier, and his state-secretary, Berthier, that the missions were allowed to teach literacy in church buildings (Berthier 1924: 317). The first permission was limited to teaching children above the age of 10 and only outside working hours. This improved the mission's opportunities for literacy work and contributed to enhanced reading skills among children and youth in the mission's congregations. In 1920, the NMS had 856 Sunday schools with 26,312 children, 33% of whom were literate (NMS 1921, : statistical attachment). Even though a large part of these children also went to primary and bush schools, some children also acquired reading skills through Sunday schools. In 1950, the number of Sunday schools had reached 1,309 with 39,818 children, 41% of which had acquired reading and writing skills (NMS 1952a, b, c: statistical attachment). In 1969, the number of children attending Lutheran Sunday schools was 66,901 (NMS 1970: 139).

I have now presented the physical and institutional literacy spaces in the mission's work, and it is clear that these spaces were contested during the 1920s. This contributed to change the context where the missionaries were working. The cases of the bush school and the Sunday school are interesting, as they illustrate well how important teaching reading skills was to the Norwegian missionaries. They show how the missionaries searched for alternative spaces to teach these skills and how they pursued their interests through political lobbying. Another important question is the content and what children were taught when they came to these institutions. I will proceed to describe the kind of literacies that were promoted through primary, bush and Sunday schools during the 1920s.

## Literacies in Sunday School

The mission was first and most interested in promoting *religious literacies*, meaning social practices involving religious texts with the aim of religious learning and conversion. Religious literacy practices are not only about reading, but singing, worshipping and praying, often involving more "emotional and embodied forms of meaning-making" (Papen 2017: 13). The Norwegian mission promoted religious literacy practices both through schools and through religious training in church, which contributed in different ways to children's literacy learning.

Sunday schools were important to promote religious literacies. This was the case for children who went to public schools, Lutheran or other mission schools, as well as those who did not go to school. Important reading materials in Sunday school were the Bible, catechism, a book with Bible stories and the songbook (NMS 1921: 133–137, 1920: 159). Before the mission got their own Sunday school magazine with four pages twice a month in 1935, they used other missions' magazines, like a Quaker magazine that came out once a month (NMS 1935: 86–89, Schaanning 1922).

Circulars signed by the NMS superintendent, aimed at employees in the Lutheran church during the 1920s and 1930s, prove how the mission promoted literacies in Sunday school similar to school literacies (see Chapter 2, p. 24). Sunday schools were expected to teach reading skills and arrange examinations prepared by the priest on what had been taught from the Bible and the catechism in Sunday school (NMS Superintendent 1927–1939). In 1922, Ole Strand, missionary in Betafo, reported that the best result from the Sunday school exam in the district that year was from a village without any schools (Strand 1923). This shows that learning effects could be quite important in Sunday schools. Strand added that the increased number of Sunday schools had contributed to increased reading skills. From the data material it is clear that it was reading skills that were important to teach in Sunday school, not necessarily writing skills. This is for instance illustrated by the quotation from the letter Bjertnes wrote to the governor-general at the start of this book where he presented reading skills as a matter of life and death for them as Christians. Sunday schools were different from place to place, and the result was very much dependent on the skills and abilities of the Sunday school teacher. In places where children also went to regular schools, it was difficult to measure what children actually learned in Sunday schools.

The ABC-book, a primer printed by the Norwegian mission's printing press, was used in Sunday schools to teach children to read. It was a little book starting with the vowels and ending with little stories (Danbolt 1929). On the cover, you could find the Ten Commandments, the Lord's Prayer and a multiplication table, which is a good illustration of material used in religious literacies. The book was popular and the printing press published 194,500 copies during the 1920s. In the 1930s, the mission revised it based on a specific method using statistical research to find the most common words in Malagasy (Stolee 1951). In 1940, the printing press published two thousand copies of the first edition for adults. This version was transformed into a wall chart during the war and 1,800 copies were published. A new edition appeared in 1946 (10,000 copies) and in 1949 the mission needed another 30,000 primers for use in the mission's literacy work.

In a letter the missionary wife Hanna Levinsen sent to the children's magazine of the mission, we can read about the role Sunday schools in remote areas played in promoting religious literacies (Levinsen 1926). A girl around 8 years old named Kolo came to Levinsen's house to buy the primer. Kolo told the missionary that she intended to learn to read in Sunday school. Her father was not Christian, but nevertheless wanted her to learn. Kolo bought the book and went "proudly away with her first book" (Levinsen 1926, my translation). The next time Levinsen met Kolo she had already learned the First Commandment, and she brought other children to the Sunday school. Levinsen reported that four teachers were teaching 85 children reading, writing and arithmetic every Sunday, Wednesday and Friday. Children as well as adults in the village started to have an interest in reading. Levinsen underlined that if children did not go to school, it was the Sunday school's task to teach them to read. Another illustration of children learning to read in Sunday school was the story of two former pupils at the mission school I met during my fieldwork in Betafo. They were born around the 1920s in a remote rural village. They described what they used to do in Sunday school:

FORMER PUPIL 6: We had that thing from the mission. The big paper with something written on it. The thing with letters. And that's what we used to learn to read in Sunday school. Especially in the countryside, but here in the city I don't think we did that. In the countryside there was a big paper that they bought from the mission.

FORMER PUPIL 5: The alphabet like A, B, D.[4]

FORMER PUPIL 6: And that's what they taught us. . .

FORMER PUPIL 5: Yes, we knew how to read from Sunday school before we came here [the mission school in Betafo]. They taught us one by one like they taught me and then you . . . One by one we learned to read in Sunday school. So we knew to read, but not good, before we came here.

(Former female pupil 5 2011, Former female pupil 6 2011, my translation)

These women remembered that sometimes the missionary living in Betafo came to visit. They had to learn things by heart, and if they managed to do their homework well, they got small pictures of Jesus. That made them very happy. Because of Sunday school, these women had started to learn to read before they became pupils at the mission's school in Betafo, where they lived at the dormitory. These accounts illustrate that people were interested in learning to read and that the mission promoted literacy learning in remote areas through making available reading books and teaching reading. This was an important opportunity in areas without schools. When villagers learned to read, these skills could be useful in various settings. From an ideological perspective, it is, however important to highlight that the way reading was taught, in which places and to whom, contributed to promoting the mission's aim of evangelisation, which will be explained in Chapter 7. I will now give some examples of how religious literacies were promoted in the bush and primary schools of the mission.

## Literacies in Bush and Primary Schools

Religious literacies occupied an important part of the school programme. The following quote is taken from an article written by teaching missionary Schaanning in 1921 aimed at mission supporters in Norway. It illustrates the crucial presence of the Lutheran religion in the school programme of the mission schools:

The Norwegian mission has not *a single* school in Madagascar where religion is not taught: and why would we need such schools! The government has never forbid us to teach religion in the schools and has never occupied itself with our schedules. It demands that French is taught and apart from that we can teach whatever we want [original italics].

(Schaanning 1921: 50, my translation)

In this quote Schaanning highlights the two-fold educational strategy of the mission: to teach Christianity and to teach common knowledge as defined by the French colonial educational policy.

The programme of mission bush schools from 1922 confirms the dominance of the Malagasy over the French language. It also shows the importance of the Lutheran religion (Figure 4.1) (NMS 1922a: 8). Ordinary school days, 4 days a week, always began with a 15-minute morning devotion. The catechism (*fotopianarana*) was taught in separate lectures for 30 minutes 2 days a week and there was singing and learning of hymns (*Hira sy Solfa*) for 30 minutes 3 days a week.

The subjects taught at the mission primary schools were based on the official curriculum, with Malagasy and Christianity as additional subjects. The subjects were the following: Christianity, catechism, Bible stories, hymnals, as well as secular subjects such as reading, writing, arithmetic, geography, Malagasy grammar and French (NMS 1924a: 94, Bjertnes 1923: 23, NMS 1922). According to the programme of mission primary schools in 1922 (Figure 4.2), the day began with a 15-minute morning devotion followed by 30 minutes of religious studies, where Bible stories

Garderie (mpampianatra iray, fizarana roa).

| | | ALATSINAINY | TALATA | ALAROBIA | ALAKAMISY |
|---|---|---|---|---|---|
| 8—8.15 | | *FIVAVAHANA* | | | |
| 8.15—8.45 | Fizarana I<br>Fizarana II | Tantara | Tantara | Tantara | Tantara |
| 8.45—9.15 | Fizarana I<br>Fizarana II | Vakiteny malagasy<br>Soratra | Vakiteny malagasy<br>Sary | Vakiteny malagasy<br>Soratra | Vakiteny malagasy<br>Sary |
| 9.15—9.45 | Fizarana I<br>Fizarana II | Soratra (copie)<br>Vakiteny malagasy | Fotopianarana | Soratra (copie)<br>Sora-tononina malag. | Fotopianarana |
| 9.45—10.15 | Fizarana I<br>Fizarana II | Marika an-tsoratra<br>Marika am-bava | Marika an-tsoratra<br>Marika am-bava | Marika an-tsoratra<br>Marika am-bava | Marika an-tsoratra<br>Marika am-bava |
| 10.15—10.45 | Fizarana I<br>Fizarana II | Marika am-bava<br>Marika an-tsoratra | Marika am-bava<br>Marika an-tsoratra | Marika am-bava<br>Marika an-tsoratra | Marika am-bava<br>Marika-an-tsoratra |
| 10.45—11 | | *FAKAN-DRIVOTRA* | | | |
| 11—11.30 | Fizarana I<br>Fizarana II | Soratra<br>Vakiteny malagasy | Soratra<br>Vakiteny malagasy | Soratra<br>Vakiteny malagasy | Soratra<br>Vakiteny malagasy |
| 11.30—12 | Fizarana I<br>Fizarana II | Sary<br>Teny frantsay | Soratra<br>Teny frantsay | Géographie | Soratra<br>Teny frantsay |
| 12—12.30 | Fizarana I<br>Fizarana II | Vakiteny malagasy<br>Soratra frantsay | Vakiteny malagasy<br>Soratra malagasy | Vakiteny malagasy<br>Soratra frantsay | Vakiteny malagasy<br>Soratra malagasy |
| 12.30—1 | Fizarana I<br>Fizarana II | Géographie | Hira sy Solfa | Hira sy Solfa | Hira sy Solfa |

*Figure 4.1* Schedule in bush schools with one teacher and two classes, 1922
Source: NMS (1922a: 8)

Ecole Primaire (1 maître. 3 divisions)

| | | LUNDI | MARDI | MERCREDI | JEUDI | VENDREDI |
|---|---|---|---|---|---|---|
| 8-8.15 | | | | CULTE | | |
| 8.15-8.45 | 3ᵉ div. | Histoire Sainte | Catéchisme | Histoire Sainte | Catéchisme | Histoire Sainte |
| 8.45 à 9.15 | 1ᵉʳᵉ div. 2ᵉ div. 3ᵉ div. | Lecture malgache Devoir de calcul Devoir de calcul | Lecture malgache Devoir de calcul Devoir de calcul | Lecture malgache Devoir de calcul Dessin | Lecture malgache Devoir de calcul Devoir de calcul | Lecture malgache Devoir de calcul Devoir de calcul |
| 9.15 à 9.45 | 1ᵉ div. 2ᵉ div. 3ᵉ div. | Ecriture Lecture malgache et Grammaire | Géographie | Ecriture Lecture malgache et Grammaire | Géographie | Ecriture Lecture malgache et Grammaire |
| 9.45 à 10.15 | 1ᵉ div. 2ᵉ div. 3ᵉ div. | Dessin Calcul écrit et oral Calcul oral et écrit | Ecriture Dictée malgache | Dessin Calcul écrit et oral Calcul oral et écrit | Ecriture Dictée malgache | Dessin Calcul écrit et oral Calcul oral et écrit |
| 10.15 à 10 45 | 3ᵉ div. | Jardin (couture) | Leçon de choses | Gymnastique (couture) | Leçon de choses | Jardin (couture) |
| 10.45-11 | | | | RÉCRÉATION | | |
| 11 à 11.30 | 1ᵉ div. 2ᵉ div. 3ᵉ div. | Repétition Langage Traduction | de la 1ᵉ trimestre Traduction | Lecture Exercices de gram. | du matin lecture Traduction | (Moniteur) 2ᵉ trimestre Traduction |
| 11.30 à 12 | 1ᵉ div. 2ᵉ div. 3ᵉ div. | Copie de la lecture Ecriture et copie Lecture française | Copie de la lecture Ecriture et copie Dictée française | Copie de la lecture Ecriture et copie Lecture française | Copie de la lecture Ecriture et copie Dictée française | Copie de la lecture Ecriture et copie Lecture française |
| 12 à 12 30 | 1ᵉ div. 2ᵉ div. 3ᵉ div. | Calcul Dessin Devoir sur la lecture | Devoir de calcul Sys. mét. oral et écrit. | Calcul Dessin Composition malg. | Devoir de calcul Sys. mét. écrit et oral | Calcul Dessin Devoir sur la lecture |
| 12.30 à 1 h. | 1ᵉ div. 2ᵉ div. 3ᵉ div. | Chant et Solfège | Chant et Solfège | Devoir de calcul Calcul oral Composition malg. | Chant et Solfège | Chant et Solfège |

*Figure 4.2* Schedule in primary schools with one teacher and three levels, 1922

Source: NMS (1922: 5)

and the catechism were the most important content (NMS 1922: 5). There was singing (*Chant et Solfège*) for 30 minutes 4 days a week. It is difficult to say which language was used in the different subjects, but the Malagasy language was mostly used in describing the content of different subjects, which indicates that this was considered the LOI (NMS 1922). At the third level, French dictation is mentioned 2 days a week (30 minutes each) and reading French 3 days a week, followed by exercises relating to the text 2 days a week. This indicates that learning French was not supposed to occupy much of the timetable in the first levels, compared to public schools. These schedules show how much time was supposed to be given to different subjects in mission schools. Which practices actually took place is more difficult to answer here since this is a reconstruction of literacies promoted in mission schools, based on archival material.

Schoolwork was of interest to the mission as long as they could teach Lutheranism. The secular colonial power allowed mission schools to do so as long as they contributed to the assimilation project by teaching a French curriculum that included French history, geography, culture and the French language. Education should make sure that candidates mastered *French-assimilationist literacies*. This was important in order to teach pupils with an aim to obtain diplomas, but also in order to educate teachers who could help expand Lutheran educational work and religious literacies. Qualified teachers were needed by the mission. In this way, the mission's primary and secondary schools, as well as their teacher training colleges, became promoters of French-assimilationist literacies. They worked hard to master those literacies and equip their students with officially recognised diplomas. Examinations are typical school literacy practices, in which pupils are measured with respect to how they comply with certain norms based on certain forms of literacies, in this case French-assimilationist literacies (see p. 24). Passing school exams was important for pupils in order to proceed to the next level or to obtain a diploma. Mission schools were, however, behind public schools with regard to educational results complying with the norms of the ruling power. This can be due to the fact that their curriculum also focused on other subjects than the French curriculum. But, mission schools were considered among the schools in the educational system in Madagascar and they were for instance invited to and participated in events that clearly honoured the history of the French colony, such as the military parade on the French national day or the honouring of former governors-general (L'Administrateur en chef des Colonies 1923, Machard 1923). Being an institution that provided education and literacies through educational institutions in this colonial context, the mission became, although not intentionally, a transmitter of a colonial ideology.

At the same time, the missionaries talked about their schools as more national or Malagasy than public schools. The concept that I use for the more adapted approach of the mission's literacy work is *contextualised* literacies. According to the *Oxford Dictionaries*, to contextualise means to study in context and take into account: "The circumstances that form the setting for an event, statement, or idea, and in terms of which it can be fully understood" (Oxford Dictionaries 2015). Even though the missions' literacies were mainly Lutheran, and therefore often universal and decontextualised in its content (the Protestant faith), the mission also promoted contextualised literacies. These literacies were, however, still part of the wider set of literacies brought to Malagasy children and adult learners by the mission. This concept should therefore not be confused with Street's focus on culturally sensitive literacy practices that attempt to focus on how people viewed as *illiterates* actually make "significant use of literacy practices for specific purposes and in specific contexts" (Street 2009: 24). Neither should it be confused with *local* or *vernacular literacies*, that are "the ways 'ordinary' people use reading and writing and the theories of literacy they hold" (Papen 2005: 49). My intention in referring to contextualised literacy practices is to show how the mission promoted literacies in Malagasy using the Malagasy contexts, villages, rice fields, geography, etc. as they were preoccupied with a concern that people should understand the content and the message.

Teaching missionary Schaanning pointed to the mission as having a "national-cultural assignment" due to its use of Malagasy as an LOI, compared to its use in public schools. She explained that they had Malagasy reading and Malagasy as a subject until the highest levels. In contrast, in public schools, most of the teaching, even the first teaching in reading, was in French. At a higher level, however, mission schools also had a lot of French teaching due to its position in society (Schaanning 1921: 52–53). Pointing to the importance of having access to literacy in one's own language, Schaanning was convinced that "if a people shall be able to fulfil their role in the larger society, it needs to be itself, which also include to know oneself" (Schaanning 1921, my translation). Schaanning argued that the different missions, both Protestant and Catholic, could take the honour for saving Malagasy history, tales and legends. The missions published adapted books where children could read about their own context:

> It is a pleasure to see with what cheers the children recognise things in these little books, which in their own language speaks to them about father and mother back home, about herding in the field outside the village, about the bulls of the boys and the little girls playing "father and mother", about rice pounding and planting, about getting grass for the fire and about going to the market when the market day is coming, and further about the mountains and valleys of Madagascar, about animals in the wood and on the fields.
>
> (Schaanning 1921, my translation)

Schaanning emphasised that every mission school had Christianity as a subject taught in Malagasy using Malagasy books. In addition to the Bible, they had a book in Malagasy about Bible stories and one that explained Luther's catechism. Some of the books referred to a Malagasy context, something that was not common in the schoolbooks used in the governmental schools which referred to the French context only. There were also questions in the books aiming to give an alternative to the culture of learning things by heart without understanding what was read. The mission wanted people to understand the message, and this was why they promoted contextualised literacies. In another article, Schaanning wrote about what children at her school were reading, most of which was published by the mission's own printing press (Schaanning 1922). She mentioned several stories in particular: among others, one story was about the Malagasy martyrs written by a Malagasy pastor, while another was a songbook for children and other tales and legends written down by missionaries. Schaanning's article shows that in the mission schools, the children engaged in a variety of literacies, many being Lutheran literacies, others being more typical school literacies, but contextualised in their content. Some books were also translated, which means the language was contextualised, but not the content. *Robinson Crusoe* was one such book which Schaanning's pupils preferred. It had been translated by a Malagasy teacher and was used as a reading book in schools. *Robinson Crusoe* was published for the first time in 1921, and reprinted in 1928 with 9,000 copies (Danbolt 1929). The moral of the story was that, in order to have a good life, one had to honour one's father and mother, as written in the Fourth Commandment. This showed that even though there were both secular and religious Malagasy books, the books that the missions made available to their pupils had been deliberately chosen. It was part of their wider literacy project and ideology and as exemplified by the story about Robinson Crusoe, the content was interpreted accordingly to Christian morals.

With regard to the school plan of 1922, it was clearly stated that Malagasy should be used everywhere possible (NMS 1922a, b: 157). Since teachers received their education in French, it was a challenge to transmit their knowledge in Malagasy, as they often were tempted to use French words. Büchsenschütz was a French pastor working as a missionary for the NMS in Madagascar in the period from 1903 to 1948, and he played an important role in the mission's educational work. He held the position as director of the teacher training college in Antsirabe. He also worked as a pastor in different districts and as acting superintendent of the mission in the periods from 1935 to 1937 and 1941 to 1948. At the NMS Mission Conference in 1930, he emphasised that it was a challenge to use Malagasy as the LOI (NMS 1930a: 147). Even though he admitted that teaching in French in public schools helped pupils pass exams, he was very clear that the use of French as the LOI in the first classes of school was not the correct pedagogical methodology:

> Another reason is that children in other schools are taught in French from the first grades. French is used as language of instruction, which gives the pupils a big advantage and a big skill. But this method is objectionable and we forbid our teachers in the first classes in Antsirabe to follow it. Teaching will be given in the mother tongue, and the children shall learn to use the Malagasy language. We will rather renounce on some skills in French than to buy it for this price. The pupils will later be rewarded through a healthier development.
>
> (NMS 1930a: 147, my translation)

It is difficult to know what Büchsenschütz meant by "healthier development", but in connecting pupils' learning in Malagasy to a healthier development, there is no doubt that he recognised the importance of using pupils' mother tongue for various reasons.

To illustrate that literacies promoted through the mission schools were different from those in public schools, I will here include a story about a native teacher written in 1925 by teaching missionary Dorthea Rugset in NMt (Rugset 1925). The article shows how religious literacies represented something specific to the mission, which was not acknowledged by the official colonial state or by local customs. It also shows that pupils were faced with different literacies in different institutions. It is important to keep in mind that this was an article within the genre intended for mission supporters in Norway. It is also important to note that the teacher that Rugset told about in the text, whose name was not mentioned in the article, exposed his life by remembering certain things from that life giving a particular meaning to the story. According to the local traditional healer, the teacher was born on an evil day, and should therefore be given away, or that the healer could help to change his future with a good one. His parents kept him, however, because they were Christians and his father worked as a catechist for the Norwegian mission. The teacher, cited by Rugset, remembered the first New Testament with hymnals that he was given:

> I loved it and I wanted to get to know it. When I started school, I brought it with me and thought that I was going to learn it there. Unfortunately, the mission does not have a school out in the countryside where we live. I had to go to the school of the government, and I did not have any use of it there.
>
> (Rugset 1925, my translation)

Reading texts from the Bible was not part of literacy practices at the public school. The first time this teacher wanted to enter the teacher training college of the mission, he failed due to missing knowledge in Bible stories. He entered the school the following year, but failed the yearly exam. He wanted to quit his studies, as people in his village and the traditional healer tried to convince him that he was a failure because he was born on an evil day. The missionaries convinced him to come back to the college, and after some years, he became a teacher who had learned to master both religious and French-assimilationist literacies and could contribute in the mission's educational work.

## Concluding Remarks

This chapter has focused on the physical and institutional literacy spaces, the public educational structure and the mission's contributions within this structure during the mid-colonisation period. It has described the resources that were applied in literacy work when it comes to administration of Sunday, bush and primary schools. The mission's education had to be in line with local educational policies. It was in their interest that their schools provided officially recognised educational diplomas. The opportunities given to mission organisations for teaching literacy depended on the colonial powers and their policies. This means that the mission could not use their resources in any way they wanted.

The 1920s is an interesting period in the Malagasy history of education due to policies that were challenging French republicanism and secularism. Director of education until 1925, Renel represented the classical approach to French colonial education. There were government regulations regarding the physical and institutional spaces intended for teaching reading and writing skills that the missions had to adhere to. Bush and Sunday schools became important alternatives of the missions when the French-assimilationist and secular policy made it challenging to run primary mission schools at the start of the century. But, also in these literacy spaces, the colonial administration had quite strict restrictions. This chapter has shown that, during the 1920s, the missions opposed quite actively and lobbied to ease these regulations and create better opportunities to spread their specific literacies. A change occurred with the change of governor-general. The bush and Sunday school controversies show how important the question of literacy space is, and how it is embedded in ideology.

Moreover, the chapter has described how literacies were promoted through the mission schools. French-assimilationist literacies were hegemonic and had to be mastered to get through the educational system. This is why the mission promoted French-assimilationist literacies in their mission schools in addition to their own religious and contextualised literacies. In the next chapters, I will describe the independence period. For this period, I had access to qualitative interviews with former teachers and pupils at the Norwegian mission school, which makes the description of literacies more detailed. An interesting question is if the policy of the government and the literacies promoted through the mission schools were different during this period of independence compared to the 1920s.

## Notes

1. The terms primary and secondary education might lead to some confusion as levels that during this period were regarded secondary might today be considered primary level. In this book, I use the term that was used during the period in focus.
2. The concept of *metropole* is sometimes used when talking about France in Europe, while the *possessions/colonies* are used when talking about the countries under French rule during the colonial period.
3. *La politique des races* was analysed by the Malagasy historian Rajaonah in two articles from 1977 and 2002 (Rajaonah 2002, Esoavelomandroso 1977). This policy consisted of conquering the Merina hegemony and collecting indigenous people into groups of origin administrated by traditional chiefs. Direct rule was to be implemented in the Highlands, while indirect rule was to be implemented along the coastal areas. A concretisation of *la politique des races* was building schools in coastal regions. One of the most important aims was to recruit local bureaucrats from all the regions, collaborators who were not Merina.
4. There is no C in the Malagasy alphabet, so it is ABD instead of ABC.

# 5 School Literacies During the Independence Period

This chapter is devoted to the independence period from 1951 to 1966. It seeks to describe educational policies and the physical and institutional literacy spaces that the Norwegian mission ran within this political context. Introduced by the educational decree of 1951, which both complicated and eased mission educational work, this political context was different compared to the 1920s. Mission education was not any longer a threat to the dominant position of public schools and the colonial government even gave financial support to mission educational work. At independence, the Malagasy Republic considered private schools as important providers of education to Malagasy children and youth. Private schools were during this period mostly owned by national churches and established as a result of mission work. One of my main questions in this book is about the literacies that were promoted through the mission. To what extent were literacies embedded in Lutheranism, the religion of the mission? To what extent were they embedded in the ideologies of the colonial power: republicanism, secularism and assimilation? In this chapter, I take a closer look at literacies that were promoted by the Norwegian mission through Sunday, bush and primary schools during the independence period. Which role did these physical and institutional spaces play in promoting *French-assimilationist* and *religious literacies* among Malagasy children and youth? To what degree were they giving Malagasy children and youth an opportunity to engage in *contextualised literacies*?

## Educational Policy During the Independence Period

World War II and a national rebellion in 1947 marked the 1940s.[1] On the one hand, the post-war era was characterised by the rise of nationalism. On the other hand, the French Union was erected in 1946 which gave indigenous peoples in the colonies the right of citizenship (Charton 1949: 368). This meant that they had representatives in the legislative bodies in France, as well as in their own countries. These tendencies increased educational demands to which the colonial government could not respond. In 1951, 9 years before independence, an educational reform changed the colonial educational structure (see Chapter 4, p. 48). It put an end to the separate systems for indigenous and European education. The colonial government underscored that schools had been European only in the sense of content of education and the sort of diplomas given, not in the sense of access (Haut Commissariat de la République française à Madagascar et Dépendances 1950: 17). Anyhow, it had been very difficult for a Malagasy to enter the European educational system. In the period from 1914 to 1951, only 150 Malagasies had been admitted to European upper-secondary schools, and only about 10% passed their baccalaureate (Goguel 2006: 39). The reform was described as revolutionary (Radaody-Ralarosy 1951–1952: 143). Members of the Malagasy elite had aspired to dissolve the dual system since its creation, as they wanted Malagasy pupils to have equal opportunities (Rajaonah 2002: 202). The reform had, however, the consequence that the former indigenous schools of the colonial administration became even more aligned with French-assimilationist policies.

The educational system was more decentralised in the 1950s compared to the 1920s. As shown in the previous chapter, previously the governor-general had to approve the provincial commissioner's acceptance of the construction of a bush school. During the 1950s, the highest central authority, now titled the high commissioner, only had to approve the construction of secondary level schools (Goguel 2006: 104–105). The provincial commissioner provided certifications to primary level schools and the district commissioner to bush schools. Regulations to open a bush school, negotiated at the start of the 1920s, were to some extent still in place (Gouvernement général de Madagascar et dépendances 1951). Now, churches and assembly houses were, however, accepted as physical literacy spaces. This was quite extraordinary when considering the controversies between the missions and the secular administration 30 years earlier. Another important change in the educational policy for the mission organisations was that they were included in examination juries. And, for the first time since the turn of the century, the missions got the possibility to apply for financial support from the colonial administration. This clearly illustrates the colonial government's change of opinion towards mission schools (Snekkenes 1950).

The 1951 decree ensured a content even more in line with assimilationist policies. The timetable in all public schools should now be based on the timetable of what previously had been called European schools, though with some modification (Radaody-Ralarosy 1951–1952: 147, Goguel 2006: 105–108). That the amount of vocational education decreased significantly to give more space for general education is evidence that education now moved towards an even more assimilationist character because the general education became even more affected by French and French values. During the 1st and 2nd years of elementary school (CP classes), the amount of vocational education decreased from 7 hours and 30 minutes weekly to 1 hour and 40 minutes and in the 3rd year (CE class) and the 4th and 5th year (CM classes) to 2 hours and 40 minutes. Geography in CM was mostly about France (18 lessons), but also about Africa and Indo-China under French possession (three lessons) and Madagascar (eight lessons). So there was some contextualised content, as the history of Madagascar, suspended from the curriculum since the 1916 decree, was reintroduced (Rajaonah 2002: 202–203). Even so, the history books were about Madagascar's relationship to Europeans and about the diversity of the Malagasy people. The story about the unity of the Malagasy people was not a subject, according to Rajaonah. It was a specific way of thinking about the Malagasy people that was put forward. Using Makoni and Pennycook's words we could say that it was the story about Madagascar invented by the colonial power for their purposes that was taught (Makoni and Pennycook 2006). Makoni and Pennycook argued that historical work must draw attention to the invention of history "as part of the process of constructing the history of others for them" (Makoni and Pennycook 2006: 5). Of 40 history lessons in the 3rd year, 16 should be about the history of Madagascar, and in the 4th and 5th year, it should be the same content as in France, although allowing the teacher to introduce some local history. For the primary school exam (CEPE), by 1956 one of three questions in history and geography was about Madagascar. Some of the French schoolbooks were adapted among others in order to avoid telling Malagasy children that their ancestors were *les Gaulois*. The book, *Joies et Traveaux de l'Ile hereuse/Eto Madagasikara nosy malalantsika*, based on the Malagasy situation and written by the former director of education, Carle, was published (Carle 1952b, 1952a). This book aimed to make a connection between the traditional world of the Malagasies and the modern world.

When explaining the reform resulting in the 1951 decree, the colonial government highlighted that pupils at primary level needed more knowledge in French in order to continue to higher levels (Haut Commissariat de la République française à Madagascar et Dépendances 1950: 18). Malagasy pupils did not use the French language outside school:

> It concerns, we have to note, pupils in European schools but who, neither in their recreational time or at home, any more speak a word of our language. From this we can easily imagine how the situation is for pupils that go to indigenous schools!
> (Haut Commissariat de la République française à Madagascar et Dépendances 1950: 18, my translation)

In the new decree, pupils should learn to read in Malagasy the first months before turning to French. The study of spoken languages (*langue vivantes*) was reduced to 2 hours and reserved to the study of the Malagasy language. Teachers used the Malagasy language, based on the

Merina dialect, in reading and writing. This was different from the 1920s, when using the written Malagasy language was out of question due to the fear of its potential to feed nationalism. Consequently, Malagasy was included in the school programme, but French was strongly prioritised in line with assimilationist policies. The predominance of the French language to the detriment of the Malagasy language clearly appears in the timetable for primary schools presented in Goguel's book, *Aux origines du mai malgache. Désir d'école et compétition sociale 1951–1972* (Goguel 2006: 106).

Goguel pointed to the fact that with about 2,000 teachers in the educational system it was logistically difficult to implement the reform (Goguel 2006: 20). And it proved to be difficult for the teachers to teach the Malagasy language. They had become professionals themselves because of their proficiency in French, and they knew that their pupils would also be dependent on French in order to reach higher levels. The teachers were suddenly expected to teach the history of Madagascar without ever having been taught it themselves at school. The consequences of the reform for the Lutheran schools supported by the Norwegian mission will be described later in this chapter.

Independence in 1960 constituted an important change in the Malagasy political context, which also influenced the mission's literacy work. Major principles for general education in the Malagasy constitution were the right to education, parent's right to choose the kind of education for their children and financial support for private education, mostly run by churches, as far as the budget permitted (Goguel 2006: 193). Primary education was restructured in 1962 into two cycles. The first cycle was 4 years (CP and CE) and the second was 2 years (CM) (Koerner 1999: 270). The policy was very ambitious, inspired by the Addis Abbeba Conference in 1961, *The Conference of African States on the development of education in Africa*. The aim was to increase the enrolment rate of school-aged children in Madagascar for the first cycle from 44% to 78%, and for the second cycle to 62% over a period of 10 years (Republique Malgache. Ministère de l'éducation nationale 1964). In order to attain these goals, a number of rural schools, in many ways similar to the missions' bush schools, were established. I will explain the concept of rural schools here, as it is a good example of how the Ministry of Education made some attempts to adapt the Malagasy educational system after more than 60 years of colonial reign.

In a speech at the inauguration of the first training centre for rural teachers in 1962, Minister of Education Laurent Botokeky described primary education in Madagascar at independence as a copy of the French system. He said it was an "almost complete application to Madagascar of French primary education" (Republique Malgache. Ministère de l'éducation nationale 1964: 2, my translation). According to him, primary education was "neglecting too much the relations between the individual and its civilisation", thereby resulting in the failure of initiating youth to contributing to development. In other words, here the minister of education is expressing lack of contextualised, or even culturally sensitive, literacy in Madagascar for development to take place. The introduction of rural schools was aimed at adapting primary education and with it literacy teaching to the local context. For the government, rural schools were a cheaper alternative than primary schools, as municipalities were expected to support teacher salaries and construction of buildings. Teachers with less education, the second year at the lower secondary level (*Sième*—year 8), were recruited, and they earned one-third of the salary of a teacher holding a lower secondary-level diploma and 1 year of pedagogical training (Goguel 2006: 193, 201–202).

The governmental rural schools were similar to bush schools in that they used Malagasy as the LOI, recruited teachers without pedagogical training and focused on local participation. Rural schools were seen as a necessity in order to achieve educational aims, and a positive outcome was said to be people's own engagement in the education of their children (Republique Malgache. Ministère de l'éducation nationale 1964: 12). The aim of rural schools was thus "To give as many children as possible a general elementary instruction", relying on the following elements; "—Reading, writing and using the mother tongue,—Practical calculation,—Useful knowledge obtained through observation" and "—Initiate knowledge about the Malagasy nation" (Republique Malgache. Ministère de l'éducation nationale 1964: 39, my translation). The Malagasy language was the LOI (Republique Malgache. Ministère de l'éducation nationale 1964: 44–51). In the 1st year, the subjects were arithmetic, reading, writing, studying the environment, moral and practical education, singing and recitation, and physical education. The teaching of French started in the 2nd year with 3 hours and was taught for 2 hours and 30 minutes in the 3rd and 4th year. The local environment should be the basis for courses in history and geography. UNESCO played an important role in the implementation of rural schools and the minister of education strongly supported it. He argued that these rural schools would contribute to fighting illiteracy:

> The development of schools of the first cycle of primary education will allow us to attain an enrolment rate of 100% in a short time (about 20 years). The National Ministry of Education cannot hesitate and I have personally engaged myself with enthusiasm to fulfil the programme, which will allow my country to rapidly fight illiteracy and through that start its way to progress.
> (Republique Malgache. Ministère de l'éducation nationale 1964:
> Avant propos, my translation)

The report from a seminar arranged by the student organisation Federation of Student Organisations in Madagascar (FAEM) in 1968 mentioned rural schools as promising and often with better results than urban schools: however, they were financially disadvantaged by being, in contrast to urban schools, dependent upon local support and finance from the municipalities (FAEM 1968: 7). Constructing rural schools was seen as an opportunity to develop an alternative to the primary school, a heritage from the colonial period when the aim was elite construction with few relationships to the rural world. In the 1966 educational reform, it was planned that the first 4 years of all primary schools should be aligned with the pedagogy of rural schools (Goguel 2006: 204–205). The implementation of rural schools experienced delays, and according to the French historian Anne-Marie Goguel, one of the reasons was that some parents were sceptical that the lack of French teaching would deprive their children of the possibility to climb the social ladder. This illustrates the difficulties of implementing educational reforms in a post-colonial society where the aims of the future are different from the aims of the past. It illustrates that changing policies and at the same time changing pupils' and parents' educational aspirations is challenging. This is especially the case when aspirations are impacted by educational success stories from former societal contexts.

Before I describe the educational and literacy work of the Norwegian mission and the FLM during the independence period, I will describe the establishment of the Lutheran Church. In this regard, I find it relevant to go back in time to provide a better understanding of the relation between the mission and the church, and the organisation of Lutheran educational work.

## Establishment of the Malagasy Lutheran Church

A Malagasy Lutheran church was the aim of the mission's work from the beginning. There were, nevertheless, disagreements within the mission regarding its establishment. Birkeli emphasised the main issue in question: Should economical self-reliance be a prerequisite for autonomy, or would autonomy help gaining self-reliance? (Birkeli 1949: 197–206). From 1879, congregations could elect representatives to church councils, and from 1890 the congregations organised themselves in larger provinces with annual meetings, but still without decision-making authority. The superintendent and the Mission Conference should be in direct relation to the districts. In 1902, a synod for the Highlands was established with 300 deputies, but was later withdrawn due to the requirement of self-reliance promoted by the mission's central board in Norway. A slower road to independence, through self-reliance, was chosen and the Mission Conference continued to be the highest decision-making body. The change of mind and the withdrawal of the Synod was a significant disappointment to the Malagasy pastors and leaders (Birkeli 1949: 197). According to Birkeli, the church structure was an arena where they could have influence after having lost, in 1896, their political independence to the French colonial power.

At a conference in 1908, the mission decided, as was mentioned in the previous chapter, to organise the church in three levels: the congregation, the parish and the district (Birkeli 1949: 220–221). A district committee consisting of all pastors from the different parishes, the missionary and two elected laymen from each parish was established. Self-reliance was an important principle and congregations and parishes became responsible for their own expenses, including expenses for educational work. The district had responsibility for pastors' salaries, the church at the mission station and various expenses that the congregations could not manage by themselves. In 1910, a Mixed Committee (*Comité mixte*—CM) with Malagasy and Norwegian missionary delegates, was established (Birkeli 1949: 222–225). Questions about educational matters were frequently discussed at their meetings. CM members were allowed to give reports from the CM meetings to the annual meetings, but annual meetings could not send enquiries directly to the CM. This was decided to ensure that the mission kept their control and responsibility. The main role of the CM was to give advice to the highest decision-making body, the Mission Conference, which in this structure could keep its authority.

The next big step towards autonomy for a Malagasy Lutheran church came in 1927, with the first indigenous decision-making body, the Church Conference (Birkeli 1949: 261–263). The number of 18 Malagasies and 13 missionary delegates were present. It was decided, as a rule, that the districts that became self-reliant should be able to send delegates to the Church Conference. The Norwegian missionaries could be among those delegates, but they were then not representatives of the mission but of the church, meaning that their membership could be withdrawn if the district stopped being self-reliant or if the district chose to send someone else. For the Western and Eastern Synods, church conferences were not established until World War II (Edland and Aano 1992: 355, Nakkestad et al. 1967). As explained in chapter one, the General Synod of the FLM was constituted in 1950. I will now return to the start of the 1950s and present how the Norwegian mission and the Lutheran Church related to the changing political context during the period of independence.

## The Norwegian Mission's Educational Work During the Independence Period

Through the 1951 educational decree, described in the beginning of this chapter, more flexible regulations were put in place for bush schools. Actually, the IPC found the regulations so liberal that they felt the need to work with their own regulations, at least concerning the curriculum and the qualification of teachers (Rajaobelina and Vernier 1952). But, running primary schools became more challenging due to the reinforcement of French-assimilationist policies. Due to the reform, a revision of the programme in the mission's primary schools was needed (NMS 1952a: 59). In 1953, a committee consisting of six missionaries presented a plan for revising the curriculum to the Norwegian Mission Conference (NMS 1953: 65–68). Even though the revision was not adapted since the Inter-missionary School Committee (ISC) on a later stage presented a joint Protestant curriculum, the discussions that took place in the conference illustrate the mission's major considerations related to educational work. The aim of primary schools was explained: to give children solid knowledge about the Christian religion, faith, and at the same time teach subjects important to pass the French primary school exams. The Norwegian missionaries aimed to implement, with some modifications, three subjects from the public curriculum: French, history and Malagasy history. In addition, they added lessons in Malagasy and Christianity. One suggestion from the committee that worked on revising the programme was that the mission schools needed to add 2 years to the 6-year programme of the public schools since they had Malagasy and Christianity as additional subjects in addition to their classes being crowded. Sending away children was not a possibility because this in practice meant that they would miss learning to read and write or that they would go to the Catholics. In spite of these arguments, the conference decided that in schools that led to a primary school exam, pupils should use 6 years. It is clear from these discussions that the mission schools struggled to make their pupils master both religious and French-assimilationist literacies.

The relation with the colonial government improved and during the 1950s, the Norwegian mission received financial support from the colonial administration to school buildings and dormitories (NMS 1954: 5–6). One persisting challenge for the mission was the recruitment of educated teachers. In order to recruit pupils in areas where people had low purchasing power, school fees had to be kept at a low level, meaning teachers were given a low salary that could not compete with that of public schools. As shown in the previous chapter, the public teacher salaries were three times higher in 1929 and, in 1950, they were even five to six times more (NMS 1950a: 6, 1929: 33).

With independence in 1960, the educational work of the churches, including the Lutheran schools, played an important role in providing education to Malagasy children and youth. At a conference for Protestant school directors, the relationship between public and Protestant education was discussed (Fampianarana Protestanta eto Madagasikara 1960). Apparently, Protestant primary schools offered good education, especially at the first levels, but public schools were more popular than church schools. One reason was that they had no school fees. It was set an aim at the conference to increase the number of Protestant schools in the countryside. If local congregations did not manage to build schools, there were possibilities for collaboration with local councils (*Fokon'olona*). Concerning schools in the cities there was a focus on ensuring the religious component through religious studies and through strengthening the relationship between the school and the church.

The Norwegian mission continued its presence and its work on the island, but in this changing political context, their priorities and cooperation with the Lutheran Church had to be revised (NMS 1963: 41). Within education, the missionaries chose to focus their financial effort on the establishment of bush schools. Bush schools were described by the former missionaries interviewed for this study that worked in Madagascar during this period as of varying quality. Gidskehaug described one bush school taking place in a church in the countryside:

> They taught in church. There were benches, a few boards. And they had a blackboard on which they wrote with some chalk. And they had a rag to dry off. But unbelievably, when I came back, many had learned to read! There were children of different ages, because everyone that didn't know to read, write or calculate came. Everybody came. Some older and some younger. They could be up to 13 years and they were together with the 7-year-olds.
>
> (Former female missionary Astrid Gidskehaug 2010)

The expansion of bush schools could meet the interest that people showed in education, and it fitted well with the public educational policy. Competition between the schools, especially with public rural schools, had, however, in some places become harder and it was a challenge to pay teachers' salaries. Thus, the educational policy of the Malagasy government at independence created opportunities, but through introducing rural schools, the policy also gave the churches and missions more competition in what had been their important instrument of evangelisation throughout the colonial period—the bush schools.

The NMS kept close relations with the FLM, and Norwegian teaching missionaries continued to work in the Lutheran schools, among them some of the teachers who were interviewed for this project. They had spent months in France to pass their French exams and worked as principals in Lutheran schools. Learning French was, as during the 1920s, a prerequisite for these teaching missionaries to do their work. But, they also worked hard to learn the local language used in school and everyday life. Teaching missionaries were missionaries and teachers; they mastered Malagasy and French, as well as religious and French-assimilationist literacies. In addition to their position as principals of mission schools, they also had the responsibility for dormitories and the work among women in the Church district, and in some places, they were in charge of selling books and magazines.

Still, after independence, there was a lack of qualified Malagasy teachers willing to work in the Lutheran schools. Since working here meant less income, it was expected that teachers, as pastors, regarded their tasks as a calling from God. In many cases, teachers did not receive their salaries for several months. School fees should help pay teachers' salaries, but many pupils came from rural families with little income-generating activities. According to one of the former teaching missionaries interviewed for this study, many parents waited for their coffee harvest in order to pay school fees. She added: "I cannot remember that I sent anyone back home if they didn't manage, but parents struggled hard to keep them in school" (Former female missionary Elfrid Søyland 2011, my translation). According to another teaching missionary, they had to send some pupils home if they did not pay until the coffee harvest was done (Former female missionary Helena Trydal 2012). One strategy to recruit candidates from the Lutheran teacher training college to work in the Lutheran school was to pay for their education and sign contracts for them to stay on until they had paid their "study debt" (NMS 1965c: 4). In spite of having a signed contract, many teachers still left. Not until the 1970s did the shortage of teachers for primary level schools become less of a worry (NMS 1970: 174).

Even though the aim was that school fees and local congregations should cover the costs of schools, the districts on many occasions received support from the Norwegian mission. The mission had received some of these funds from other channels. During the 1960s, the NMS received some funds from the Malagasy Republic (NMS 1962: 19, 1960a: 5). The mission was grateful for this support, although they were afraid that too much financial support could end up dictating their work and make them dependent and vulnerable. In 1960, the Catholic mission negotiated with the Malagasy Republic to have the government to pay the salaries of teachers in private schools (Snekkenes 1960: 49). The Norwegian and other Protestant missions were reluctant, as it would mean that their schools could become more dependent on the state, while at the same time it would loosen the relationship between teachers and congregations. The mission put great value on being independent and maintaining a link between the church and schools in order to ensure their religious literacies. From the 1960s onward, the mission also got support from the Norwegian government and the LWF to build dormitories, schools and an agricultural school (The archives of the superintendent of the mission. 1950–1959, Bøe 1969b: 58).

The political context during the independence period was improved compared to former years. It was a great demand for education and an enhanced recognition of the educational work of the churches and the missions. For the Norwegian mission's literacy work, the eased regulations and recognition of bush schools, their most important instrument to promote their religious literacies, were important in creating an enabling political context. In addition, financial support from different channels helped to develop Lutheran educational work on the island. An important element during this period was the transmission of responsibility from the mission to the FLM, also within education. This changed the working environment for the missionaries, but the close relationship was kept alive. In the next pages, I will describe how literacies were promoted in the schools of the mission and the church during this period.

## Religious Literacies

I found some indication in the archives on how religious literacies should be promoted. An interesting quotation in this regard is from a pastor in Antsirabe, Rajaona (Rajaona no date). He made suggestions to the Church Conference on how to strengthen the faith of the members in the Lutheran Church. Teaching Christianity to children in Lutheran schools should strive to make children understand *in their hearts* what faith was about in order to live like Christians, and not only learn it by heart like other subjects. Here, Rajaona intended that in Christianity lessons pupils would not just read, recite or memorise but that they would discuss the content of what they read. He also argued that there should be a closer relationship between the Church and the school (e.g. by doing the morning devotion in church). From an ideological perspective on literacy, these statements are interesting. What was taught in school, and the way it was taught was influenced by Lutheranism and the missionaries believed that Christianity was different from a school subject like maths, in that the faith would have an impact on the children in a different way than the imparting of secular knowledge via subject lessons would have.

The accounts of former missionaries widened my understanding of how religious literacies were promoted in mission schools. Former missionary Trydal mentioned that the catechism (Figure 5.1) was something pupils were expected to be in position of:

> We had the catechism. Even if they did not have any other books, they at least had that book. The price was two Ariary at that time. The principals sold books. That was part of the job. We had a bookshop, and I remember we needed a lot of copies of that book.
> (Former female missionary Helena Trydal 2012)

In the mission literature, I found some descriptions of religious literacy practices in Norwegian mission schools where religious books were in use. In 1951, missionary Alfhild Haus wrote for instance a story about a visit by the Norwegian mission's superintendent to a school in the forest (Haus 1951). The story was published in the mission's children magazine

*Figure 5.1* The catechism in Malagasy, 1956

and it is important to keep in mind that it was intended for children in Norway. Haus described, from her point of view, how pupils could have felt during the visit. The school building was very simple and the pupils were dressed in traditional clothes always wearing a knife, a necessity in the forest. Before the examination begun, the superintendent asked if they had books. The teacher counted how many of the pupils who had the catechism, Bible stories, songbooks, the New Testament and school-books in French. The superintendent then asked if they had general reading books. "They do not have any", the teacher answered, "We use the catechism" (Haus 1951: 10, my translation). Haus explained that everyone could afford the catechism and the songbook. Those who had newly started school were to show that they could read:

> all the catechisms appear on the desks in front of the pupils from the first level. They start from the beginning, the 1st Commandment and the explanation. Some manage well, others mumble and stutter and repeat wrong things over and over again. One becomes so confused when those white people are sitting there watching with small, blue eyes. "Fortunately I know this by heart, so I do not need to read letter by letter", Solo thinks, and keeps on reciting. Oh no, don't imagine that the smart teacher does not understand that he is actually not reading in the book, and in addition he was unlucky to say a wrong word, and has to take the shame to spell it like some fool. "Why do they always need to be so accurate about those unimportant things!"
>
> (Haus 1951: 7, my translation)

This is an excellent example of how religious literacy practices could take place in the mission schools and how religious texts were used to teach reading. It also illustrates how the engagements between teachers and pupils could be and the importance given to written texts, recitation, remembering by heart and at the same time be in position to read.

## French-Assimilationist Literacies

I will here quote a section from the article mentioned previously, in which Haus described French teaching in a rural school during the superintendent's inspection (Haus 1951: 6–7, 10). This section describes literacy practices in French and touches on issues of authority and hierarchy in the classroom. It describes how some pupils' difficulties with French made them feel stupid, whereas others mastered it well. Solo is the same character who had to read from the catechism described previously. The author named one of the other pupils *Brysom*:

> "Brysom, please rise!" the teacher says in French, and at the last row a big boy rises. "What are you doing?" is said in French. "I rise," Brysom answers in clear French. "What is Brysom doing?" asks the teacher a little girl. "Brysom rises," she answers. "Brysom, leave the desk!" the teacher says, and Brysom stands beside his desk. "What is Brysom doing, Solo?" asks the teacher. But Solo, the poor one, was

not prepared on being asked so suddenly. He partly rises and strives to get his arms out of his sweater before he answers. In the confusion he makes a mistake, and puts his left arm out of a hole in the shirt behind the armhole, so it is a lot of trouble to get it back again and put it in the right hole. "Brysom, Brysom," he stutters. "Brysom, he, he rises." To understand this French language, that's not easy—and there are surely also other pupils that stumble both in words and sentences. But Brysom, he is standing there as steady as always, like there was no inspection or white bishop at all. He knows after all that he masters this, and he walks slowly over the floor to the black-board and writes what the teacher tells him to. For sure, Brysom has no problem with the inspection!

(Haus 1951: 7, 10, my translation)

Using French as the LOI was challenging. The former teaching missionaries interviewed for this research highlighted the fact that students were strug-gling with the foreign language (French): "No wonder that they didn't pass their exam. How they struggled! And the teachers struggled. And we strug-gled" (Former female missionary Astrid Gidskehaug 2010, my translation). Another said, "Those who did not learn language easily never passed. They never passed exams in French. It was always only a little group that passed and it was not because the others were stupid" (Former female missionary Anne Marie Reimers 2012). The mission had, however, to adhere to official regulations in order for their pupils to get their diploma. French continued to be the LOI, although teachers ended up using Malagasy in order for chil-dren to understand. This says something about the assimilationist aim of education. As highlighted by Street and Street, the LOI used plays a role in the pedagogisation of literacy in school (Street and Street 1991: 150–151). The LOI used in school can be distant from the pupils' everyday language. When the LOI is a foreign language not used in the everyday life of the pupils, reading and writing, and thus literacy learning, become even more distanced from the pupils' lives and experiences.

Using the French language as LOI was also challenging for the teach-ers. Superintendent for the Norwegian mission, Snekkenes, recognised the difficulties faced by Malagasy teachers when asked to teach in a lan-guage that was not their own:

That is in itself not so bad, but one has to remember that everything will be in French, and the Malagasies are not French speaking, but have their own language, which is not at all related to the French. That is why the demands towards a Malagasy teacher are higher than what is the case in Norway. Imagine that Norwegian teachers should take their exam in French. This would ask much more work than is the case right now.

(Snekkenes 1954: 74, my translation)

Sandvik argued that the Catholic school in the village where she was working was the most popular school (Former female missionary Tordis Sandvik 2011). The main reason for this was that they had European teachers (nuns) with French as their mother tongue.

As explained earlier in this chapter, also the content became more aligned with the French-assimilationist approach during this period. The Norwegian teaching missionaries interviewed for this study, commented upon how French history and geography, in place of Malagasy, dominated schoolbooks. Andersen, who was a member of the Protestant Educational Committee, said most schoolbooks were ordinary French schoolbooks used in France (Former male missionary Anders Martin Andersen 2011). The books were not adapted to the local setting; Andersen pointed to the example of the half-moon, which looks different in Europe in comparison to Madagascar. Another issue was the high price of imported books. Teaching missionary Trydal said: "We sold the nice French books in natural science and geography. They were so nice, you know, but who could afford them?" (Former female missionary Helena Trydal 2012). Søyland found it inappropriate to teach Malagasy pupils about French history and geography when they for instance said *our* rivers, meaning French rivers (Former female missionary Elfrid Søyland 2011). Sandvik described the particular feeling of teaching Malagasy students French geography and history in French in the late 1950s:

> Something that I still remember . . . after all, this was only 10 years after independence in Norway, and I came to Madagascar to teach French history—"Nos ancêtre les gaulois". French geography. French history. Everything was French at that time. This is something that I still remember very well. And for the students the goal was to be able to repeat without too many faults, so that they could pass the exam. And to take the exam they had to travel a couple of miles to Ambositra, which is situated near the main road.
>
> (Former female missionary Tordis Sandvik 2011, my translation)

This is an illustration of how the missionaries were obliged to promote in their schools French-assimilationist content and writing in French, not in Malagasy. Sandvik here makes references to the Norwegian context and refers to the quite strong, and well-known, example of how these lessons even used phrases such as *our ancestors* pointing to the French history. She promoted, however, literacy practices such as dictations and exams embedded in French-assimilationist policies in order for pupils to reach educational goals set by the ruling power. This was a question of survival for the schools. The main aim for the exam was to avoid too many faults in French because that was an important measure of success according to the colonial government. It was not primarily about understanding what was read.

When Gidskehaug was principal of a Lutheran school in the 1960s, geography and history books were still written in French, but they were now at least telling the story about Madagascar, including Malagasy geography and history (Former female missionary Astrid Gidskehaug 2010). Gidskehaug and Søyland showed me geography books about Madagascar written by French authors in French, which were used in their schools. One of the authors, G. Bastian, was teaching history and geography in Madagascar at higher secondary level (Bastian 1955). The title of one book, *Madagasacar. Les Hommes. Le pays. La mise en valeur* can be translated to *Madagascar. The People. The Country. The Development*. The title clearly indicates that teaching of history and geography was regarded as an instrument for a certain kind of development.

## Contextualised Literacies

The Norwegian mission education was contextualised by the use of children's language rather than the French language. Habberstad wrote in 1965 that the Lutheran schools, in contrast to public schools, where all teaching was based on the French language, always focused on the mother tongue (Habberstad 1965: 56). During the first 3 or 4 years in mission primary schools, the LOI was Malagasy (Habberstad 1965: 56). The level of Malagasy in the mission school was higher than in the official schools, and they preferred to use their own books in Malagasy. A Malagasy holding a high position in the educational administration in the capital visited former missionary Søyland in her school on the East Coast, where she was working in the period from 1953 to 1970 (Former female missionary Elfrid Søyland 2011). He was impressed by the teachers' knowledge of Malagasy at the mission school, and said that teachers in public schools would never perform that well. According to Søyland, the reason was that teachers in her school had studied at mission schools where they learned the Malagasy language well in contrast to public schools. Aamland mentioned how teachers naturally used their own language, but at the same time had to relate to the official policy:

> The Malagasy language was important and it was natural for them to use it as much as possible at the same time as they were conscious, the teachers, that they should lead them to a public exam where French was demanded. They could not ignore that.
> (Former female missionary Eldrid Aamland 2012, my translation)

The book *Lala sy Noro* (see Figures 5.2, 5.3 and 5.4), written by Prosper Rajaobelina and printed by the Lutheran press, was important in promoting contextualised literacies (Rajaobelina 1955). It was sold at a low price, which meant that quite a lot of the pupils could afford to buy it (Former female missionary Helena Trydal 2012). The book took the local context into account and was widely used as a reading book. In the

*Figure 5.2* Copy from the reading book *Lala sy Noro*, 1955, front page

Source: Rajaobelina (1955: front page)

book's front page the boy Lala and the girl Noro are walking on a road in a Malagasy landscape, with typical palm trees and cactuses on each side of the road (Figure 5.2). Inside the book there were insects, animals and situations familiar to Malagasy children, at least for those who lived in the Highlands. On page 15, there is a drawing of a woman carrying

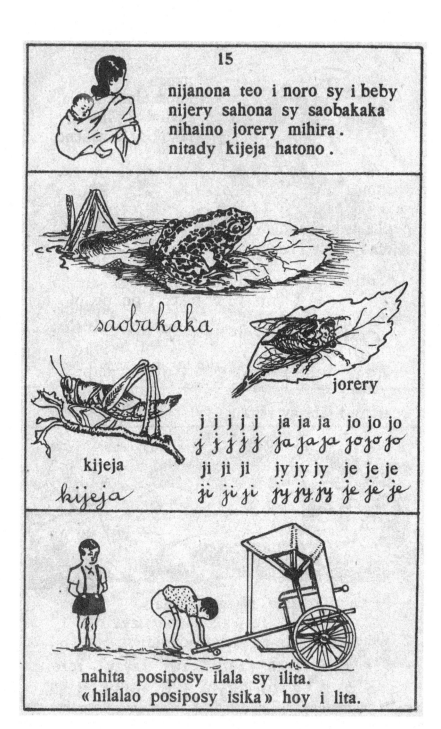

**15**

nijanona teo i noro sy i beby
nijery sahona sy saobakaka
nihaino jorery mihira.
nitady kijeja hatono.

saobakaka

jorery

kijeja

j j j j j   ja ja ja   jo jo jo
j j j j j   ja ja ja   jojojo
ji ji ji   jy jy jy   je je je
ji ji ji   jy jy jy   je je je

nahita posiposy ilala sy ilita.
«hilalao posiposy isika» hoy i lita.

*Figure 5.3* Copy from the reading book *Lala sy Noro*, 1955, page 15
Source: Rajaobelina (1955: 15)

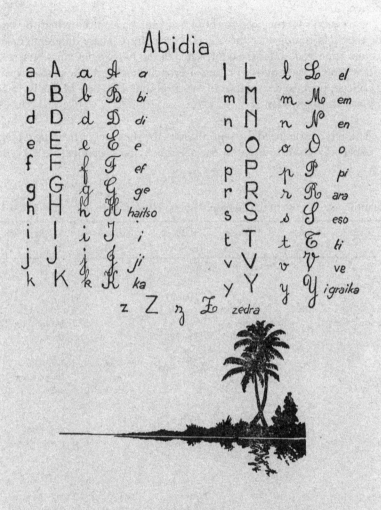

*Figure 5.4* Copy from the reading book *Lala sy Noro*, 1955, last page

Source: Rajaobelina (1955: last page)

a baby on her back (Figure 5.3). On the same page there are also insects and a drawing of what is called *posiposy*, the Malagasy rickshaw. Reading such a book in school can be described as a contextualised literacy practice.

The mission saw the need for books in Malagasy, although at the same time they had to consider the official curriculum. These different considerations appeared under the conference of the Norwegian missionaries in 1950 when Georges-Sully Chapus, a French teacher at the teacher training college, proposed to elaborate on a bilingual French-Malagasy reading book for his students:

> There is a large need for schoolbooks for the teacher training college, especially because those in use are much too dependent on a French

*Table 5.1* Schoolbooks for use in the mission schools, 1964. Source: Jacobsen (1964b)

| Class | Bible | Songbook | Bible History | Catechism | Malagasy Reading | Malagasy Grammar | French Reading |
|---|---|---|---|---|---|---|---|
| CPI | - | - | - | - | Lalas sy Noro Tsingory | - | - |
| CPII | The New Testament | The hymnal | Vogt: Histories from the Bible | Catechism (the small one) | Tantelin-jaza I Tantelin-jaza II | - | Carle: Livre de lecture française |
| CEI | --//-- | --//-- | --//-- | --//-- | | Rajaobelina: Gramera Malagasy I | Rakotozafy: Irango et ses amis |
| CEII | --//-- | --//-- | --//-- | Johnson: Explanation of the catechism | Robinson Crusoe Ny any nahabe Zava-boahary I | --//-- | Rakotozafy: Izy mianadahy (Frère et Soeur) |
| CMI | The Bible | --//-- | --//-- The New Testament | --//-- | Zava-boahary II Ravelomanana: Ny amboarako | Rajaobelina: Gramera Malagasy II | Dumas: Le Livre Unique de Français, CM |
| CMII | --//-- | --//-- | --//-- The Old Testament | --//-- | Ravelomanana: Ny amboarako | Rajaobelina: Gramera Malagasy II | Dumas: Le Livre Unique de Français, CM |

environment. There is a need for books especially developed for the Malagasy environment. On the other hand, however, we also have to consider what is demanded for exams; our books need to be part of the whole so that the pupils are not put in a worse situation because they are examined by other guidelines.

(NMS 1950b: 49, my translation)

Towards the end of the colonial period and during the first years of independence, the status of the Malagasy language was reinforced, and the NMS/FLM's experience with printing of Malagasy schoolbooks became a resource also for the government. In 1964, a list of schoolbooks that should be used in Lutheran schools was distributed to Norwegian teaching missionaries (Table 5.1) (Jacobsen 1964b). This list is interesting, as

| *Divers* | *Math* | *Malagasy* **History** | *World History* | *Malagasy Geography* | *World Geography* | *Science* |
|---|---|---|---|---|---|---|
| - | - | - | - | - | - | - |
| - | - | - | - | - | - | - |
| Ravelomanana: Thèmes et versions I | Rajoalisolo: Fianara- marika CE | Rakotomamonjy: Fianarana Tantara I | - | Hatzfeld: Anivon'ny Riska | - | - |
| --//-- | --//-- | Rakotomamonjy: Fianarana Tantara II | Bastian- Croison: Histoire des Civilisations | --//-- | Hatzfeld: Geographie CEII | ??? |
| Ravelomanana: Thèmes et versions II | IPAM Calcul CM | Fagereng- Rakotomamonjy: Ny Tantaran'ny firenena Malagasy | --//-- | Dorian: Géographie de Madagascar | ??? | IPAM: Sciences d'observation CM |
| --//-- Souché- Mánard: Exercices de français | -//-- | Bastian: Histoire de Madagascar | --//-- ??? L'Antiquité? | Bastian: Géographie de Madagascar. Bastian; Cartographie de Madagascar | ??? | --//-- |

it shows the diverse amount of material that the Lutheran schools possessed. The list included religious books (the Bible, the New and Old Testament, hymnals, catechism and an explanation of the catechism), the Malagasy reading books published through *Salohy*, an Inter-protestant edition, Malagasy grammar, French reading books and grammar by both French and Malagasy authors, Malagasy and world history and geography books in both Malagasy and in French.

After independence, Protestant converts continued the missions' focus on the local language. Among others, they had expectations that the primary school exam (CEPE) would be in Malagasy, and the Protestant Education Council (CEP) worked hard for its implementation. This would drastically change the norms that pupils would have to comply with in order to obtain a diploma based on their knowledge. The Protestant school authorities were convinced that this change would take place, and when this did not come through in 1964, the CEP decided to have their own primary school exams in Malagasy while waiting for the government's decision (Jacobsen 1965, ISC 1964d, c, b, a, Jacobsen 1964a). The Protestant CEPE exam did not have any official value, but could act as practice before the official exam. The Educational Council encouraged every pupil at the CMII level to sign up for the exam. The pupils were examined in arithmetic, both written and orally, geography, history, natural science, French (a few questions that the children should answer), and Bible stories (a story about Jesus with some questions). Norwegian teaching missionaries were part of the exam commission, and 50% of the pupils passed the exam in the 1st year. I did not find an overview of the percentage that passed the public CEPE in mission schools in the archives in order to compare, but this was presented as a very good result. The school secretary of the Norwegian mission, Alfhild Jacobsen explained that the level of the tests was the same as the official CEPE exam, but in Malagasy, and they also included questions about Bible stories. Documentation about the period of time this exam existed was not found in the archival material, but missionary Eikeland remembered that it was used in the school where she started to work in 1969 (Former female missionary Helga Eikeland 2010). She got the impression that the Malagasy exam was there in order to show that pupils had the knowledge. When they were able to use their own language, the results were very different. Even though it was not an official exam, the pupils got a proof of their knowledge, and the diploma could be used within the church structure. In other words, this exam complied with the norms of the church and the mission and could be used within those institutions. The fact that two primary school exams, one in Malagasy and one in French, existed at the same time clearly illustrates the difference between French-assimilationist, religious and contextualised literacy practices. These exams, which are typical literacy practices, had different contents, ways of learning and values in different institutional settings. They complied with different norms that were on one hand embedded in Lutheranism and on the other ideologies on republicanism, secularism and assimilation.

## Concluding Remarks

This chapter started by describing the political context that the Norwegian mission had to relate to during the period of independence, 1951–1966. The political context at the end of the colonial rule and the 1st Malagasy Republic was more supportive for the mission literacy work than during the 1920s. Financial support was given to develop educational structures and opportunities to promote religious and contextualised literacies through bush schools increased. There were also challenges during this period, especially due to the fact that French-assimilationist policies were reinforced in primary and secondary schools challenging the mission and Church's educational work.

The Norwegian mission's educational strategy was two-fold, relating to the mission's aim of itself and the aim of the French colonial power. On the one hand, by being part of the colonial educational system, the mission promoted French as the LOI and taught pupils to read and write in French. On the other hand, the Malagasy language was promoted as the LOI as part of religious literacies. In the bush schools and Sunday schools, Malagasy was used to teach children to read and write, which was an important reason why the mission focused their energy on these alternative institutions. By providing opportunities for contextualised literacy practices, in the local language, the mission made room for an education that acknowledged the children as Malagasy learners. Alternative literacies to the dominant colonial French-assimilationist literacies are interesting because their very existence showed the Malagasy pupils that literacy could be done in different ways. You could learn to read and write without the use of the French language. The Protestant missions offer an interesting case of the history of literacy in Madagascar. Their existence ensured that the hegemonic literacy during the colonial period was challenged, which provided the Malagasy state with a choice between promoting literacies in French or in Malagasy in the post-colonial era. In the next chapter, I will describe the case of Betafo. The goal is to get a better understanding of how the literacy work of the mission could look like and how Malagasy pupils and teachers experienced literacy practices in the schools of the Lutheran Church and the Norwegian mission.

## Note

1. See an analysis of the Norwegian mission's educational work in Madagascar during the 1940s in Rosnes (2017).

# 6 Betafo

## A Case Study of the Mission's Literacy Work

The city of Betafo was chosen as a case for this study as it has a long history connected with Norwegian mission literacy work. The Norwegian missionaries started teaching activities when they arrived in Betafo in 1867. Gradually, a public and a Catholic school were put up in addition to the Lutheran school. The town is situated in the centre of Madagascar, 25 km west of Antsirabe. Antsirabe is the capital of Vakinankaratra, a region in the Highlands. The population in the district surrounding Betafo, which carries the same name, was 10,927 in 1965, of which about 2,000 lived in the urban centre of Betafo and were considered as non-farmers (Bied-Charreton 1968: 15–16). They worked in a rice mill, as mechanics, carpenters, store staff, hotel staff, employed by the municipality and traders, and some were also employed by the Catholic and Norwegian missions. In 1968, there were a total of 2,574 pupils in the district of Betafo, of which 700 belonged to public schools, 518 to Lutheran schools, 1,212 to Catholic schools and 144 to independent schools (Bied-Charreton 1968: 16).

This chapter is primarily based on the qualitative interviews I conducted with former pupils and teachers at the mission school of Betafo during the 1950s and 1960s. As explained in Chapter 3, I collected life stories of 10 former pupils in this area. These life stories, in addition to qualitative interviews with former pupils and teachers, provide an understanding of the kind of pupils who came to the mission schools, their perceptions of formal education, motivation, the sacrifices made by their parents in order to let children go to school and the relevance of literacy for their lives. I will also discuss factors that hindered children's access to school, such as distance to school, lack of interest in education, gender and school fees. The collection of life stories and interviews provided me with a deep understanding of people's experiences of the mission's literacy work and its influence on people's lives.

## Mission Education in Betafo

The first Norwegian missionaries to Madagascar settled at a hill north of the city of Betafo in 1867, next to the local aristocracy (Birkeli 1949: 62).

This region, Vakinankaratra, was under the control of the Merina Kingdom, and at that time Betafo was the capital in the region, housing Merina governors from 1882 (Esoavelomandroso 1989–1990: 308). Betafo lost its position as the capital of the region to Antsirabe during the 20th century. When the French colonial administrator came, he settled not far away from the mission station. Thirty years after the Norwegian missionaries had started educational work in the area, the colonial administration put up a public school. Due to the colonial demand in 1906 that all schools needed to have French educated teachers and that all school activities had to be run in dedicated school buildings, the number of the Norwegian mission schools was dramatically reduced. According to Birkeli, 100 out of 104 schools had to be closed down in the district of Betafo (Birkeli 1949: 212). They were left with only four schools. As in many other places, the mission then started to focus on establishing Sunday schools (Bjertnes 1927).

In 1927, when the number of Norwegian mission primary schools in the district was still four (with 399 pupils), there were 65 Sunday schools with 2,050 pupils (Bjertnes 1927). The district of the Lutheran mission Church Betafo covered most of its own expenses. Half of the expenses to run the schools were covered, and it was expected that in the very near future the district would be able to cover the total amount. If they managed, they could send a representative to the Church Conference in the Highlands. The mission also had bush schools in the countryside, and the number of these increased, especially in the 1940s and 1950s. In the district of Betafo, there were three bush schools registered by the Norwegian mission in 1939, whereas the Catholic mission had 12 (Colonial administration 1939). In 1960, the number of NMS bush schools had increased to 22, and the Catholics had 48 (Colonial administration 1960).

The former pupils and teachers interviewed in this study used several names for the mission school in the town of Betafo: the Norwegian school/at the Norwegians, the mission school/at the mission, the Lutheran school/at the Lutherans and the upper north side. Today the name of the school is Kolegy Loteriana Malagasy (Lutheran Secondary School—KLB). In 1921, the school had 280 pupils and offered the first years of primary school (Lovise Haug in Bjertnes 1921). I had the opportunity to interview the last Norwegian principal at the school, Kari Johanne Honningdal (Former female missionary Kari Johanne Honningdal 2011). She was the principal from 1967 to 1971. The principal was responsible for reporting to the government, and she worked closely with a Malagasy colleague, the principal assistant, who was responsible for financial and disciplinary affairs. During the 1950s, the school had expanded its work and taught all levels of primary school. In the late 1960s, there were 350–400 pupils. Today, the school has around 1,150 pupils from the primary to the upper-secondary level (Principal Assistant KLB 2012). When I was visiting the school in 2011–2012, the number of pupils was decreasing due to the political crisis that started in 2009 and that made it difficult for parents to pay school fees. Christianity was one of the subjects, and pupils still participated in the ritual of morning devotion, as well as praying before going home in the afternoon.

## Who Came to the Mission School?

From the life stories collected within the framework of this research, I will draw a picture of who came to the mission school and peoples' view of education during the 1950s. This will help answering the question of whom had access to mission schools and what effect the mission's literacy work had on pupils' lives. Moreover, this is an important aspect regarding the impact of the mission's literacy work on power relations between the educated elite and the people in general in the Malagasy society. By providing education and the possibility to obtain official educational diplomas, the mission contributed to form the educated elite of the country. The pupils interviewed within the context of this study lived both in the town and in rural areas in the district. They have in common that they all went at one time or another to the mission school in the town of Betafo.

The interviewees felt that life was easier when they were children. Land was available since fewer people shared the same land. But they had to work hard, as expressed by Patrick:

> Life was hard for my parents. Very hard. At that time they were really . . . mum and dad worked non-stop to get enough food. Cultivating, raising livestock, cultivating . . . the cows and the small pigs had to be taken care of. At that time it was not like . . . if you had an outfit, you used it. We didn't even have a hat. That was life before. It was quite hard.
>
> (Former pupil Patrick 2012, my translation)

Pupils told they woke up at 3 a.m. to cook the rice, potatoes, manioc or corn, eat and be able to reach school before 8 a.m. (Former pupil Patrick 2012, Former pupil Rolland 2012). School finished at 1 p.m. and then they went home to eat again. Teaching missionary Honningdal emphasised that most of the children at the mission school were children of farmers (Former female missionary Kari Johanne Honningdal 2011). The parents of the interviewees had various occupations such as farming, vocational, bureaucratic and church work. The salary was often insufficient to support the whole family. Occupations other than farming were often combined with some farming and other income-generating activities such as embroidery and craftwork. The former pupils highlighted that they often helped their parents at home doing agricultural work, herding the livestock and taking care of smaller sisters and brothers. Haja had to do his homework while herding the cattle: "We had to do exercises at home, but things we could learn while herding, we did while watching the cattle" (Former pupil Haja 2012, my translation).

Some parents, like Patrick's parents who were farmers, had not acquired reading and writing skills, as opposed to those who were bureaucrats or worked within the church. The participants said that in the village where they lived, there were both people who had acquired reading and writing skills and those who had not. They also had friends of the same age who did not go to school. An important question when analysing who had access to the schools of the mission and its consequence in society is if people valued the literacy skills that the mission offered. What was people's view of formal education? There is a word called *bado* in Malagasy, meaning people that are not too intelligent, who cannot read and write. When telling that her grandmother did not go to school, Honorine said, "She didn't even know her age" (Former pupil Honorine 2012, my translation). "It's hard not to know", Honorine's grandmother told her and she urged Honorine to go to school. When her grandmother died, however, she stayed with other family members who did not value formal education:

> They had a daughter. She didn't go to school any longer. And they said: "Stop schooling, you should rather learn to do things." So they didn't let me go to school and I quit. I cried when I had to quit, and the teacher asked, "Where is Honorine, she is not in school," "She is not going to school anymore," the children from my village replied. He then said that I should go to school. "No, me, I'm not going to school anymore." The consequence was that I wanted to get married because I didn't want to stay, and then I got married. And that's the story.
>
> (Former pupil Honorine 2012, my translation)

Honorine was forced to quit school in order to "learn things". This gives a good example of how some people viewed education as not relevant to the life of the villagers. She was very vulnerable since she was an orphan, and possibly also because she was a girl and marriage could become a way out. Others put a lot of effort in getting an education for their children. Rolland's parents managed to educate all of their 11 children. Others in the village were encouraged to do the same: "They wanted their children to have knowledge. So they did everything they could in order to be able to give us that. That's why we also helped them. We didn't have any holidays, but we helped our parents" (Former pupil Rolland 2012, my translation). Patrick also said his parents wanted their children to acquire more knowledge, even if they didn't go to school themselves:

> They didn't know much before, and they wanted their children to go to school in order to know things. People can fool you if you don't

have knowledge. So they pushed us to school, my younger and older siblings all went to school and I went to school. Everyone had to go to school for at least some years.

(Former pupil Patrick 2012, my translation)

In the quotation, it is evident that Patrick's parents regarded education as helping their children to better live their lives and not to be tricked into something they did not understand in a society where reading and writing skills came to be more and more required. To learn basic reading and writing skills were, however, seen as sufficient, and he went to school for only a few years.

Some of the former pupils interviewed for this study went to other Lutheran primary schools or bush schools in the countryside before continuing their education at higher levels at the mission school in Betafo. Some also went to a public primary school, like the one in Betafo, for some years before coming to the mission school. Others went to the mission's primary school in Betafo for the entire period. Former pupils participating in the life story approach lived up to 7 km away from the Lutheran school, and they went by foot every day. A few of them remembered the walking distance, and that they were tired and hungry on their way back home. To be closer to school, some lived in the dormitory, while others stayed with relatives. Daniel lived with his grandmother and later in the dormitory (Former pupil Daniel 2012).

## School Fees

The financial aspect of educational work is a recurring theme in the documents that I have searched, but also in the interviews I conducted. One former teacher in Betafo said school fees were very low at the Lutheran school, which made it possible also for poor children to enter (Former male teacher 4 2011). Difficulties in paying school fees were, however, a recurring factor that was mentioned as a reason for quitting school by some of the former pupils. A few pupils were supported through the missionaries and through being children of church employees. Some of the children of pastors and teachers within the Lutheran Church did not pay school fees at lower levels. This gave an opportunity to their children to go to school even though their parents did not have very good salaries. One former pupil and teacher said he was very happy for that, because his parents could never have afforded to pay (Former male teacher 3 2012). Jean remembered that he was sent home to get money:

We could say that life was cheaper at that time: however, it was difficult to pay the school fees. "Go home and get the school fees!" And I went home. "Why did you come home? Oh, the school fees!" And then I got the school fees and I went to school. "Here are the school fees". Yes . . . but school fees were difficult, and at the public school there were no school fees. There weren't. We just studied. That's how it was, and when you didn't pay school fees, you had to go home.

(Former pupil Jean 2012, my translation)

During the last years of primary school, the school fee was higher, which was the reason why some did not manage to pay, so therefore had to take their children out of school. Sarah was one of those whose father was a pastor and did not pay school fees at lower level. When reaching her 6th school year, she had to quit due to her age and views on education for girls:

So, I had to stop there at the age of 15. But they continued to send one of my siblings to school because he was a boy and it was very sad if he didn't have any knowledge. Rather let the girls stop schooling. I was sad. Very sad. But there wasn't any help from my parents so I stopped because it would be sad for my brother not to have any knowledge. I then stayed at home helping my parents farming. That's life. And when I grew up, when I got old enough, when I got old enough to get my own home, I got married.

(Former pupil Sarah 2012, my translation)

Families consisted of many siblings, and when some were able to read and write, younger sisters and brothers got a chance to go to school. As shown in Patrick's story (Figure 1.1 in Chapter 1), he quit school after seven years: "The parents didn't manage. Those who got some knowledge had to quit. They had to quit. That's enough. You can quit now so that the others can go to school" (Former pupil Patrick 2012, my translation). Avoiding paying school fees was one reason why some chose to go to the public school. The public school could not, however, accept many pupils. One former pupil at the mission school went to the public primary school but did not get a place on the lower secondary level, even though he passed the primary school exam. He then started at the mission school (Former male pupil 8). He revealed that only about one-fourth of the pupils at the public school could continue at the secondary level, while about half continued in private schools and one-fourth quit school. This comment illustrates how the education provided by the churches acted as an alternative option for those who did not have access to public schools.

## Teaching in the Mission School

The Protestant, and also Lutheran, focus on understanding the text, not only read it or learn it by heart, would give expectations that the pedagogical approach in mission schools were different from public schools. As shown by Harries, Swiss Protestant missionaries in South-East Africa were annoyed by the "parrot-like learning of words and sounds" with no emphasis on a deep understanding (Harries 2001: 416, 418). But teaching in the mission school of Betafo was not, according to some of the former pupils, much different from others. It was described as passive by one of the former pupils, who later worked as a teacher (Former pupil George 2011). The teachers were talking most of the time and the children received knowledge without any dialogue. They often had to learn things by heart. Daniel said they could not argue with the teacher, and the teacher taught them to be polite, to respect other people, to behave and to greet people (Former pupil Daniel 2012). There were both male and female teachers, young and old. All of them were Lutherans. Corporal punishment was used to make pupils behave. Naivo said the threats of one teacher in particular made him afraid:

> There were nice teachers with good hearts, of whom we were not afraid. And there were teachers who were very strict with the pupils, of whom we were afraid. I was afraid of them, and even when I should have known the answer, I couldn't answer and then I was taken.
> *And what happened when you didn't answer?*
> They hit. If I didn't know the answer, I was hit with the ruler.
> (Former pupil Naivo 2011, my translation)

Patrick revealed that they were 50 pupils in one class with only one teacher: "They hit us if we were not quiet. Yes. And 'Sit!' when we had finished the praying, 'Sit!' The teaching went on. We were not allowed to say anything again before the break" (Former pupil Patrick 2012, my translation). Another former pupil, who also went to a public school, said he preferred the Lutheran school because the teachers were nicer at this school (Former male pupil 8). However, his parents could not afford the school fees, so he went to the public school until he was refused at the lower secondary level. These accounts show that teaching during this period in mission schools, as in public schools, involved strong means to establish order, hierarchy and control.

## Educational Achievement

The former pupils interviewed in the framework of this project started school at different ages. There was no age limit in the mission school as in the public school. One former teacher said that, due to no age limit, some of the pupils were even the same age as he (Former male teacher 4 2011). Passing the yearly exams was a challenge for many, and they used a different number of years to achieve the same educational level. The high failure rate was one important factor for the large dropout rate. Many of those who reached the level of the primary school exam failed and had to retry several times. This was discouraging for both the pupils and the parents who had to pay. At the end, some just quit. Rolland quit secondary level in order to let his younger siblings go to school because they did not know how many years it would take him to get a diploma (Former pupil Rolland 2012). Jean's story illustrates well how difficult it was to get through the educational system (Figure 6.1).

The lack of schoolbooks was given as one reason why the exam results were low by the former teaching missionaries interviewed in this study (Former female missionary Tordis Sandvik 2011, Former female missionary Kari Johanne Honningdal 2011, Former female missionary Elfrid Søyland 2011, Former female missionary Helena Trydal 2012). Even though books published by the Lutheran printing press were sold at a lower price than imported French books, many pupils could still not afford them. Former pupils said that they bought schoolbooks from the principal. Even though this was an extra economic burden, the books were theirs to bring home whereas the books available for free to pupils in the public school had to stay at school. One advantage was that siblings could inherit books. Haja said:

> Our parents bought books for the oldest child who gave them to the next one, who gave them to the next one, who gave them to the next one. That's why it was not that difficult to ensure that all the children had books.
>
> (Former pupil Haja 2012, my translation)

---

Jean grew up in a village close to Betafo. He was born in 1941 and was the oldest of eight siblings. He went to Sunday school as a child. He remembered they had a blackboard in church, but does not remember if they learned to read. After 2 years in a local public school he moved to study at the mission school in Betafo. He repeated some levels twice, and one even three times as far as he remembered. He got his primary level diploma, but chose to leave school after the second year of secondary school. He liked school, but said it was not for him, as he didn't pass the exams. His father, though, encouraged him to get an education. After quitting school, he was recruited by a pastor to work as a teacher in a bush school in the countryside. After 7 years as a teacher he got another job in Betafo, and since then has been employed by a company. He has 11 children and talked about the importance of education nowadays, as there is not enough land to feed every family.

*Figure 6.1* Jean's story

Source: Former pupil Jean (2012)

## Education for What?

Some quit school after leaving the school in Betafo, while others continued their education in other schools. Olga, George and Rolland continued at the mission's schools in Antsirabe. Some also mentioned that being too educated could involve the risk of becoming a bureaucrat and having to move from the village and the agricultural land. Bloch also revealed in his study of literacy in a Malagasy village that parents could be afraid of losing their children due to education (Bloch 1998: 179). The following quotation from the interview with Jean illustrates why basic reading and writing skills could be considered sufficient:

> When the collector of rice came, some people had good harvests. And some of them who came to the collector had tons of rice. Tons! There were those who had 10 tons, five tons, six tons . . . like that. That was life before, so education . . . if the children knew to read . . . if they knew quite well . . . the children seemed to want to stop.
>
> (Former pupil Jean 2012, my translation)

A good alternative to paid jobs that required reading and writing skills existed at that time, as it was easier to live from the land. According to Jean, there has, however, been a change in people's opinion about education since Jean's childhood due to the amount of land available and that people have also become more used to the idea of leaving the land of the ancestors.

The participants in the life story approach had done various things after school, such as farming, vocational work and working as bureaucrats. Naivo, who had done different kinds of vocational work, found it important to know arithmetic and to be able to read (Former pupil Naivo 2011). Sarah and Honorine contributed to the family's income through sewing clothes, a craft they learned in school (Former pupil Honorine 2012, Former pupil Sarah 2012). Jean, who passed primary school exam, was recruited by the pastor to work at a bush schools in the countryside where he worked for 7 years (Former pupil Jean 2012). This is a good illustration of how the church recruited teachers from their own schools to work in their bush schools. George, Haja and Olga trained to become teachers and worked mostly in public schools until their retirements (Former pupil George 2011, Former pupil Haja 2012, Former pupil Olga 2011). Rolland got a career within the military and supported his sisters' and brothers' education. Patrick argued that school made him more capable of receiving advice from development organisations to improve his harvest:

> There were benefits. Like you can see better what is the best way to do things, like agricultural techniques. You manage to follow the

training because those agricultural technicians come and it's easier to learn. Then you can learn to plant new things. Our parents only had potatoes, wheat, rice and that's the only thing they had.

(Former pupil Patrick 2012, my translation)

Some of the pupils also focused on becoming more independent when knowing to read and write, like Daniel:

> Education is useful. Yes. The reason is that we should learn in order not to . . . in order to know things better, to be educated. When things have to be done you don't need to ask others. No problem, you just use what you learned and then it's okay . . . Like when there is . . . things that you don't want people to know about, that you want to do . . . like something that could be good for yourself. However you have to send it by letter. Then you have to get someone to write it for you . . . and ask what it means. . . "That's what I want to do . . . could you please help me with this?"
> *Did anyone ask you for help?*
> Yes, to write letters and for instance when they receive an answer they ask me to help again. And that's shameful. . . . "Mister, what does this mean?", "I'm going to do this and that . . .". That's not how it should be.

(Former pupil Daniel 2012, my translation)

This farmer obviously used the knowledge he learned at school, and others in the village came to him for help. Haja argued that in a district where the mission worked, more people knew to read and write compared to other places, for instance in a region in the north of Madagascar where he was working as a teacher:

> You come there, and in addition to being a teacher you have to be the secretary . . . you do everything that has to do with writing because people don't have the skills. . . . But in the districts where the mission worked people know how to read and write because the teacher taught them in church as well as in school.

(Former pupil Haja 2012, my translation)

This quotation says something about the impact the mission schools had in terms of supporting literacy. Haja was president of the area where he lived (*Président Fokontany*), and he said he used the skills he learned at school, especially through religious studies, to solve problems between different parts in a conflict. The participants mentioned some of their voluntary work, especially in church committees, at local as well as national level. Some were treasurers and secretaries, others children and youth workers, and women were engaged in women's work (for instance, women's meetings and raising money to church work). The literacies the mission brought, including teaching in Malagasy, had the potential to allow people to take up new roles and responsibilities in their communities. It is important, however, to be aware that with the literacies that the mission brought, also religion in the form of Lutheranism came.

Up until now in this chapter, I have focused on the pupils who went to the mission school in the city of Betafo and their opinion about teaching in mission schools and the value of education. I will now take a closer look at how literacies were promoted and experienced in the educational institutions of the mission in the district of Betafo during the period of independence.

## Literacies in Sunday Schools

The story of former pupil Daniel (Figure 6.2) is interesting with regard to Sunday school experiences during the 1950s.

The participants in the life story approach came from Lutheran families, and some of the parents worked as catechists and pastors. Sunday school was believed to have an impact on children's behaviour and being a good Christian parent involved making sure children got religious training. This obligation, illustrating the link the mission created between the church and the home, was apparent in the qualitative interviews. When asked who made her go to Sunday school, Honorine said: "There was no

---

Daniel was born in 1941 and was the only child of his mother. A catechist became his father, as he married his mother when he was a little boy. Daniel went to Sunday school where his father was the teacher. There he learned to read with other kids. All the children were in one class, and the smallest ones looked upon the older and learned. Daniel went to the Lutheran school in Betafo at the age of 10 or 11. They didn't have to pay school fees due to his father's work as a catechist. The school was about 6 km from the village. He first lived with his grandmother in Betafo, but when she moved he stayed at the dormitory. He got his primary school diploma and CSD, but quit school after he failed a lower secondary exam. After primary school he worked as a teacher for the smallest children at the school of Betafo for a few years. However, since he was the only child in his family, he had to take care of the family land. He quit school and settled down in his village of origin, got married, had seven children and worked as a farmer.

---

*Figure 6.2* Daniel's story

Source: Former pupil Daniel (2012)

one who made me go, I was born in a Christian family" (Former pupil Honorine 2012). Jean remembers the poetry, preparation and celebration at Christmas, which gave him a lot of good memories (Former pupil Jean 2012). He said Sunday school helped children to find faith and keep their relationship with God throughout their lives. At Sunday school children learned to pray, sing, respect their parents and not to use bad language, according to Patrick (Former pupil Patrick 2012). They also learned discipline, which made it easier for them to start school. It was mostly the catechist who was responsible for Sunday school, but sometimes, like in Betafo, Sunday school teachers could be the same teachers as in the primary school (Former pupil Haja 2012). This meant that teachers would use their pedagogical knowledge from teacher education in Sunday school. From the 1950s onward, Sunday schools were also equipped with age-specific educational material with pedagogical and practical information to teachers about running Sunday schools, printed by the Lutheran printing press (Former female missionary Tordis Sandvik 2011).

In some places, Sunday school was on Sundays. In other places, such as in the city of Betafo, it was two times a week. In Sunday school there were school-aged children who went to primary school, as well as those who did not go to school. Rolland said they followed the curriculum for Sunday schools elaborated by the church and there were examinations where they were asked questions according to this curriculum (Former pupil Rolland 2012). According to Olga, the Bible was in focus in Sunday school:

> We learned the Bible, they taught us hymns, they taught us . . . they taught us to look in the Bible . . . things like that. This was in addition to what we learned about the Bible at the Lutheran school. Because in the Lutheran school there had to be Bible studies in the schedule. There was reading from the Bible and they said: "You have to learn this by heart: For God had such love for the world . . .", like that. And that's how it was in school and in Sunday school.
>
> (Former pupil Olga 2011, my translation)

This talks to how literacy practices, both in Sunday school and primary school, were based on regular repeated activities involving reading parts of the Bible and learning verses by heart. Daniel remembered the stories from the Bible:

> We learned the Holy Scripture and we learned the stories from the Bible by heart. There were books before with stories from the Bible. We used them . . . there were quite a lot of pages. The story changed every month because we didn't have many books, only one, and next year it was the same book. Catechism, Bible stories and the

New Testament. We didn't use the Bible, but books with stories. We learned those stories about Joseph in Egypt.

(Former pupil Daniel 2012, my translation)

Patrick mentioned the catechism as being important for teaching in Sunday school: "In the catechism, there were things from the Holy Scripture, and the Ten Commandments. We learned everything. We learned, 'Our father who is in heaven' and then we knew it" (Former pupil Patrick 2012, my translation). Pictures were also used in Sunday school, and Olga remembered that sometimes they used a Flannelgraph with characters and objects from the Bible story to stick to the board and move around while telling the story: "They put things on it . . . there were pictures. This is Jesus. This is Mary. This is . . . they took Jesus with them because the king could take him" (Former pupil Olga 2011, my translation). In some places, small books and magazines, such as the Lutheran youth magazine, were distributed to the children. Jean was given magazines at Sunday school: "I remember that they gave us a Sunday school magazine. So we could learn things. This made us happy. Yes. At Sunday school" (Former pupil Jean 2012, my translation).

Several former pupils interviewed through this study emphasised that reading skills were taught in Sunday school, especially in the countryside. One was born in the mid-1950s and lived in Betafo. Sometimes he went to Sunday school in his family village only 1 km from town. He said that at Sunday school in the village they learned the alphabet, and some learned to read, but this was not the case in Betafo (Former male pupil 2 2012). Daniel, whose story is included previously (Figure 6.2), talked about the reading material they used:

There was a poster with the letters . . . things like that . . . It was at Sunday school that I started to learn reading. And with the teacher in primary school I already knew how to read but learned things like counting, we did dictation before, copying and things like that. . .

*But you did not know how to write before you entered school?*
Here? No, but I was able to read.

*Were there any other kids who learned to read here at Sunday school?*
If they were in our class . . . in our class, they would be able to read. Because the little ones looked at what the elders did and then they knew that this is like that and this is like that.

(Former pupil Daniel 2012, my translation)

A pupil's experience with the difference between Sunday school and primary school is described in this quotation. Reading was part of Sunday school, whereas literacy practices like counting and dictation took place in school. In the interview with George we get a glimpse of how literacy practices focusing on the alphabet could be in Sunday school:

> We had . . . what do you call it . . . a poster, with the alphabet. We used those to learn to read and write. Little by little. We learned the A for instance, then we wrote it afterwards, and then we put the letters [A,B,D, E. . .] together. So the teaching was like that, little by little. And when we had learned some letters, we learned to read a word. And to write it.
> *In Sunday school?*
> Yes, in Sunday school. Little by little, but in school I think we learned to read faster.
> (Former pupil George 2011, my translation)

Tests are similar to how Papen describes dictations. It is a typical school literacy practice where pupils are measured as to how they comply with certain norms, based on certain forms of literacy (Papen 2005: 45). Exams in Lutheran Sunday schools were based on the norms of Lutheranism. Still, in the 1950s, students were tested in the Sunday schools of the mission. If the church did not have a pastor, but only a catechist, the pastor in the district would come to ask the children questions about the bible and the Lutheran understanding of the Bible. It also happened that the Norwegian missionary at the nearby mission station came for an inspection. Daniel remembered how they were tested in Bible knowledge during the exam:

> For instance, we had to say things by heart. Like what was written in John and we had to answer . . . what is written in the psalms . . . tell us about . . . tell us about the life of Moses, or Joseph or Jacob . . . things like that. What's the name of the father of that man and who was the child of Abraham?
> (Former pupil Daniel 2012, my translation)

One woman who grew up in a village outside Betafo in the 1950s and 1960s worked as a Sunday school teacher in the 1970s, when she was about 15–16 years (Female Sunday school teacher 2011). Even if this is beyond the period of study for this research, I chose to include it, as it describes well the practice of reading in Sunday school. From the view of a Sunday school teacher, she described how they taught the children:

> Many of the children could not read or write, but they could hear. They were good at listening when we explained. And they understood. They wanted to learn to read and write also, at least their names. They learned to read their names first. And when they had

learned that, we went through the alphabet. Yes, we taught the alphabet in Sunday school in those times, with the catechist. And we used coal to write on the trees . . . they had to step forward one by one. First to write their names. When they knew how to write their names, they started to understand what was written on the blackboard. They listened. They listened.

(Female Sunday school teacher 2011, my translation)

Rolland argued that Sunday school could act as a passage to school, giving the children a taste of education and familiarising the parents with the idea of educating their children in an institutional establishment (Former pupil Rolland 2012). I will now proceed describing religious literacies in Lutheran schools in the Betafo region.

## Literacies in Primary Schools

The former pupils I met remembered some of the teaching in religion in the primary school in Betafo. Their accounts give a picture of what religious literacies could be in a Lutheran school during the 1950s and 1960s. Sarah said that continuous Bible study was what made it a Lutheran school (Former pupil Sarah 2012). Patrick maintained that they had to read small books in Malagasy with Bible stories, the New Testament and the catechism (Former pupil Patrick 2012). They also had morning and afternoon devotion:

We had to do the Lord's prayer every morning. And we learned "Our Father in Heaven" and those things. When school was finished . . . we took turns praying. Today it was my responsibility, your turn . . . before we could go home.

(Former pupil Patrick 2012, my translation)

This quotation shows the repetitive character of religious literacy practices and that pupils actively participated. Honorine, who also went to a public school for some years, thought the praying was the main difference between the public and the Lutheran school:

What was different between the schools was that at the Christian school we prayed before studying. Yes. And they raised the children. Even if we wanted to be mean, we should remember that "I am at the Christian school". At the public school there was no praying but straight away "Bonjour Madame, bonjour Monsieur!" And the lesson started. We started to study. There was a difference. And at the Christian school we also prayed before going home. When going home, we also prayed. That was nice. It was not like that at the public school. We only took the things, said goodbye and took off.

(Former pupil Honorine 2012, my translation)

This quotation speaks to the difference, in content and purpose, between a public school promoting French-assimilationist literacies and the mission school, where religious literacies were promoted. In the quotation, Honorine also raised the issue of a specific Christian upbringing that took place in mission schools. Patrick stated that their parents preferred the Protestant school, despite the school fees:

My parents were Christians so they were not very eager towards the public school, we could become mean if we went there. We wouldn't know God. So they sent us all there, even though school fees were hard they preferred to send their seven children to the Protestant school.

(Former pupil Patrick 2012, my translation)

This quotation demonstrates that by some of the church members the Lutheran school was regarded as important in cultivating a Christian morality among the children.

A quotation by former pupil George reflects the appearance of subjects in the mission school in Betafo:

In order to be a school, we had to follow the public programme, and in addition we had Bible studies. But it was much like public schools, we had math, French, history, sciences. . . . What was in the public school, we also learned.

(Former pupil George 2011, my translation)

According to George, geography and history were mainly about France, and they learned by heart about their ancestors *les Gaulois*:

In primary school there were also things about Madagascar, but in French. In secondary school, there was French history. We learned it very well, the length of La Loire, La Rhone, La Seine . . . by heart . . . the Jura, the different mountains, that's what we learned a lot.
*Did you learn anything about Malagasy geography?*
It was not until the last years of primary school we learned . . . it was like we learned the history of Madagascar in the middle of primary school . . . And in the last year of primary school there was less, there was not much about the history of . . . you know . . . why we were colonised, but the history of France. When learning history

in primary school, we said, "Our ancestors the Gauls" . . . that's
what we learned by heart, by heart "Our ancestors the Gauls". In
the caves. . . .

(Former pupil George 2011, my translation)

This quotation illustrates that lessons were strongly focussed on
France, so in that sense teaching was assimilationist. Pupils who studied at the mission school in Betafo also learned the songs of the colonial administration at school. Former pupil Jean started to sing during
the interview when he described a performance they had at a yearly
gathering in the district (Former pupil Jean 2012). Jean and his classmates, wearing the colours of the French flag: blue shorts, white t-shirt
and red caps, made a pyramid and Jean was at the top when they were
singing:

Do you know the three colours
the three colours of France
That makes the heart dream
about hope and glory

(Former pupil Jean 2012, my translation)

Jean started to sing this song, which he remembered very well, because
he was thinking of a good memory from his years at the mission school.
From an ideological perspective, the meaning of the song is rather strik-
ing: a colonised singing about the colours in the flag of the coloniser.
Another former pupil, Rolland, still remembered the first words of the
French National Anthem, La Marseillaise, *Allons enfants de la patrie*,
and revealed that he had to sing during the oral examination in primary
school:

When I took my primary school exam we had to write in French,
a small text. And at that time we had to sing during examination.
You had to have a notebook with five songs and there you go . . .
and there was an oral exam. You went to take your notebook, the
hymnal and there you go. "Sing this song to me", and there you go.
*In French?*
In French. Yes. Yes. We had to learn them, it was the French
national songs at that time, like "We have a fatherland." Because we
were still colonised, it was not until 1960 that Madagascar became
independent.

(Former pupil Rolland 2012, my translation)

This quotation reveals that pupils had no choice but to learn the songs
of the colonial power, because singing these songs were among the skills
students were tested for to get through the exam. This was a strong

mean to promote the policy of the colonial power. It really speaks to questions of identity. One former teacher, who was a pupil at the school during the 1950s, revealed that some teachers also tried to make children speak French, and he remembered that at one time there were sanctions against those who spoke in Malagasy (Former male teacher 3 2012). The mission school was, however, generally known to be open to the use of the Malagasy language. Rolland said they were met with understanding, while describing how they struggled with French-assimilationist literacies:

> There were books in French, and in Malagasy, like "Avancer le matin", "On se lève de Bonheur". Yes, things like that. Since the exam was in French, all had to be in French. All of the questions, because writing was in French at that time. There was like: "Edit a text in French". It was like that . . . unbelievable, but everything had to be in French. And we tried . . . There was a difference at the mission school. When they saw that it was difficult, they explained it in Malagasy.
>
> (Former pupil Rolland 2012, my translation)

As explained in previous chapters, what I mean by contextualised literacies are literacies in Malagasy that to some degree took the Malagasy context into account. The former pupils and teachers did not talk much about that, but some mentioned that they used the Malagasy language in the mission school. One former male pupil, who went to the Lutheran school for only the 1st year and 2nd year of primary school during the 1960s, said they only used Malagasy in school: "We only spoke Malagasy. French was barely used. Only a few words. No grammar, only words. We only had Malagasy at that time" (Former male pupil 7 2011, my translation). When asked if the pupils at the Lutheran school were better in Malagasy than the pupils at the public school, George replied that was true and truly an advantage. The fact that pupils were not able to use the Malagasy language to show their knowledge for the exam was, however, a challenge for many of them. One of the former pupils interviewed in this study said:

> For the pupils in this school it was difficult to pass the primary school exam in French, as the teaching was in Malagasy and even if you knew things, it was difficult to write it in French. That was very difficult. When they did it in Malagasy, it was easy to show the knowledge. But, when it was in French, when we had to tell it with French words, the children really had problems. In the public school, there were more pupils who passed. It was a big burden not to know French.
>
> (Former male pupil 2 2012, my translation)

This pupil possessed the Protestant primary school diploma. As explained in the end of previous chapter, this was a diploma for having passed the primary school exam in Malagasy. It was not recognised by the government, but it showed that the candidate had the knowledge, it could be used within the church structure and its existence promoted contextualised literacies.

## Concluding Remarks

This chapter aimed, based on the narratives and interviews of former teachers and pupils of the mission's primary school in Betafo, to describe the kind of pupils who went to the mission schools and how they experienced school. The case of Betafo gives a good insight into the mission's literacy work in the period around independence. It draws a picture of the society in which the mission promoted reading and writing skills. Based on what I have discussed here, we can imagine some possible long-term consequences of the mission's literacy work. The identity of pupils who had followed teaching at the mission school had the potential to be different from those who successfully passed the French-assimilationist public educational system. This had the potential to challenge French-assimilationist literacies. At the same time, it should not be forgotten that these literacies were embedded in an institution promoting religious literacies and a Malagasy Christian identity.

In the previous chapters, the broader literacy policies in Madagascar during the two periods under study have been described, as well as the role played by mission schools. These chapters constitute a more descriptive part of the book on which literacies were promoted and how these were experienced by former pupils and teachers in mission schools. In the coming chapters, I will analyse why these literacies were promoted. I will do this by discussing the ideologies in which these literacies were embedded.

# 7 Secular and Religious Literacies

In previous chapters, I have shown that at times the colonial government appreciated and, at other times, they were sceptical of the missions' efforts to promote literacy. From an ideological approach to literacy, this is not difficult to understand. As stated in Chapter 2, literacy is not only about reading and writing skills, but it is ideologically embedded. In this chapter, I will explain educational goals from both perspectives: from the colonial power and the Norwegian mission. In this way, I will better be able to describe the ideologies behind the literacies that were promoted and experienced in the mission schools.

First, I will describe how the colonial educational policy was rooted in Republican traditions and a secular discourse, and how this impacted on the way they related to the missions. Second, I will analyse the dominant and alternative discourses that the Norwegian mission drew upon in their literacy work. Further, I will describe the Norwegian mission's collaboration with likeminded institutions. The Protestant missions were important collaborators in the mission's literacy work, whereas the Catholic mission was looked upon as a rival throughout the period focused on in this research. The sources are primarily based on the Norwegian mission's archives and Norwegian missionaries' perspectives.

## Secularism Imported to Madagascar

According to Republican visions, education had to be secular and universal with a desire for a secular state freed from the Catholic domination (Daughton 2006: 9). *Anticlericalism* as a concept appeared in France in the 1870s as "an indication of how politicians considered the church to be their main political, social, and cultural adversary" (Daughton 2006: 8). Moderate Republicans had won legislative power and started the fight to ease the grip the Catholic Church had on the nation. With Republican values, the society should become modern and organised according to abstract, meaning scientific, principles (Chafer 2007: 444). Education became one important area to ensure the dissemination of Republican values instead of religious and monarchist ideas

(Chafer 2007: 439). Secularism in education was based on Republican decrees of 1882, 1886 and 1905 (The Director of Education 1943). The 1882 decree removed religious education from the curriculum in primary schools, while the 1886 and 1887 decree did not mention children of pastors and their delegates among those who should have free access to public schools. The 1905 decree specified that based on the 1882 decree, religious education could not be taught to children between the age of 6 and 13 years in public schools. This had to be done outside school hours.

Anticlericalism was also exported to the colonies. James Patrick Daughton has described the fight between the religious Catholic and the secular Republican France at the dawn of the colonial period (Daughton 2006). Daughton asserted that a great paradox was apparent in the heart of French colonial policy. On the one hand, it was built on Republican secular ideas and anticlericalism. On the other hand, the implementation of these policies in the colonies depended on the Catholic mission due to the lack of resources. A discussion at the National colonial conference held in France in 1889, before Madagascar had become a French colony, described by Martin Deming Lewis, serves as an example to this ambiguous relation:

> Finally, with regard to Madagascar, where French control was not yet complete, the congress seemed most concerned that the government "should energetically maintain the political supremacy of France. . . *vis-à-vis* foreign powers". Assimilation came into the picture only in the request that France should "give as much support as possible to the French missionaries and their *mission civilisatrice*" in the island [original italics].
>
> (Lewis 1962: 146)

The same support should be given to missionaries who taught French in Indo-China, which is a clear indication that French politicians considered missionaries as instruments in their colonial project (Lewis 1962: 145–146). With a case from Madagascar, Daughton illustrated an ambiguity in that French citizens had different views of colonial policies at the same time as they shared common interests. A local colonial administrator wanted to make charges against a Catholic priest in his area of administration, but he was ordered by Governor-General Galliéni not to pursue any charges. When the administrator and the priest in the end made peace, the priest wrote a conciliatory letter where he asked, "Are we not Frenchmen working for the greater good of our common mother, dear France? *Vive, vive, vive la France*!!!" (Quoted in Daughton 2006: 5). Republicans with anticlerical views could fight against Catholic influence at home and at the same time argue for including the Catholic mission as allies in the colonial conquest.

Thus, in spite of the dominance of Republican values, mission schools continued to play an important role in the colonies, keeping a religious orientation in their school curriculum (Farine 1969: 52–53). The colonial government considered the arrival of the French Protestant Mission (MPF) to Madagascar as an important contributor in promoting the French language and civilisation, and also in helping Protestant schools owned by non-French mission organisations. The first missionaries were even given buildings for free by the government (Guitou 1925). Rakotoanosy emphasised that since many, often of notable origin, had already been converted to Christianity when the colonial power came, opposing the missions would be too dangerous (Rakotoanosy 1986: 84–88). It was a challenge for the secular French government that many members of the Merina bourgeoisie were Protestants and educated by British missionaries. For the Malagasy elite, Protestantism was associated with the British, whereas Catholicism was associated with the French (Vigen and Tronchon 1993: 328, 331). To show that also French could be Protestants, the government strived to collaborate with the Protestant missions. The colonial government became, however, disappointed of the MPF missionaries. Instead of supporting the colonial policy, they seemed to ally with the Protestant missions in opposing governmental decisions (Guitou 1925). One example to this is the bush school dispute, described in Chapter 4. According to Daughton, even though the government strived for good relations with the Protestants, more decisions were in favour of the Catholic mission (Daughton 2006). Faced with the domination of Protestantism in Madagascar, the Catholic mission became an ally even though they were fierce opponents in the metropole (France).

In Chapters 1 and 4, I mentioned some of the decrees introducing secularism in the colonial educational policy in Madagascar. In the following pages, I will describe the reflections behind these policies, with a special focus on the reasoning behind the 1906 decree. Discussions related to educational reforms illustrate that there were different opinions among French politicians and colonial administrators. The first colonial decrees on education introduced the secular school in Madagascar. Article six in a decree dated 1899, issued under Governor-General Galliéni, was clear that religion had no place in public schools, but had to be practiced outside school (Galdi and Rochefort 1960a: 651). But the missions were allowed to continue their educational work with religious content in their own schools. Minister of the Colonies Gaston Doumergue played a role in putting an end to the missions' dominant position in educational work. In a 1903 confidential letter to the governor-general, he argued in favour of secularism to avoid that the missions, through establishing schools of different denomination, divided the population (Doumergue 1903). In Galliéni's last decree the following year, it was stated that support to religious schools would stop due to the complete separation of the church and the state in France (Galliéni 1904).

As explained in Chapter 1, Augagneur took over as governor-general after Galliéni in 1905. This was part of a strategy by the French government to strengthen secularism in Madagascar. He was a franc mason and socialist known for an authoritarian temperament (Vigen and Tronchon 1993: 326, 345). In a speech in the capital in Madagascar in 1907, Augagneur argued that secular education meant teaching "what was proven to be the truth for every human being", and that which was scientifically approved (Augagneur 1907a, my translation). Augagneur is in this quotation promoting the universality of secular literacies by pointing to its *scientific nature*, hiding its inherited ideologies. This is a good illustration on how governments promote literacy as something neutral, building on neutral competencies and hiding their ideological roots. Regulations and circulars were issued, some of which were explained in Chapters 1 and 4. At times regulations were, according to the Malagasy historian Monique Irène Rakotoanosy, illogical and absurd, such as forbidding natives to teach their neighbours to read (Rakotoanosy 1986: 96–97). The mission organisations perceived the policy as an anticlerical and even antireligious fight.

In 1905, the colonial government mapped which schools they could recognise as schools according to colonial educational regulations. Recognised schools used separate educational buildings, not a church or religious assembly house, and they were registered in the name of a qualified teacher. Table 7.1 shows the statistics on schools and pupils in public (colonial) and mission schools. What is interesting in the table is that it also shows the number of schools and pupils who were not recognised by the colonial administration. Only 1,070 of the pupils of the Norwegian mission and 7,677 of the pupils of the LMS were considered as attending recognised schools. As many as 41,326 of the NMS pupils, roughly double the number of LMS pupils (20,321), attended schools that were

*Table 7.1* Unrecognised and recognised public and private schools in Madagascar, 1905

|  | Unrecognised | | Recognised | |
| --- | --- | --- | --- | --- |
|  | Schools | Pupils | Schools | Pupils |
| **Public** |  |  | 371 | 28626 |
| Catholic | 938 | 45693 | 73 | 6533 |
| MPF | 300 | 12748 | 108 | 8017 |
| LMS | 403 | 20321 | 75 | 7677 |
| FFMA | 172 | 9216 | 9 | 830 |
| Anglican | 66 | 4012 | 31 | 1772 |
| NMS | 944 | 41326 | 15 | 1070 |
| **Private** | 2823 | 133316 | 311 | 25899 |

Source: Gouvernement générale de Madagascar et dépendances (1905)

unrecognised by the French administration. These numbers are a clear indication that the missions' most important instrument for literacy work was heavily threatened.

With the help of French deputies, the MPF lobbied the government in Paris. This dispute is important to understand the history of the relation between the missions and the colonial power. I have described this dispute more in depth in a chapter of the book *Empire and Education in Africa* (Kallaway and Swartz 2016).[1] Here, I will only give a short explanation to illustrate that there were different opinions within the French society on how secularism should be implemented in the colonies.

Deputies sent letters to the minister of the colonies and Governor-General Augagneur in Madagascar, arguing that the decree violated the freedom of thoughts (de Pressensé 1907, Siegfried et al. 1907). They argued that Augagneur's policy was not in line with the policy in the metropole and the heritage of the French Revolution. Governor-General Augagneur replied that the missions were protesting not because they were afraid of their educational work, but rather because they were afraid of losing their "power of evangelisation" (Augagneur 1907b, my translation). Education that took place in church buildings was described as "ridiculous parodies of real schools". In contrast to the *neutral literacy* taught in colonial schools, Augagneur is here clear about his opinion of the missions' literacies as being embedded in religion. Augagneur considered mission schools as only transmitting religious literacies and not managing to transmit French-assimilationist literacies, considered by the colonial administration as the basis for "real schools". Augagneur recognised, however, that the teaching of the missions that had taken place in church buildings could have a *moralising role*. Consequently, he allowed them to exist under the name *garderie*: bush schools. In these bush schools, as explained in Chapter 4, teaching could be done in the Malagasy language, but had to be done in separate buildings for educational purposes, not in a church. The protests of the missions were unsuccessful (Guitou 1925). Augagneur did not bow for the lobbying and stated that he intended to continue the French secularisation work in Madagascar. As explained in Chapter 4, the missions raised these issues again during the 1920s and they got some release under Governor-General Olivier's administration. Olivier's views on the implementation of secularism were more in line with the deputies that lobbied Augagneur in 1907.

As it has been shown here, French colonial education and literacy work were embedded in ideologies of republicanism, anticlericalism and secularism. There were different opinions about these ideologies, leading to different colonial educational policies and opinions on the literacy work of the missions. Now, I will analyse discourses and ideologies on which the mission based its argumentations for their educational work.[2]

## Discourses of Evangelisation and Development

In his book *Missions and Empire*, Etherington has argued that evangelism was the main aim of mission education:

> Few missionaries treated education as an end in itself; schooling was ancillary to the primary object of Christian evangelism . . . The great majority of Protestant missionaries, however, understood Bible-reading to be an essential tenet of their faith. This had driven remarkable spread of basic literacy through England, Scotland, and Wales and caused even the poorly educated missionaries first sent out by the London Missionary Society to make schooling, along with translating and printing Bibles, the first business of their missions to the South Pacific islands and southern Africa.
>
> (Etherington 2005a: 261–262)

How did the Norwegian missionaries regard their involvement within education? Why were they so eager to spread literacy, and how did they regard the function of literacy in the societies they were working in? Was education seen as an instrument in their evangelical work, or was it seen as something that provided people with a new capacity they could make use of to improve their lives more generally? There are several answers to these questions, related to different discourses that were relevant for the mission to draw upon and relate to. These discourses were rooted in both international and local mission movements.

At the World Missionary Conference in Edinburgh in 1910, Commission III focused its energy on education. The work of this commission was later published as the report *Education in relation to the Christianisation of National Life*, which will be referred to here in order to identify major discourses on mission education at the beginning of the 20th century (World Missionary Conference 1910). These discourses were relevant to various mission bodies through different periods of time. The commission was convinced that missions had made an important contribution to education and that education played a crucial part in evangelisation:

> The subject of education in missionary work is of special and far-reaching importance. No one, who knows the history of missions, can doubt that missionaries were pioneers of education wherever they went, and it is hardly possible to exaggerate the debt of gratitude which is due to them for their labours in education, nor can it be doubted how important a part education has played in the process of evangelisation.
>
> (World Missionary Conference 1910: 5–6)

The report of the commission on education was based on questionnaire responses from missionary workers, representing various mission bodies in different countries. In his book on the conference, Brian Stanley analysed the work of Commission III (Stanley 2009: 167–204). According to him, the survey was primarily concerned with Anglophone mission fields and the report was "the product of a process of negotiation between British and American educationalists and ecclesiastics" (Stanley 2009: 173). The commission was primarily concerned with education as an instrument for developing native Christian churches and promoted education as a subject of inter-missionary cooperation. In the conclusion, the commission presented several arguments for missionary educational work (World Missionary Conference 1910: 369–370). The motive of educational work should above all be *evangelistic*, viewing education as an instrument in evangelisation. It should be *edificatory*, promoting native church building, and *leavening*, aiming at the dissemination of Christian ideals and influence in the society at large. A *philanthropic* motive was promoted by liberal views of some of the commission's American members, especially Professor Ernest Burton (Stanley 2009: 177). A majority of the commission agreed that mission education could and should also have a philanthropic motive:

> d) The motive of missionary education may include the philanthropic desire to promote the general welfare of the people. There may be occasions in which the members of a Christian nation, confronting the situation in another nation, shall be compelled in obedience to the spirit of Jesus to recognise that the needs of this people are so various, so serious, and so pressing, that as Christians they cannot limit their efforts to evangelistic, edificatory, or leavening ministries, but must, to the measure of their ability, extend to them the hand of help in every phase of their life.
>
> (World Missionary Conference 1910: 370)

According to Stanley, most of the respondents to the questionnaire had not talked much about "mission education as a disinterested act of philanthropic service" (Stanley 2009: 177). The promotion of the philanthropic argument also easily led to disagreements within the commission. A minority, arguing that the first three aims were sufficient, were afraid that the philanthropic argument would distract them from their primary objective: "the vaguer philanthropic aim would be to direct them upon a path in which their efforts would lose in intensity, and the definite Christian motive would be weakened, and the positive Christian fruit would be likely to be found wanting" (World Missionary Conference 1910: 371). The main arguments for mission bodies to be involved in educational work should be religious: "the aim of true education is necessarily a religious one. The best educator is the best missionary" (World Missionary Conference 1910: 383).

Purposes, intentions and actions are intertwined and are difficult to separate, in the mission's policy as well as in reality where the missionaries performed their missionary duties. Since disseminating their universal faith was the assignment of missionaries, it can be argued that they never did what Stanley referred to as "a disinterest act of philanthropic service" (Stanley 2009: 177). Tjelle presented education as part of "indirect evangelization work" or "civilizing mission work" (Tjelle 2014: 50–51). According to Tjelle, civilising mission work was "based on the idea that the Christian mission would lead to an improvement of the totality of people's lives, including materialistic conditions, social structures, and political systems" (Tjelle 2014: 51). In order to analyse the aim of education within the Norwegian mission, I have identified two major discourses: one discourse of *evangelisation* and one on *development*. The evangelistic discourse is very evident in mission literature and has from the start been the dominant discourse. The discourse of development has been there from the start and evolved to different degrees in different periods of time. In a study on the spread of Christianity, missionary and historian Emil Birkeli argued that as a consequence of the mission movement during the 19th century also "home mission, philanthropy, charity and a sense of responsibility flourished" (Birkeli 1935: 79, my translation). The mission concept included caring for people's general well-being, which inspired different forms of involvement in society. Confronted with people's needs in the field, missionaries had to work to improve people's social and mental well-being.

In order to see how the Norwegian mission related to the evangelistic and the development discourse on an organisational level, it is relevant to look at the different revisions of the NMS missionary mandates concerning educational work. In the 1867 revision, article 12 of the NMS missionary mandate concerning education was formulated: "§12. As far as other activities permit, mission-assistants should offer school for the heathen children, as long as the parents give their consent. One should also give one's attention to people's general well-being and cultivation as a whole" (NMS 1867, my translation). In the missionary mandate of 1933, it was made very explicit that schools and Sunday schools should be created at every station, and that education should always be an instrument in the service of evangelisation. Christianity was to be taught, and the moral pledge to contribute to the general well-being and cultivation of the people as a whole still remained:

§13. Schools and Sunday Schools should be created at every station, where first and foremost Christian children have access, but where also non-Christian children can be accepted as far as possible. Mission schools always have to be an instrument in the service of evangelisation. Teaching Christianity and the personal influence to embrace the Christian faith must therefore as far as possible have a prominent place in schoolwork. In addition to that, any missionary should also give his attention to people's general cultivation and well-being as a whole.

(NMS 1933a, my translation)

During the 1960s, the formulation of the NMS missionary mandate was very much the same as in 1933, except that the sentence about people's general well-being was removed and a sentence about striving, if possible, to teach Christianity in public schools was added (NMS 1965a). I could not find in the archives who suggested this quite important change, but it appeared after the mandate was sent for consultation to the NMS districts in Norway and the mission fields. In the mandate of the 1960s, this pledge was taken away and substituted with a motivation more in line with the aim of *leavening* from the World Missionary Conference in 1910 that is the dissemination of Christian ideals and influence in the society at large, building upon an *evangelistic discourse*. Christianity was looked upon as universal and was to be shared with every human being. An individual relationship with God was important for conversion and therefore all members of a congregation should individually be attached to the *Holy book* by acquiring reading skills. Church members should also use their literacy skills for the purpose of developing a native church that could participate and later take the lead in evangelisation work.

## Norwegian Missionaries' Views on Education

In order to keep its function as an instrument in mission work, educational work had to stay in line with the evangelistic discourse, and show that it contributed to evangelisation. In addition, the mission's educational work was also evaluated by educational outputs. These kinds of considerations were apparent in strategy papers and discussions about planning the educational work in the mission field. Evangelistic and educational outputs related to different discourses that the mission drew upon, and the missionaries' concerns were different within different field of actions.

The aims of mission education are here described by analysing what missionaries wrote and discussed about their educational work. By pointing to how they mainly related to the mission's discourses on education, the hegemonic *discourse of evangelisation* and the alternative *discourse of development*. These discourses were not, in the view of the missionaries, necessarily contradictory, but rather complementary. The aims of mission education were manifested through archival material, mainly yearbooks, magazines and conference reports of the NMS. Some of the cases that were discussed at the conference had already been discussed in different committees, like the CM, an advising committee for the Mission Conference with both Norwegian and Malagasy members, and the Educational Committee. Their views on different issues were presented in the conference reports. In the following pages, I will also make some references to the qualitative interviews I conducted with former Norwegian teaching missionaries.

When reading NMS yearbooks and journals aimed at mission supporters in Norway, it clearly appears that schools were regarded as *an instrument for evangelisation*. It is apparent, however, that educational work was an indirect instrument in evangelisation and not a direct instrument, such as preaching the gospel. There was a continuous need to define education as a duty of the missionary and as a basic part of missionary work. In other words, it seems like not everyone agreed to promote mission educational work, which made it vulnerable and not likely to be prioritised. When presenting the challenges of teacher education to the NMS Conference in 1930, Büchsenschütz for instance argued against looking at schoolwork as something different from ordinary missionary work. Everything that strengthen a Christian school would eventually have impacts on the development of Christianity (NMS 1930a: 148). The school was promoted as the founder of the congregation, and teaching subjects such as French and mathematics should be considered as part of the missionary duty.

The NMS magazine for children and youth published several stories about Malagasy children who got the opportunity to go to the mission school. They were intended for Norwegian children, and the mission was certainly also aware that parents read those stories to their children. These articles were impacted by the need of publicity; the missionaries' concern of giving an advantageous account of their work, to ensure and increase moral and financial support. Some of the stories, which occurred in both periods under study, revealed children who were the first in their family to get to know Christianity and be baptised.[3] In this way, education was presented as a good instrument in evangelisation. This is illustrated by the last drawing in a cartoon about Koto, published in 1951 in the children's magazine *Kom og Se* (see Figure 7.1). Life in a Malagasy rural village was described very lively in the story. Koto meets his cousin Mino, and she shows him she prays. The text in the last drawing is as follows:

> "I would really like to know more about that God of yours", said Koto to Mino. "I wish you could teach me to pray to him". "I will rather take you to the mission school so that you too can learn to talk with God as well", Mino answered. Then Koto went with Mino to the school, and he was a glad and satisfied little Malagasy boy.
>
> (No author 1951, my translation)

**14.**

«Jeg vil gjerne vite mer om den guden din,» sa Koto til Mino. «Jeg skulle ønske du ville lære meg å be til ham.» «Jeg skal heller ta deg med til misjonens skole så du kan lære å snakke med Gud du også,» svarte Mino. Så ble Koto med Mino til skolen, og han var en glad og fornøyd liten gassergutt.

*Figure 7.1* "Koto"

Source: Kom og Se (No author 1951)

In several yearbooks from the 1950s and 1960s it was emphasised that bush schools were an instrument in evangelisation work. They were described as the best instrument of evangelisation, also in the coastal areas, as many pupils came from non-Christian homes (Torbjørnsen 1960: 64, Dahl 1957: 62). When the same teacher taught the children in school during the week and in church on Sundays, the teacher would have an important impact on the children. Bush schools were considered as door openers to areas that were difficult to reach. The local congregations needed, however, financial support and to neglect this part of mission work was to let precious opportunities slip away. Bush schools were regarded as important instruments of evangelisation also after independence, in the Norwegian mission's collaboration with the FLM, as described in Chapter 5 (p. 77).

Education was seen as *an instrument in shaping children and youth*. At the beginning of the 1950s, the schools were described as a condition to teach Christian belief and learning (Snekkenes 1954: 74). During the period from 1954 to 1957, the schoolwork expanded on the West Coast. It increased from 16 to 21 schools (Dahl 1957: 62). Fifteen of these schools were bush schools run by teachers without pedagogical training, but children still learned literacy skills, the catechism and Bible stories. Pupils in mission schools got values that they did not get in public schools, "the word of eternal life into their hearts" (Sjursen 1957: 54, my translation). To *educate future church leaders*, was a recurrent argument for schoolwork. In the yearbook for the period 1948–1951 it was stated that schoolwork was an important part in the institutionalisation of the church with Malagasy nationals. Even though the number of pupils, especially on the West Coast of Madagascar were not too many, the missionaries believed they would see the fruits of this important work in the future (Sæveraas 1951: 116). Schoolwork and the education of children and youth was seen as a central part of the life of the church: "Any church needs a backbone of knowledge, that can grow and develop in relation to the growth of the church" (Nielsen 1957a: 41, my translation). Education was also regarded as *an instrument in the competition between various mission bodies*, especially between the Protestant and Catholic missions (Sjursen 1960: 58–59). I will later in this chapter describe in more depth how the Catholic mission represented a threat to the Norwegian mission and how schoolwork was considered an important instrument in recruiting adherents.

The discourse of development was less apparent in the discussion of educational matters in the archival material. One example can be taken from an article in NMt from 1921 written by teaching missionary Schaanning (Schaanning 1921: 52). She was quite clear with regard to the emancipating effect of literacy. In spite of the fact that the number of public schools increased, she argued that the mission schools were needed since there were still too many Malagasy children that did not know how to read. Reading skills were, she added, "one of the best weapons primitive people can be given in the fight against ruthless exploitation from higher ranking people and tribes" (Schaanning 1921: 52, my translation).

The discourse of development appears clearly in some documents from after independence, and in the interviews with former teaching missionaries. The new Malagasy State was strongly challenged in regard to meet the needs of education for children and youth, which constituted 50% of the population. In this regard, *the mission's moral responsibility* was addressed, but it was also considered an opportunity (Torbjørnsen 1964: 35). Former missionary Honningdal focused on the educational situation in Madagascar when asked about the aim of the mission's educational work (Former female missionary Kari Johanne Honningdal 2011). She argued that it was a poor country and that many of the schools were in the hands of churches. According to her, the aim was to give education, educate teachers and leaders to the Malagasy society, and it was important that children and youth received this education. Children had to learn to read, write and do simple arithmetic, but the mission also had to help those who wanted to study further, who could among others become teachers. Former missionary in the period from 1961 to 1975, Anders Martin Andersen, worked at the dormitory of the Lutheran secondary education institution in Antsirabe, Mangarivotra, and at the teacher training college in Fandriana (Former male missionary Anders Martin Andersen 2011). He argued that education was essential if one wanted to contribute with anything in a country at a low level of development. According to him, both evangelisation and development were aims of the mission's educational work, which illustrates how these discourses were complementary. Reimers also argued that caring for the whole human being was a reason why the mission did educational work as part of their missionary mandate. Further, she focused on the potential of education in building societies as a reason why the mission should invest in it: "Without knowledge we do not go forward. You do not have any future prospects if you cannot read, write or do simple arithmetic. You have few, if any, possibilities to gain new knowledge" (Former female missionary Anne Marie Reimers 2012). In this quotation, literacy is clearly regarded as a prerequisite for individual and social development. Former missionary and principal in different schools on the East Coast from during the 1960s and 1970s, Helena Trydal, said she came to Madagascar as a teacher with a teacher's perspective:

I had been working as a teacher in Norway. And I was going to work at a school. I suppose I was thinking as teachers normally do, that pupils should learn what they had a right and a need to learn. But, I was a missionary, and I was conscious of that. It was a matter of cause that our school . . . as it was a school of the Malagasy Lutheran Church it was a Christian school and in opposition to a public school, which did not teach Christianity, we taught Christianity.

(Former female missionary Helena Trydal 2012)

According to Trydal, the aim was two-fold: helping pupils to become good citizens, and develop their knowledge about Jesus and become Christians. This illustrates again how the discourse of development and of evangelisation was not contradictory, but complementary. She further revealed that some pupils did convert, especially among those living at the dormitories.

In Chapter 5, I described that the mission during the independence period received financial support to their educational work from different institutions. In asking for funds from institutions such as the Norwegian government, the mission had to re-interpret their goals and roles of the mission's development work. Egil Eggen, who had been a missionary to Japan, was aware of critics accusing the mission's development work only to pave the way for soft evangelism:

We may also meet the view that the mission's social effort in reality is just kind of a bait. What we really want is to preach the gospel and the purpose of our hospitals, schools and other institutions are just to trick people into Christianity. At best, they are understood as contact surfaces paving the way for the spiritual efforts of the mission.

(Eggen 1969: 21–22, my translation)

Eggen argued that it was a common misunderstanding that the mission was only interested in the salvation of the soul. Helping the needed was just as important as preaching the gospel, and it should be a natural part of Christian mission work. From his point of view, the mission's social work was different from other understandings of development work in the sense that it offered something more. The mission's true interest was to gradually evolve in terms of care for the whole human being, in keeping with broad Christian principles.

## Inter-Missionary Collaboration

I have now looked at the discourse behind the Norwegian mission's educational work. These discourses were shared with other missions that were present in Madagascar. The missionary movement was international in its nature, as expressed in the following quotation from Porter: "Missionaries were conscious that they were part of a global enterprise and often found in that involvement additional sources of support to offset the waywardness of their own national governments or other authorities overseas" (Porter 2002: 567). This resulted in collaboration between mission organisations from different countries with various religious affiliations, such as Moravians, Anglicans, Lutherans and Reformed. During the 19th century, there were several disputes about territories and influence between Protestant missions in Madagascar, described by Gow as "The struggle for souls and territory" (Gow 1979: 50). The 20th century was, however, characterised in general by closer collaboration between Protestant mission organisations from Britain, France, America and Norway. The 1910 World Missionary Edinburgh Conference (see p. 116 in this chapter) advocated for more collaboration between Protestant missions. Other reasons for the closer collaboration were the challenging relation with the colonial power and the increased activity of the Catholic mission, to which Protestant missions at times had quite harsh relations. Catholicism and Protestantism were struggling for religious hegemony in a secular colony. At independence, the structures of mission organisations changed due to the establishment of Malagasy churches. Two Protestant churches were the result of the presence of Lutheran and Reformed mission societies. The FJKM was a merge of different religious orientations with the French and British Calvinists being most influential, and the FLM was Lutheran following on from the Norwegian and American missions. In terms of theology, Protestants agreed on many aspects, but on some main issues they strongly disagreed.

The first inter-missionary Protestant Conference was held in Madagascar 3 years after the 1910 Edinburgh Conference with representation from seven missions: the British and French Calvinist Protestant missions (LMS and MPF), Anglican SPG) and Quakers (FFMA) as well as two Lutheran American (United Lutheran Church of America—ULCA and the Lutheran Free Church of America) and the NMS. The collaboration between the Evangelical missions, mainly through the IPC and Conference, was described in annual reports of Norwegian missionaries in general as good. The importance of *the written word*, the Bible, was the common basis for the Protestants.

As already described in previous chapters, one important area of collaboration between the Protestant missions was lobbying the government on education.[4] The IPC functioned as a representation of the missions and was regularly lobbying and negotiating with the colonial administration. The cases to be promoted, however, had to be agreed on by the different missions. As shown in the bush school dispute in the 1920s, described in Chapter 4, it was especially important to have a French representative who could relate to the French colonial government. It was somehow more complicated in the Sunday school dispute, described in the same chapter, when the Norwegian mission did not get support from the French superintendent, Mondain. He did not support lobbying for the case probably due to different opinions about strategy, timing and which cases to be prioritised. In the same period, Mondain supported, after some hesitation, the NMS superintendent Bjertnes on his intention to influence the Government's work on religious decrees to further restrict religious freedom (NMS 1920: 5–8). A short description of this case is included here as an example of how the IPC lobbying could be and the impact it could have on mission work.

In January 1920, the missions wrote a document entitled *A Statement on the Necessity of a Revision of Legislation in regard to Public Worship in Madagascar. Limitations, Restrictions and Abuses under the Present Regime*, which was signed by the seven Protestant missions (IPC 1920). The missions presented the difficult situation especially since the 1906 decrees and asked for better working conditions in the future, among others concerning receiving authorisations to open new congregations. This joint effort of the missions seems to have given some fruits. In a January 1921 circular, Bjertnes reported to his missionary colleagues on how the Protestant missions had been involved in negotiations around a new church decree with the administration (Bjertnes 1920). At the start, Governor-General Garbit promised to inform local administrations to be less strict in practicing church decrees, but afterward he decided the decrees to be re-edited. According to Bjertnes, the Norwegians saw an opportunity to be involved in the process and pushed the inter-missionary Conference to lobby for that. The IPC members and other delegates were positive, but reluctant. They preferred to wait for the church decree to be issued. Bjertnes, however, was of the opinion that they wouldn't have anything to say on a decree that already was accepted by the French government. As a Norwegian, he felt he could not interfere, and he therefore asked for Mondain's support. Mondain went to the governor-general several times arguing that the missions could not tolerate less freedom of religion and that through collaboration, future troubles would be avoided. In the end, they were allowed to read through and comment on five drafts before it was sent to France for approval. In the circular, Bjertnes mentioned one suggestion they made: when the overall number of churches that could be built within one region was limited, consideration should be made to the confessions of those churches. In some regions, the Norwegian mission had experienced that the Catholics had already build so many churches that there were no longer room for any Protestant church. Bjertnes did not attach the whole text to the circular he sent to the Norwegian missionaries around on the island, since he was afraid that local administrators, sceptical towards the missions, would interfere if it came into their hands. This refers to the different opinions of French citizens on colonial policy and the sensitivity of the matter in question, as was described by Daughton referred to in the beginning of this chapter (Daughton 2006).

In 1926, the third Inter-missionary Protestant Conference took place, where all the seven missions were represented, in addition to Malagasy representatives. Missionary to Madagascar in the period from 1916 to 1932, Ole August Kopreitan, wrote in the Magazine NMt, that the IPC had achieved many things, especially in lobbying the colonial government (Kopreitan 1927a). At the Conference, several subjects related to education were discussed. A challenge for all missions was the lack of educated teachers and schools. The ISC, with two representatives from each of the missions, was to be established (NMS 1927: 91–95). The ISC's mandate was to give advice and information to the missions, visit schools, work to coordinate primary school and teacher exams, coordinate the curriculum, schoolbooks, schedules, publish a pedagogical magazine, collect statistics and finally the school committee should document their experiences. The Norwegian missionaries expressed some scepticism about the coordination of teacher training due to the fact that their salaries were below those of other missions, and they were afraid they would lose students to other missions. Even though they decided to be part of the ISC in 1927, the ISC did not do anything in practice until the 1950s, as far as I could find in the Norwegian archival material.

The educational reform in 1951 (see Chapter 5, p. 69) increased the missions' need to collaborate and through the ISC the missions got suggestions on how to relate to the reform (Snekkenes 1954: 81). Another reason for increased collaboration was the opportunity to ask for public financial support and they needed to find out and inform each other about what they could ask for and how to apply (ISC no date). In 1958,

Hermann Ravelomanana, a former school director of MPF and an author of Malagasy schoolbooks, was hired as general secretary of Protestant schools (Fagereng 1958). His mandate was to be the representative of Protestant schools towards the government, inform Protestant schools about new regulations and decrees, visit schools and follow-up the publishing of schoolbooks in collaboration with a CEP that had replaced the ISC (Ravelomanana 1961). In the meetings of CEP they discussed publication of schoolbooks, public support for education, exams, holiday courses for teachers and curricula (Conseil d'enseignement protestant 1958). In 1958, the CEP arranged a conference on common issues in Protestant educational work (NMS 1958: 134–135, Rajaobelina 1958). The secretary of CEP was for a period Rajaobelina, former director of French Protestant schools and also the author of several Malagasy schoolbooks. In 1959, the name of the Protestant Educational Committee changed their name again to *Affair Scolaire Protestants* (ASP) where the members represented churches rather than mission societies. Members should be Lutherans and Reformed, and representation from different districts and synods on the island was to be ensured (NMS 1959: 96). Norwegian missionaries saw the benefits of a Protestant collaboration. They were, however, very much aware of their Lutheran affiliation. There were times when the Lutherans felt overrun by the Reformed, the strongest partners in the collaboration. At independence, there were some efforts made to create one Protestant church, which was not supported by the Lutherans, as this was believed to take away their distinctive character (NMS 1964b: 58, 1966: 10). The Protestant Committee consisting of 12 Reformed and nine Lutheran members meeting annually, replaced the IPC (NMS 1960b: 18).

A conference for directors of Protestant schools took place just after independence in July 1960 (Fampianarana Protestanta eto Madagasikara 1960). There was a question about the necessity for religious schools at the time of independence and the answer pointed to the dominant discourse of evangelisation, but also to the discourse of development when talking about citizenship: "YES, because the schools of the church are instruments in teaching the gospel to the children so they can develop into good and useful citizens" (Fampianarana Protestanta eto Madagasikara 1960, my translation). Protestant schools were needed in order to raise the children into the Christian faith from a young age. An important factor that made Protestant schools Protestant was first of all the teachers. They were employed by the church and should be Christians. Teachers in Protestant schools were expected to pray and preach in school, and cooperate and support each other. Their work should be more than just a way to earn a living; teaching should be considered *their call*. From the report of this Conference, it seems like Malagasy Protestant converts were now in charge of the Protestant schoolwork, both as directors of schools and in school departments. They had adapted and now promoted the specificity of religious literacies embedded in Protestantism in opposition to public secular literacies.

## Catholicism as a Threat

During the periods under study, the relation between Protestant and Catholic missions was tenuous. The Catholic mission was very active, and what the missionaries referred to as the *Catholic propaganda* was seen as very threatening to the Lutherans. Missionaries reported the loss of congregational members to the Catholic Church and also the loss of pupils to Catholic schools. One of the first French Lutheran missionaries helping NMS in the colonial period, and who worked in Madagascar until 1946, Abel Auguste Parrot, represented a religious minority in France where the majority of the population was Catholic. He was especially active in putting the challenge of competition with Catholicism on the agenda in mission conferences. Additionally, other missionaries around the island expressed concerns in reports about the Catholics gaining ground.

In the NMS Conference in 1920, Parrot described what he called the *Catholic propaganda* (NMS 1920: 31–38). Hundreds of Lutheran church members had converted to Catholicism, and Parrot encouraged the missionaries to wake up and react. According to Parrot, the Norwegian missionaries were ignorant about Catholicism. He was also of the opinion that there was a lack of knowledge among their church members about the differences between Protestantism and Catholicism. Further, Parrot argued that the NMS should resist mixed marriages and prevent parents from sending their children, especially girls, to Catholic schools. In addition, they should also provide a form of short-time unpaid work, *engagements*, which is what the Catholics intentionally did to convert Lutherans into their faith. Engagements were popular as they could be a reason for exemption from forced labour imposed by the colonising rulers.

In 1922, Parrot again presented the struggle against Catholicism at the Mission Conference, arguing that their converts turned surprisingly easily to Catholicism (NMS 1922: 96–100). Catholics were more active and better organised, and Parrot could name many former pupils of Norwegian mission schools who had become leaders in Catholic congregations. When some missionaries expressed their fear of attacking the Catholics and start a church war, Parrot replied that they had to defend themselves and avoid being eliminated as Protestants experienced in France. It was decided to write a little information booklet about the difference between Catholicism and Protestantism.

In the mixed advisory committee to the missionary conference consisting of Malagasy and Norwegian missionary delegates (CM), they agreed that Catholics were quite active in recruiting members to their congregations. Their strategies were said to be hiring more European personnel, door-to-door visits, accepting mixed marriages only when they both converted to Catholicism, engagements and talking, in this inter-war sensitive context, about Lutherans as German friendly. The CM suggested reacting to these by promoting door-to-door visits and informing their church members and workers about the difference between them and the Catholics, especially in "owning the gospel". This argument, pointing to the Protestant approach to read the Bible in one's own language, is interesting seen from a literacy perspective. It shows that the ability to read is important for the Protestant missions, more so than for the Catholics. At the same time, CM also argued that parents should be banned from putting their children in Catholic schools. And, as long as the Catholics promoted mixed marriage, the Lutheran Church should try to avoid that their church members married Catholics.

This was apparently a theme that interested the missionaries as it initiated significant discussion. There were for instance disagreements if parents should be *denied* or *warned* from sending their children to Catholic schools. According to missionary Ole Strand, they could not as Lutherans expel those who sent their children to Catholic schools from their congregation because they did not believe in forcing people. He would rather focus on school building; mainly primary schools as bush schools could be closed down if a Catholic school was built nearby. As explained in Chapter 4, a common strategy was to build primary schools recognised by the government to force bush schools of other denominations to close. In Strand's opinion a major challenge was that the Catholic mission paid for both school buildings and teachers as long as there were pupils, whereas NMS only gave some support towards the costs. Catholics also built bush schools near their churches, and members of their church were expelled if they sent their children to Protestant schools. This account is interesting as Strand clearly insists on increasing the mission's opportunities for transmitting Protestant religious literacies as a response to the expansion of Catholic educational facilities promoting Catholic religious literacies.

At the Inter-missionary Conference in 1927, the *Catholic propaganda* came up in the discussions, as it was a common interest for the Protestant missions to find ways to relate to it. What is interesting, from a literacy perspective, is again the way in which the missionaries highlighted the main difference between Protestants and Catholics with the Bible. The Protestants owned the Bible: "—Lift up high the Bible, let the word of God win.—Protestantism, that is the Bible, Catholicism, that is the rosary. Teach people to read and love their Bible" (Kopreitan 1927b, my translation).

Competition with the Catholics was a common argument for involvement in educational work during the 1920s. Missionaries argued that they needed to invest in schoolwork if they did not want to leave the children to the Catholics (NMS 1922: 28). Missionary Parrot was in no doubt that schoolwork was the reason for the Catholic success (NMS 1930a: 150). Parents followed after their children and he was afraid that if they did not invest in schoolwork, the district where he worked would soon be taken over by Catholics. One challenge for the Protestant schools was that Catholic schools were known to have better results than Protestant schools in the exams. Catholic missionaries were often French speaking and they had good knowledge of the French educational system. Catholic educational work was often described in Norwegian missionaries' reports as flourishing. They put up new school buildings, dormitories and modernised old ones. In the 1923 conference report, it is stated that the Catholics understood the importance of education as part of missionary work (NMS 1923b: 37).

Also during the 1950s, missionaries expressed concerns. In 1955, the Catholics were described as very strategic at the West Coast, since they, in response to the 1951 reform (see Chapter 5, p. 69), had put up several bush schools (NMS 1955: 14). If the Norwegian mission did not follow-up with more bush schools, it would probably be the end for the Lutheran church on the West Coast. In the Highlands, the problem in the 1950s was that Lutheran bush schools disappeared as a consequence of Catholic primary schools being built nearby (NMS 1962: 10). Those schools were more popular. On some occasions, missionaries emphasised that due to their schools being overcrowded, children had to go to the Catholic school. As late as in 1957, it was mentioned in the yearbook that membership in the Church was sometimes demanded in order to enter a Catholic school, with the consequence that Lutheran congregations lost them (Sjursen 1957: 54). A former teaching missionary said in her interview that the Catholic Church expected their pupils to attend their church (Former female missionary Anne Marie Reimers 2012). When asked about the difference between the Catholic, Lutheran and public school in Betafo, a former pupil at the Norwegian mission school in Betafo during the 1950s, George, mentioned the exam results:

> There was a difference. The curriculum was probably the same, but the Protestant school, the Lutheran was like . . . how can I say this . . . forsaken . . . when it came to making educated people. What they did in the upper north and in St. Louis . . . because in St. Louis there could be 100% passing, but if there were 10% over there. . .
> *At the Lutherans?*
> Yes. You know the exam results were low at our place.
> (Former pupil George 2011, my translation)

George argued that the main reason for the Catholic school's good results was the language, as the Catholics had French teachers. *Good results* and *educated people* are here evaluated according to the norms of the colonial school system.

Even after independence, the relation with the Catholics was strained, as for instance reported from the East Coast in 1965:

> The relationship with the Catholics is outwards very sincere, but inwards filled with tension, and for the Protestants characterised by an inferiority complex. We are all the time bothered by the fuss: "Look at the Catholics. Look what they manage to do". Nice schools and big churches with sounds of bells from morning to evening. White fathers and nuns increase from one year to another, as far as we can see. They are numerous whereas we Lutheran missionaries can be counted on one's fingers. It is not strange that our Christians become thoughtful and sad.
>
> (NMS 1965b: 15, my translation)

When asked about the relation between schools of different religious affiliations, former missionaries interviewed for this study said that, during the 1960s, there was not much collaboration between Lutheran and Catholics at a local level. In Betafo they invited each other to services once a year (Former female missionary Kari Johanne Honningdal 2011). Søyland said that they met each other for soccer matches (Former female missionary Elfrid Søyland 2011). In a period during the mid-1960s with a focus on ecumenical initiatives, such as common youth meetings, and unity, there were several attempts from Catholics for collaboration with Lutheran congregations (NMS 1966: 10). These initiatives were on some occasions by Norwegian missionaries interpreted as another tactic to attract Lutherans into Catholic congregations.

## Concluding Remarks

This chapter has presented some explications of the ideologies that the Norwegian mission met in the political context of the French colonial administration in Madagascar. With the history of French secularism and anticlericalism in mind, the way the colonial government put in place restrictions to control literacies makes sense. On the one hand, the dominating discourse for the mission's involvement within educational work was the discourse of evangelisation. Education played an important part in the aim of church building, which necessitated educated church members. It was also considered an important instrument in the competition with other missions. On the other hand, there was an alternative discourse of development, or a secondary aim, to care for *people's general well-being*. The former missionaries interviewed for this research were clear in how they related to the discourse of development, which illustrate that this discourse had gained terrain. As educated teachers, they saw the value of education in itself, at the same time as they recognised the aims of mission educational work based on a discourse of evangelisation.

As argued in previous chapters, bush schools were at times regarded by the French administration only as an instrument for the missions to recruit church members and did not contribute, according to the norms of the French colonial policy, to attain educational aims. This chapter showed that missionaries themselves regarded bush schools as an important instrument in evangelisation. The role of bush schools was indeed to transmit religious, and not French-assimilationist, literacies. At the same time, the programme in bush schools was based on contextualised literacies that gave Malagasies an opportunity to read in a Malagasy language. From a discourse of evangelisation this can be seen as a by-product. Education was also indented to meet the mission's expectations, that people were able to understand God's word, as well as acquire literacy skills for individual and social development, so a discourse of development was also evident. This issue will be touched upon more closely in the next chapter, where the language used in schools will be analysed in more depth.

The Norwegian mission shared part of its educational aims with other Protestant missions whereas the Catholics were looked upon as competitors throughout the period of research. The sources presented here about the Norwegian missionaries' attitudes towards the Catholic mission are important in the context of this research, not only because they describe the context that the missionaries were working in, but because at the same time they illustrate the aim of mission education. Missionaries recognised the success of Catholicism in Madagascar, making the link between how they better mastered French-assimilationist literacies in addition to their Catholic religious literacies. Even though the Norwegian missionaries underlined their purpose of education for conversion, through the Catholics they acknowledged that offering *successful* education, in the eyes of the ruling power, was an advantage and even helped conversion. For the Norwegian missionaries, the 1951-decree created more collaborations with other Protestant missions at the same time as the Catholic competition in some regions became more intense.

## Notes

1. See Rosnes (2016)
2. See also Rosnes (2013)
3. See for instance: Kallekleiv (1970), Løtveit (1961), Fagereng (1949b), Meling (1954), Fagereng (1949a), No author (1929).
4. See for instance: Snekkenes (1951: 108).

# 8 Literacy in Whose Language?

This chapter contributes to an understanding on how the mission's literacy work impacted on power relations between the educated elite and the rest of the population in the Malagasy society through developing and using a Malagasy language. This chapter also contributes to an understanding of the importance of the choice of language for mission literacy work.

Makoni and Pennycook have argued that "all languages are social constructions" and have encouraged researchers to search for social processes; for example, "the development of colonial and nationalist ideologies through literacy programs" that lead to their construction (Makoni and Pennycook 2006: 1). The effects in societies of these inventions are, however, real. With this perspective, it is important to bear in mind how the missionaries, when creating writing systems for some languages and publishing literature in these languages, contributed to the creation and standardisation of these languages in specific ways. As explained in Chapter 1, it was Protestant British missionaries who created the writing system based on the Latin script for a Malagasy language that previously, with the exception of a few documents written in the Arabic script, had been oral. The Norwegian mission contributed to further develop this written language when they arrived on the island, and the mission's printing and publishing press was of great importance in the promotion of what I have called contextualised literacies (see Chapter 4, p. 64). Important questions are what pupils read, who wrote what they read, and who decided which literature they had access to. The literature provided by the mission was rooted in the evangelistic discourse and restricted by the aims of religious literacies.

The mission's involvement with language made them an important contributor to the way the standard written language developed in Madagascar. There are two important issues to this. One is the choice of which dialect of Malagasy to choose and base the standard writing system on, which was dictated by the kingdom in power in the pre-colonial context, the Merina regime. The other is that the standard written language primarily developed further according to the needs of religious literature.

The status of the standard Malagasy language on the West Coast is a good example of how the mission, through its religious literacies, promoted a specific church language. This socially constructed standardised Malagasy language, based on a dialect in the Highlands, was difficult for some people to understand, especially in the coastal areas. Some words could, if pronounced slightly in the wrong way, have very different, and in some cases offensive, meanings. This was a reason why some missionaries were in favour of also developing written languages based on other Malagasy dialects. This chapter will present a case on Bible translation that is opposite to what happened in many African contexts, where evangelising missions developed several languages out of dialects (Prah 2009). In addition, this chapter describes one case from the mid-colonisation period and one from the independence period, that challenged the dominant linguistic policy. During the 1920s, a disputed educational decree was issued making Malagasy the LOI in government schools. At independence, part of the Malagasy society, including Protestant converts, argued that the Malagasy language should become the main LOI, and the language used in exams in primary schools.

## Providing Religious and Secular Literature in a Malagasy Language

The Malagasy researcher Jeanne Dina argued that: "With the help of missionaries, the Malagasy is a well-established written language at the dawn of the colonisation, a language used for administrative communication everywhere where the central administration is represented" (Dina 2006: 2, my translation). The fact that there were books written in Malagasy helped preserve the language, and made it harder for the colonial power to introduce French as the only option for schooling (Gueunier 2004: 2). Raison-Jourde questioned, however, the way missionaries and the Merina power standardised the Malagasy language, arguing that "the language is a mirror of social relations" (Raison-Jourde 1991: 529). The missions and the regime in power were guardians of how the language should be written in the correct way. Raison-Jourde focused on the relation between the spoken Malagasy used in everyday life, and this written *religious* language. In helping to make Merina the official language, Protestant missions reduced the importance of dialects. Some missionaries did research on local dialects and wrote stories in different dialects, but it was the standard Malagasy language based on the Merina dialect that they used, also in Bible translation. Raison-Jourde's argumentation fits well with Makoni and Pennycook's perspective that languages are socially constructed. The Malagasy language was not a thing to be discovered, but it was created and formed by the interests and ideologies of the institutions working for its creation. The aim of the Highland Merina king who ruled over a large part of the island was to unite Madagascar into one nation and the interest of Protestant missions was evangelisation. A standard written Malagasy language was in the interest of the Merina kings and queens because it was believed to help promote nationalism. For the Protestant mission, a written local language was an instrument to promote evangelism. For the colonial power, the French language was an instrument in their colonial assimilationist policy. In addition, fighting against the standard Malagasy language and instead promoting many dialects was in the interest of the colonial power as an instrument to divide the population, promote regionalism and thus to hinder nationalism.

During the period from 1870 to 1880, the Norwegian missionary Lars Dahle took part in the joint Protestant translation work of the Bible (Dahl 1984: 4–6). He also conducted research on the origins of the Malagasy language. He was the first researcher to prove grammatical similarities between Malagasy and the Austronesian language family, and he developed hypotheses about the appearance of African words in the Malagasy language. Another important contribution by Dahle was his 457-page book *Specimens of Malagasy Folk-lore* (Dahle 1877). This book, written in different dialects and not standard official Malagasy, was a collection of fairy tales, proverbs and other literary treasures. Still, Malagasy pupils read these stories. During his work in Madagascar between 1927 and 1959, missionary Otto Christian Dahl wrote a book with fairy tales in the Sakalava dialect (Dahl 1968). Dahl also conducted research on the connection between the Malagasy language and Austronesian and Bantu languages, and the origin of the Malagasy people. In an article about the many contributions made by Norwegian missionaries to the preservation of the Malagasy language, Dahl sought to answer criticisms that missions only destroyed the culture in which they were working (Dahl 1984: 5). He mentioned several books written by Norwegian missionaries.[1] Missionaries wrote about Malagasy language and culture, and textbooks for studies in different fields such as theology and medicine. What is not discussed here, however, is that the missionaries by writing about Malagasy language and traditions, did not only preserve those languages and traditions, but they contributed to their further development.

Only 10 years after their arrival, in 1876, the mission established a publishing house and printing press. Written material played an important role in transmitting ideas. Through reading what the mission chose to publish, they believed that individuals were transformed according to what they read. The British Bible Society had already been printing the Bible and the New Testament, so the Norwegian mission's, and later the Lutheran printing press, printed other kinds of religious and secular material. The mission had a literature committee, elected by the Mission Conference, with both Norwegian and Malagasies members. They received, studied and proposed manuscripts to be published, which had to be approved by the Mission Conference. These publications encouraged writing and reading, and they were seen as an important instrument to spread the Gospel and a Christian moral. Publishing also became an instrument in the competition between different mission societies. About 50 years after its creation, the printing press was described as modern "spreading literature throughout the whole country" (Strand 1928: 40, my translation). The importance of the printing press to the mission could not be valued enough:

> We get our schoolbooks from our printing press. We cannot ignore that, now when our work is remembered. For over 50 years, it has sent out hundreds of thousands of catechisms and thousands of Bible stories. We have our congregational magazine: "Husvennen (The visitor)" [Mpamangy], probably the best way to translate it in Norwegian, is in its 48th volume. The interest in reading is increasing to such a degree among youth and old in Madagascar, that our printing press is very occupied providing what is needed. What our books and magazines do around in thousands of homes, in church and at school every day can hardly be appreciated enough.
>
> (Meling 1928: 36, my translation)

On the one hand, the mission published religious books, such as bible stories, the catechism, hymnals and books about Christian morals. On the other hand, the mission published secular literature that should raise literacy, which of course shared the mission's moral or gave an ethical message. This literature consisted of stories, both translated from other languages and written by Malagasy authors, poetry or informative books (NMS 1922a: 151–156, 1920: 150). Books for missionaries and other foreigners to learn the Malagasy language were also printed by the Lutheran printing press (Bøe 1969a). In 1922, the printing press printed 1,000 copies of a Malagasy textbook aimed at French high-ranking officials to learn Malagasy (NMS 1922a: 155). Every year, they

*Table 8.1* A selection of literature published by the NMS, 1921

| Literature | 1921 |
| --- | --- |
| Book explaining the catechism (96 p.) | 2,000 |
| Bible stories (94 p.) | 5,000 |
| Christian morals/ethics (240 p.) | 1,000 |
| Raozina (a story) (32 p.) | 3,000 |
| Robinson Crusoe (128 p.) | 4,000 |
| Reading book ABC (18 p.) | 20,000 |
| Catechism (18 p.) | 10,000 |
| Mpamangy (16 p.) (monthly) | 2,300 |
| Mpamangy Christmas | 3,500 |

Source: Bjertnes (1921: 97)

published practical material, such as diaries and registers for schools and Sunday schools and account books (Bjertnes 1923b: 28). Shortly after their arrival to the country, NMS started a monthly magazine for adults, *Mpamangy*, which became an important channel to inform church workers and members. From 1936, they published a four-page magazine for Sunday school children twice a month (NMS 1935: 86–89). In 1951 a weekly Lutheran newspaper, *Firaisana Kristiana* (Christian unity), was launched (NMS 1958: 18, Nielsen 1957b: 75, NMS 1955: 45–47). They closed this newspaper in 1957 and decided instead to participate in a joint Inter-protestant newspaper, *Fanasina*.

The mission sold a lot of books, and they could not always keep up with demand. Only in 1921, for example, the mission's bookshop attached to the printing press in the capital distributed 4,940 hymnals, 7,720 catechism, 2,169 Bible stories and 25,967 ABCs (a primer) (Bjertnes 1921: 98). According to Schaanning, owning a book was something new to many people, and the primer was so cheap that parents gladly bought new ones when they were well used (Schaanning 1922: 163). The hymnal, one of few songbooks they had in Madagascar, was very popular (Schaanning 1921). Missionaries made this printed material in standard Malagasy language available in remote areas. They sold books at their mission stations, on the weekly market and on their mission trips. In 1921, missionary Isaksen confirmed that there was a large interest in the books that he brought for sale on his journeys (Quoted in Bjertnes 1921: 87). When we take into consideration that a book often is read by several people in these areas, the amount of people attained through this literature was quite important.

At the beginning of the 1950s, Enok Gramstad, who ran the bookshop in Antsirabe and who sold Christian literature on the market, said missionaries should promote other Christian literature than the Bible, catechism and songbook (Snekkenes 1953). The best period to do this was apparently after the rice harvest, which speaks to how the missionaries considered the rural context in their work:

> 1. Not before all the other needs are met, do people buy Christian literature. Therefore, it is only in the months of April, Mai, June and July, when the rice is harvested that we can sell anything of importance. 2. First and foremost, people buy songbooks, the Catechism, new-testaments and Bibles, they have little awareness of other Christian literature.
>
> (Snekkenes 1953, my translation)

To illustrate people's access to written material, I will include some of the accounts of former pupils and teachers at the school of Betafo, described more in depth in Chapter 6. These former pupils stated that they had limited access to written material and that religious literature dominated,

particularly the Bible, hymnal and catechism. The bookstore in Betafo
was one of the mission's bookstores in Madagascar that sold most books.
Honningdal, former teacher missionary and headmaster at the school,
said the bookstore was part of her apartment, and people came knocking
on her door from 6 a.m. to buy books (Former female missionary Kari
Johanne Honningdal 2011). She sold schoolbooks to her own pupils,
and to pupils at smaller schools and bush schools in the countryside.
They had all the books needed for school, like French reading, Malagasy
reading, French and Malagasy grammar, arithmetic, geography and history. They also brought schoolbooks, Bibles, new testaments and hymnals for the Monday market. Missionaries recruited people to subscribe
to magazines, individually or through the church. According to former
pupil Haja, they were popular, and included practical and educational
information, for instance cooking advice, which made them relevant to
buy also for those who were not attending church (Former pupil Haja
2012). George, with a father and a grandfather who were pastors, had
access to Lutheran magazines:

> Before, it was possible to . . . for instance to have subscription to
> magazines. Such as subscription to *Zakaizan'ny tanora* [youth maga-
> zine]. That came every month. And *Mpamangy*. And what else . . .
> the church's newspaper. . . *Fanasina*. We subscribed to those maga-
> zines and the Lutheran bookstore in Antananarivo sent them to us.
> (Former pupil George 2011, my translation)

Daniel and Sarah, whose fathers were catechists, remembered that
they received magazines every month (Former pupil Daniel 2012, Former pupil Sarah 2012). One former pupil mentioned that he used to read
the *Mpamangy*, which his mother got through her engagement as the
president for women in church (Former male pupil 9 2012). Another
former pupil said that his grandfather, who was a bureaucrat, subscribed
to magazines for youth (*Ny Zakaiza'ny tanora*), adults (*Mpamangy*) and
the Protestant newspaper *Fanasina* (Former male pupil 7 2011). This
pupil particularly enjoyed reading the Christmas edition that included
new songs. Haja remembered that they were given religious books, like
books with the word of the day, from the Norwegian missionaries for
Christmas (Former pupil Haja 2012). In some families, this religious literature was the only written material they had. As Rolland expresses:
"In our house there was nothing else to read except for the Bible and the
stories . . . the church stories" (Former pupil Rolland 2012, my translation). Jean remembered a little red religious book that he used to read:

> I think it was a book from Farimena [the centre of a revival move-
> ment]. It was the little red book. When I wanted to read, it was
> *Lalam-pamonjena*. That was the book I read when I was at home.

Then I could read something. And when I knew how to read a little bit, I got the catechism, and the Bible stories.

(Former pupil Jean 2012, my translation)

These accounts of former pupils at the mission school of Betafo illustrate that the printing press of the mission ensured that there was written material available in children's homes. The mission also stimulated the writing culture in Madagascar, by encouraging Malagasy authors to write books and articles for their magazines and newspaper. Native converts got an opportunity to express themselves in writings that could be distributed to many people. What they wrote, however, had to be accepted by the editor/literature committee with both Norwegian and Malagasy members, and it was discussed at the Mission Conference. The registers and account books contributed, as well, to stimulate writing among church employees. Even though written material in the Malagasy language contributed to allowing texts to be read that dealt with local themes, this form of contextualisation remained limited. The stories and magazines were written by Malagasy authors who had become Christians. It is important to highlight that the literature provided by the mission had to be in line, at least not in opposition to, religious literacies. On the next pages, I will present controversies related to the specific written Malagasy language the mission used in its publications. What should be the characteristics of the language used in religious literature? And what effects would this language have in the larger society?

### Did the Language Used in Religious Literature Promote Regionalism or Nationalism?

Derek R. Peterson described the challenges of liberal Scots missionaries in Kenya who translated the Bible into the Gikuyu language, and preached the gospel using "what they took to be an already-existing Gikuyu religious grammar" (Peterson 2004: 43). He described well the problems related to finding concepts with the intended connotations to important Christian concepts such as "God", "sin" and "law". In Madagascar, this challenge appeared not only between the missionaries' language and the local language, but also between different dialects.

A discussion in the Mission Conference in the Highlands in 1923 on how to increase the interest of the mission's magazine *Mpamangy* on the coast illustrates that the dominance of the Merina dialect could be a hindrance in mission work (NMS 1923a: 184–185). Converts all over the island should be encouraged to write and they should search for contributions in a language understood by people in different areas. Writers often became disheartened when their contributions were not published due to the language, which apparently was not good enough to the editor. They were reminded about that: "it is the average people in the countryside who is going to read, and they do not know the language of the capital. Our working field is not Imerina [the land of the politically dominant group Merina]" (NMS 1923a: 185, my translation). The most important book, the Malagasy Bible, was also considered by some as not applicable to every dialect and culture in the different regions of Madagascar. Some missionaries questioned in whose dialect the Gospel should be written and preached. One complicating factor was the existence of many dialects existing side by side within different ethnic groups. There was no obvious alternative. Who was to define what language the FLM was to use?

On the West Coast, the Sakalava dialect was the most widely used and presented as an alternative to the Merina dialect. Already at the end of the 19th century, there had been suggestions to publish literature in the Sakalava dialect (NMS 1930b: 45). Only the catechism was published in 1909, but it was not widely used. During the 1920s, missionaries discussed vividly and frequently how to deal with the question of dialects, but no consensus emerged. On the one hand, Alfred Andresen, who worked as a missionary in this area between 1920 and 1946, argued that the mission should not publish Sakalava literature because it was difficult to sell. On the other hand, the nurse and midwife Martha Kristine Fagereng, whose career spanned 40 years between 1893 and 1937 argued: "We have to do all we can in order for the Sakalavas to have God's word in their own language. They do not consider Hova [Merina] to be their language" (NMS 1926: 92–93, my translation). In 1922, her son, Edvin Kristian Herbert Fagereng, joined her as a missionary. He worked in different periods until 1960 and fought for the translation of written material into the Sakalava dialect.

Two years after his arrival, Fagereng argued in the Mission Conference that the Hova language, being used by pastors and evangelists from the Highlands, was one of the obstacles for the ethnic group Masikoro to be evangelised (NMS 1924b: 32–36). Congregations led by Hova-speaking pastors mostly had members who were Merina migrants. Many of those who originated from the area did not come to church, because they did not understand what was preached. It was decided that pastors from the Highlands should pass an exam in the Sakalava dialect after they had worked in the field for 3 years. In addition, they should teach evangelists in Sakalava, even though the Sakalava dialect was not spoken in the entire district. When it comes to language skills of the missionaries, the dialect in which they should do their Malagasy language exams was frequently a subject of negotiation (NMS 1929: 51–56, 1926: 94–95, 1923b: 90–97, 1922: 43–51). Missionaries on the West Coast had to pass an additional exam in the Sakalava dialect. Being close to the people was said to be the reason. The exam was quite demanding, and some of the missionaries did not have any use of the Sakalava dialect at their mission station. In 1929, this additional exam therefore became voluntarily.

Edvin Fagereng worked on a dictionary Sakalava-Merina-French, together with a former Malagasy pastor Denis Mahavere (NMS 1929: 57–61, 1928: 51–54, 1926: 53–55, 1925: 53–54). In 1927, the translation from Sakalava to Merina was finished, but there was still a long way to go. The expenses of the project became higher than expected, which made the central board in Norway sceptical. It seemed, however, that the board was not only sceptical due to financial costs, as Fagereng had to struggle for permission to work on it in his spare time, but to the idea in general. In 1938, this work was still not finished and Dahl, linguist of education, got to work on the dictionary with Mahavere in his spare time (NMS 1938: 56–58). The dictionary Sakalava-Merina-French was never published, and the manuscript is to be found in the *Mission and Diakonia Archives, VID*.

Fagereng admitted that many Masikoro could learn by hearth in the Hova dialect, but argued in line with Protestant thoughts that: "they shall read it with reflection and understanding" (NMS 1924b: 33, my translation). Even pupils in the course for catechists misunderstood many of the Hova words, and how should other non-educated Masikoro understand? One opinion against publishing religious literature in Sakalava was the disadvantage of reading texts that were too different from the Bible:

> if they only read the catechism and the Bible stories in Sakalava, they will be strangers in their Bible when they are going to read it, since it is published in the Hova dialect. And the Bible should be the treasure of every Christian.
>
> (NMS 1924b: 35, my translation)

In 1928, Fagereng suggested to translate the New Testament into Sakalava in order to "give the Sakalava what they need the most: God's word in their own language" (NMS 1928: 55, my translation). A primary reason to do this was that many words in the Merina dialect had totally different meanings, which in many cases were embarrassing. For instance was the meaning of the Merina word for oil, *menaka*, a name for the female genital in the Sakalava dialect? This word was for instance used in John 11.2, in the story about Mary who poured perfume on the Lord and wiped his feet with her hair. Fagereng asked, again in the Protestant spirit, if it was satisfying for them that only the educated could read the Bible? The discussions that followed Fagereng's proposition illustrate very well the mission's involvement in translating the Bible in local languages, and its intended and unintended consequences.

The CM, consisting of Norwegian missionaries and Malagasy converts, rejected the idea as they thought this would create a conflict between Hova and Sakalava:

CM is in doubt if it is good to translate the New Testament to Saka-lava or another dialect, as the Hova dialect is the one common for all the tribes, and is best known by everybody. Therefore, it is not necessary to translate the NT to another dialect.

(NMS 1928: 57, my translation)

In addition, the British Bible Society would not accept other dialects than the Hova. Missionary to the West Coast in the period 1897–1931, August Østby, argued strongly against the proposition:

If Hova words have a bad meaning in Sakalava, then Sakalava words also have bad meanings in Hova. The bad words are understood and are not offensive. During 50 years, we have worked without any use for a N.T in Sakalava. If this translation should take place, then N.T. also would have to be translated to other dialects.

(NMS 1928: 58, my translation)

Fagereng argued that "the government supports willingly other dialects to challenge the Hova's influence, following the principle: split and reign" (NMS 1928: 60, my translation). Fagereng is here refereeing to a ten-dency of the colonial administration to rather focus on different dialects than contributing to establishing one standard Malagasy language. He is well aware of the aims behind the colonial government's approach: to "split and reign". The use of different dialects was believed to contribute to regionalism and thus to hinder nationalism, which was in the interest of the colonial power.

A missionary in the period from 1925 to 1962, Thorvald Foss reacted to this argument and pointed to the effects language policy could have:

The Bible has been a language-unifying instrument. Even though sal-vation of souls has to be our biggest aim, we have to watch out not to do a disservice to the Malagasies by splitting them in two when it comes to language.

(NMS 1928: 59, my translation)

Anyhow, Foss supported translating part of the New Testament to see if it was a reasonable project. Missionary to Madagascar in the period from 1922 to 1933, Sjur Sjursen Fykse, was also sceptical of the project. On the one side, if a people were of a certain number and their language was enough developed, they had a right to have the Bible in their mother tongue. On the other side, if a language could be used for many groups, that was the solution to follow. Due to the political sensitivity of the issue, it was decided to postpone a decision and ask for the opinion of other missions. Fagereng also suggested publishing the translation of the Lutheran liturgy and which verses from the Bible to be read every Sunday during the year *(Perikopa)* to Sakalava (NMS 1928: 62). The answer from the CM was clear about what should be the characteristics of the language used in religious literature: "As the Lutheran church already has the liturgy and the perikopa in Malagasy, it is unnecessary to translate them to remote dialects" (NMS 1928: 62, my translation).

NMS general secretary in the period from 1923 to 1957, Einar Amdahl, wrote about the language question on the West Coast in an article about his journey to Madagascar, published in the NMS magazine in 1929 (Amdahl 1929). He was very understanding of the difficulties connected to the Sakalava dialect, but also very clear in the solutions that he suggested. He agreed that the language barrier was a reason why evangelisation work in the coastal areas met so many obstacles:

> How can then the bearer of the Gospel proceed? Is Hova going to be the church language everywhere? Or should some dialects—namely those most different form the Hova—become church languages—and literature languages within their tribes? For the extensiveness of the Gospel, it is necessary that the Christian message is preached in the language that people use. Only then will people understand and evolve a dedicated belief. This is the goal of the evangelical mission. Therefore, it [the evangelisation] is highly interested in the living word, the language that people use.
>
> (Amdahl 1929, my translation)

Sakalava was, however, not a language, Amdahl explained. To him, it was one of many dialects of the Malagasy language, and this put the situation in a very different light. He maintained that languages were barriers between tribes and peoples. It was the biggest hindrance for Christianity dividing Protestants in national churches. They should not split Malagasies, but unify them in one church society, with a common literature and language. Further, he argued that the Hova was well advanced towards being the unifying language in Madagascar, and the mission and church should contribute to this through preaching and spreading literature in Hova: "It can collect and unify" (Amdahl 1929, my translation). Amdahl also considered the Protestant collaboration and mentioned that the British Bible Society did not accept any publication of the Bible in other dialects than the Hova out of fear that it would hinder the construction of a native independent church: "The Christian mission should never follow the principle: 'split and reign!' It should collect and unite to one shepherd, one herd, one church" (Amdahl 1929, my translation). This was also the view of the Mission Conference in the Highlands, other missions and the Church Conference (NMS 1932: 75–82). Critics of missions, by contrast, argued that the missions' involvement in the process of creating writing systems other places in Africa created confusion both with regard to standardisation of languages and with regard to identity, as described in Chapter 2 (Prah 2009).

In the case of Madagascar, there are no doubts that Protestant missions supported the development of a national identity as Malagasy people through their literacy work. This case from the Norwegian missionaries on the West Coast illustrates well the different needs, considerations and also consequences that were taken into account in the mission's literacy work. From a Protestant point of view, people should have the opportunity to read the Bible in their own language. The question was to what degree the standard Malagasy language, based on the Merina/Hova dialect, was a language that people understood, and could identify with. Protestant missions promoted a language, via the writing system they used, that was to some degree contextualised to the Malagasy society. This written language or literacy was, however, closer to some Malagasies' realities than others. With an ideological perspective on literacy, it can be argued that the mission, like the colonial power, contributed to making standard written Malagasy, based on Hova, a dominant language, and, in so doing they also contributed to the construction of a particular identity, which in many ways was Merina-dominated instead of French-assimilationist. On the one hand, the missions were careful not to construct several written versions of the Malagasy language, and by that they probably also avoided contributing to construct/reinforce ethnic divisions in the Malagasy society and a divide-and-rule policy. On the other hand, missions contributed to defining the standard Malagasy language, and by that they also contributed to the development of a Malagasy identity.

## Language Policy as an Instrument of French Assimilation and Regionalism

In 1949, Inspector General of French West Africa Albert Charton described teaching in a classroom in a rural area (Charton 1949). French was spoken; there was a text of La Fontaine and pictures of France and Africa. At secondary school, there were black and white pupils in the same class, with a French curriculum aiming for the same baccalaureate. Abdourahim Saïd Bakar, subjected to colonial education in the Comoro Island, wrote about his personal experience:

> Since we were considered as 'French à part-entière', nothing but French was taught. The whole curriculum was based on France and anything that was French, whereas Comorian, our mother-tongue, was never considered to be a suitable medium of instruction. It was forbidden to speak Comorian and if by hard luck we were caught whispering a Comorian word to a friend, we were sorely punished. We never studied anything which related to the Comorian way of life, its traditions or history. For the Colonial settlers, as the teaching

of history (French history) was to prove, 'We were French and our ancestors, the Gauls, lived in a country called Gaul'.

(Bakar 1988: 184)

*Equality* was one of the central Republican values that in line with discourses of assimilation were part of the ideology behind French colonial educational policy. Centralisation and ideally a universalistic treatment of all students were important elements (Clignet 1970: 428). Through education Africans should "think like Frenchmen" and "acquire loyalty to the French State" (Frazier 1956: 93–94). Even though there were some experiments with the use of local languages "all instruction had the mastery of the French language as its ultimate goal" (White 1996: 11). According to Gail P. Kelly, a "good" student was one that spoke French and accepted French authority (Kelly 1986: 173).

The first governor-general to Madagascar, Galliéni, acknowledged that the language was "one of the most powerful elements of assimilation" (Galliéni quoted in Chapus 1930: 236–237, 275, my translation, Rosnes and Rakotoanosy 2016). The school programme should therefore insist on the French civilisation, "le culte de la France", and half of the timetable was to be used on learning French. Indigenous bureaucrats were required to know the colonial language. Even though half of the primary school programme was to be in the standardised Malagasy language until 1906, the level of French was the main indicator of pupils' knowledge, as it was the language used in exams (Koerner 1999: 153, Rakotoanosy 1986: 271). The place given to the Malagasy language in primary education was a point of discussion during the entire colonial period. Malagasy researchers have shown that the specificity and the complexity of the Malagasy context did not allow an absolute and stable linguistic policy (Rakotoanosy 1986: 298, Esoavelomandroso 1976).

Governor-General Augagneur, who followed Galliéni, was of the opinion that people in the colony ignored *la Mère-patrie* (the motherland) and did not understand French (Esoavelomandroso 1976: 106, 124, Rakotoanosy 1986: 265). At arrival in 1905, Director of Education Renel promoted French as the LOI, arguing that the Malagasy language was too poor, inadequate as an instrument of abstract/complicated thinking and there was almost no literature written in Malagasy. Renel was responsible for the 1916 decree that was issued after a nationalistic revolt. (Gouvernement général de Madagascar et dépendances 1931: 17, Rakotoanosy 1986: 276). History and geography, as well as Malagasy as a subject based on the Merina dialect, were suspended from the school programme. When teaching first-year pupils, the teacher should start using the local dialect before using more and more French (Galdi and Rochefort 1960b: 1078, Esoavelomandroso 1976: 127). In his book from 1922, Renel recognised similarities between the dialects (Renel 1922: 15). The difference between the dialects was, anyhow, put forth as an argument against the use of standard Malagasy. Evidently, the ideology of regionalism following a "split-and reign" policy suited the colonial project. The LOI was French, but Malagasy dialects, not standard Malagasy based on the Merina dialect, was used to explain things. In the following way, Renel described the place of Malagasy and French in school:

> A preeminent place is reserved to the study of the French language, which is first and foremost taught by conversation exercises and by explaining lectures. There is no methodological teaching of the Malagasy language. In the beginning, the teacher uses local dialects in order to explain, but progressively, and as soon as possible, he substitutes them with the French language.
>
> (Renel 1922: 20, my translation)

This educational policy was to be challenged by the governor-general in Madagascar from 1924 to 1929, Olivier. He expressed an admiration for the quantity of pupils Renel had managed to put in school, but questioned the quality of education (Olivier 1931: 211). Olivier was more a supporter of the Malagasy language within education. He had dialogue with the Protestant missions who explained that they preferred using the local language as the LOI, at least the first 3 years in order for children to understand (Bjertnes 1925, IPC no date). In contrast, French was used at higher educational levels, admitting its usefulness and advantages in a French colony. This is a good illustration of the literacies that were transmitted through the mission schools. The missions had to teach French-assimilationist literacies and promote the French language; otherwise, the pupils would not have passed the exams. But, the missions argued for more contextualised literacies in Malagasy schools. In order for pupils at lower levels to develop and learn other subjects better, including the French language, they argued in favour of the Malagasy language as LOI. A few years later, Olivier was to implement this policy also in public schools.

## The Short-Lived 1929 Decree: A Threat of Nationalism?

One year before the 1929 decree, General Inspector to the Colonies Pegourier was in Madagascar (Pegourier 1928). He supported the use of local languages as LOI at lower level arguing that the French colonial government, due to pedagogical consequences, should not impose the French language as LOI in first levels. According to him, "the intelligence of the child is without any doubts more easily discerned when judged based on notions received in the mother tongue" (Pegourier 1928: note attached to page 3, my translation). The local language was not taught as a subject, the report admitted, "for political reasons, to avoid giving a new instrument for hegemony to one of the ethnic groups by exclusively using their dialect" (Pegourier 1928: notes attached to page 3, my translation). From this statement, it is clear that the colonial power was well aware of political consequences and implications of language. The Malagasy language was, nevertheless, regarded by Pegourier as a useful language to transmit knowledge, for instance in subjects like hygiene, moral education and civic education.

The educational reform of 1929 did not touch upon the organisation of the educational system as such, but on the content. French was still given priority as a subject, but one important change was that Malagasy gained status as the LOI in primary schools (Rakotoanosy 1986: 278). Olivier's opinion of the educational policy of his predecessors was that: *"the gaps in native education should be assigned to the premature use of French as language of instruction in the schools* [original italics]" (Olivier 1931: 211, my translation). Primary education had until then been nothing else but a step to get access to higher levels. Through a new decree, Olivier aimed to make primary education complete in itself, and secondly a step towards higher levels of education (Olivier 1931: 218). As long as the LOI was French, primary education did not respond to that aim, as all the energy was put towards learning a new language. By introducing Malagasy as LOI in primary school, Olivier promoted more contextualised literacies. This had, however, after all, the ultimate aim to transmit certain morals and an education based on the needs of the colonial power. This transmission would be more successful if pupils were taught in their mother tongue, instead of only repeating sentences in a language they did not understand.

The decree was quite radical and met resistance from French administrators and colons. They feared that Olivier's administration had endangered French influence on the island. In response to this, Olivier pointed to the knowledge in French of pupils in mission schools. They were taught in Malagasy during their first years, and Olivier said that he himself often was struck by their knowledge of French. He also pointed to research on the Gold Coast, arguing that children educated in their own language learned the English language faster. Olivier was clear that, "the influence of schools at primary level on the propagation of the French language in Madagascar was zero, or close to zero. The fact is that this propagation cannot be done by anyone but the indigenous elite" (Olivier 1931: 220, my translation). Olivier's point is here that the elite is able to learn the foreign language well, whereas the population in general have difficulties to master the foreign language not used in their environment. The Education Department admitted the failure of linguistic assimilation in the colony (Gouvernement général de Madagascar et dépendances 1931). Due to the lack of qualified teachers and schools, "the experience aiming at linguistic assimilation did not obtain the expected results" (Gouvernement général de Madagascar et dépendances 1931: 15, my translation).

In 1933, Inspector of the Colonies Moretti visited Madagascar (Rako-toanosy 1986: 281–282, Esoavelomandroso 1976: 108–109, 118, Moretti 1934). He admitted that pupils' progress was faster when using Malagasy rather than French as LOI (Rakotoanosy 1986: 290). Still, he asked if it would be right to sacrifice the elementary knowledge of French to the profit of the local culture. Here, Moretti recognises the pedagogi-cal advantages of using the local language as medium of instruction, but argues that they are to the detriment of the French-assimilationist aims of the colonial educational system. In 1933, a decree reversed Olivier's policy. It became again compulsory to use local dialects instead of stand-ard Malagasy based on the Merina dialect, before changing as soon as possible to the French language (Esoavelomandroso 1976: 108, Galdi and Rochefort 1960b: 1087). The aim of primary education was to make pupils able to use the French language, to give them essential elementary knowledge and to teach manual skills related to agriculture, art and sew-ing. Education should again be assimilationist in terms of language, but in terms of the structure of education, it should be adapted. In her article on the language policy during the inter-war period, Esoavelomandroso concluded by characterising it as inconsistent and filled with contradic-tions (Esoavelomandroso 1976: 155–156). This makes this period very interesting when it comes to the history of education and literacy pol-icy in Madagascar (Rosnes and Rakotoanosy 2016: 52–54). The other period that was chosen for this research had some of the same character-istics with the appearance of conflicting policies, aims and interests when it came to language policy.

## With Independence Comes Not Necessarily Malgachisation

In 1944, a conference in Brazzaville discussed the future of the French empire, reaffirming the ideal of assimilation to the French nation (Goguel 2006: 57, Koerner 1999: 238–239, White 1996: 12, Lewis 1962: 129, No author 1958). French was the only accepted pedagogical language and local languages were not to play a role in education. A conference of directors of education in Africa and Madagascar, held in Madagascar in 1950, affirmed that local languages could not, and should not, be used in education (Goguel 2006: 96). The French culture was to be kept united throughout the entire Republic, including the metropole, the depart-ments and the overseas territories. Parts of the local elites in Madagascar supported the policy of assimilation, and in 1944 native members of an economic and financial delegation asked for equality and an end of the dual educational system, the divide between European and indigenous education. European and indigenous education were both impacted by a content based on French-assimilationist policies, but the systems differed most importantly in their educational structure and opportunities given to the pupils, as explained on page 48 (Esoavelomandroso 1976: 156). They wished that the primary school exam should be the same for every pupil, and that French should be used as the LOI, both of which were rooted in their aspirations for access to higher education.

Even though assimilation was the dominant discourse until independence, there were discussions about adapting the Malagasy educational system, building on liberal discourses of association. In 1958, Carle, who had a position in the Department of Education, gave a presentation about the challenges regarding the LOI (No author 1958: 337–339, Carle 1958). As a previous director of education and the author of books adapted to the Malagasy context, he argued that the language issue was the main element in the adaptation of education to the Malagasy context (Carle 1952a, 1952b). Even though Madagascar was a special case with a united and rich language, French authorities tended to interpret problems in Madagascar having in mind other African colonies where the language situation was one of multilingualism. Carle was of the opinion that there was a linguistic unity in Madagascar in spite of different dialects. The richness of the language, both with regard to its role in practical life and ability to express abstract concepts and ideas, was indisputable. In fact, this situation made it possible to develop a primary education with the same quality as in the metropole, without using the French language. Carle actually argued that Malagasy pupils by using their mother tongue could obtain the same knowledge as they do in France, a quite radical argument to be expressed by a French colonial administrator of education. Carle further explained that even though many scientific words did not exist in the Malagasy language and it was easier to directly use "the big languages of civilisation", it was possible to develop the vocabulary through starting to use it in education (Carle 1958, my translation). Carle emphasised, as Olivier had done during the 1920s, that even though French should play an important role in the Malagasy society, it was a mistake to believe that the school would ensure that Malagasy people learnt French fluently. He highlighted, "Indeed, I think I have shown that the existence of a widely used language, the Merina language, constitutes permanent barriers to the massive dissemination of French" (Carle 1958: 13, my translation). Carle's conclusion illustrates the context when it comes to the language issue that the colonisers in Madagascar were faced with during the whole colonial period. The position of the Malagasy language was too important to neglect.

In 1958, the director of academic service in Madagascar, Bergeaud, arranged a conference for the CEP to inform about a new educational reform (Vialle 1958). This reform aimed to add the two last years, the 4th year and 5th year CM classes, to all primary schools and educate the maximum of children. In the debate that followed, the question of, "the Malagasy language, which is extremely important to most of the members of CEP" was raised (Vialle 1958, my translation). The arguments of CEP members focused on the failure of education in French, and how it negatively impacted on the intellectual development of the Malagasy child. Malagasy pupils did not have enough knowledge of French to develop intellectually in that language. They focused on the fact that French was not widely used: "Finally, when education is given in a foreign language, which is not the language of everyday life and of the family, the school appears like an artificial environment" (Vialle 1958, my translation). Bergeaud's arguments were the well-known arguments against the use of the Malagasy language: the diversity of the Malagasy language, its poor vocabulary and the opposition of the coastal population to the use of the language of *Ambaniandro*, literary meaning *under the day* referring to the population of the Highlands, as national language. According to Bergeaud, "the French language can and have to be the language of reflection" (Vialle 1958, my translation). He admitted that Malagasy should play an important role, but had to be enriched. It could, however, never become a world language that was needed in a modern world, Bergeaud argued. Disregarding the arguments of Bergeaud, members of CEP argued that Malagasy should be considered for use in the primary school exam. And again, when the question of development of schoolbooks came up, the language question was raised. The colonial government worked on developing adapted schoolbooks in French whereas the CEP was concerned about publishing schoolbooks in Malagasy. The Protestant missions and their converts were still promoting Malagasy as LOI, and they continued to lobby for an extended use of the local language during the first Republic that came into being a few years later.

The Malagasy government was more willing to use the Malagasy language; they ordered Malagasy schoolbooks and supported teaching in Malagasy in the first years of schooling (Habberstad 1965: 58). There was, however, no real change in the language policy. Former missionary Aamland revealed that the Malagasy language was given greater value after independence, but its use in the educational programme was not really implemented (Former female missionary Eldrid Aamland 2012). The fact that the primary school exam continued to be in French speaks to the continuing dominance of French-assimilationist literacies in Malagasy schools also after independence.

In a conference for Protestant principals in the year of independence, it was argued very clearly that: "Malagasies should know that 'CEPE' [the primary school exam] in fact is a level of knowledge that has to reach everybody. This should be in French in FRANCE. And it should be in MALAGASY here in MADAGASCAR [original capital letters]" (Fampianarana Protestanta eto Madagasikara 1960, my translation). A political argument was also put forth as a reason why teaching should be in the mother tongue: it contributed to the independence of the country. In addition, it made learning easier and helped children understand and not only memorise. Protestant converts at independence acknowledged their role as preservers of the Malagasy language and they argued that contextualised literacies provided the best approaches for learning and for the development of a new nation. Also at secondary level, Malagasy language and content were to be strengthened. Parents should be informed that, "In taking care of the child, it is more important to focus on developing the heart and reflections, than to, for any cost, obtain the diploma" (Fampianarana Protestanta eto Madagasikara 1960: 11–12, my translation). This quotation speaks to the core of the fight between French-assimilationist and contextualised literacies. They were different in content, relating differently to the Malagasy identity, and they had different consequences. French-assimilationist literacies could be perceived more easily to have socio-economic benefits whereas there was a need to inform parents about the importance of contextualised literacies that was rooted in other aims and ambitions.

In the archives, I found a document where the ISC explained their position towards the use of languages, Malagasy or French, at independence (ISC no date [between 1955 and 1963]). The *tenin-drazana*, literally meaning the language of the ancestors, was to be the basis for learning for first-year students. It was easier to teach children in a language they understood, the teacher would not lose time preparing lessons in French and the children would not lose time on memorising French. But, it was also stated that foreign languages, particularly French, was needed, especially for those students who wanted to reach higher levels of education.

From the part of the Malagasy government, a decree came out in 1960 expressing a need for examination at primary level in the Malagasy language (CEPE) (Goguel 2006: 193–195). In a 1962 decree, this was taken away, and examinations in the Malagasy language were not introduced until 1968. The diploma should be valid in all the states of *the French Community*. The political choice was, according to Goguel, that, "an elite has to be educated, an elite as French as possible" (Goguel 2006: 195, my translation). Another reason was that politicians from the coastal areas were afraid coastal children would perform poorer than children from the Highlands if the language based on the Merina dialect was used in schools.

A UNESCO report written by three experts on the situation of education in Madagascar from 1963, argued for, "an integral malgachisation, a uniting factor for planning and for the union of the nation" (Goguel 2006: 256, my translation). According to Goguel, the report was confidential and remained so for many years, probably because of its open support to malgachisation as a unifying factor, which could be used by the political opposition. Malgachisation of the educational system was considered in the report as more of a political issue than a technical problem.

Political and pedagogical arguments for malgachisation, concerning language use as well as content, were promoted. The report maintained that the question of language was one of the main problems of education in Madagascar, in addition to a lack of contextualisation of the content of education (Goguel 2006: 260, my translation). Goguel emphasised, however, that the report probably underestimated the ethnic dimension of the issue, the fear of "merinisation". The government did not implement the propositions regarding the LOI promoted by the UNESCO report. As described in Chapter 5, they put up some rural schools, but these were not part of the main and dominant educational system. Malagasy was used in ordinary schools the 1st year, not as a subject of importance in itself but rather as a mean to access the French language. Goguel raised the question if the government was too closely attached to the French government by financial and technical aid to do radical changes, as 43% of expenditures on education was said to be foreign aid.

That Malagasy did not become the LOI was contrary to what the Protestants had expected to happen at independence. NMS School Secretary Alfhild Jacobsen had been told that Malagasy was believed to become the LOI and that French would be taught as a foreign language from the 2nd or 3rd year. Jakobsen wrote in vivid words about a meeting with Rajaobelina, the secretary of the CEP, and member of a committee working for a Malagasy school reform: "For years, he has fought to make education in Malagasy, so now he was delighted like a little boy. 'The victory is ours'" (Jacobsen 1964, my translation). A new programme, where Malagasy was the LOI the first years in school, was to be implemented, and the Lutheran printing press had already been instructed to print books in Malagasy that were needed for public schools. As already mentioned, Malagasy as LOI was not implemented as expected, but schoolbooks in Malagasy was demanded and the Lutheran printing press experienced a boom in the demand for schoolbooks to be used in public schools. They had among others published Malagasy schoolbooks through the Inter-protestant publishing series *Salohy* (Rajaobelina 1973, 1968, 1964, 1966, NMS 1962: 112). They had also published several books about Malagasy history (Rakotomamonjy 1964, Fagereng and Rakotomamonjy 1963, Rakotomamonjy 1961). The printing press had to expand in order to respond to demands and for this purpose the mission asked and got support from the Norwegian Development Aid (Fagereng and Rakotomamonjy 1963). They argued that they were in position of schoolbooks in Malagasy in spite of the colonial educational policy, due to their continuing focus on using the Malagasy language.

## Concluding Remarks

This chapter has shown how Protestant missions insisted on using the standard Malagasy language, which the missions had contributed to construct and further develop through their publications. The case on initiatives for translating the Bible into a dialect on the West Coast illustrates that this decision was firm, in spite of different opinions about the effectiveness of the standard Malagasy in evangelising work in different part of Madagascar. On the one side, by insisting on this language the missions ensured that more adapted alternatives to the French-assimilationist literacies were present and challenged the dominant literacies in Madagascar. On the other side, by insisting on this language that was based on one of the dialects in the country, they indirectly contributed to develop a certain kind of a Malagasy identity. Protestant missions made a choice concerning which language to be used in Madagascar. To have a standard unifying language for the national churches was based on the missions' own aims and perspective. This fitted well with the ideology of malgachisation promoted by the opposition at independence. The opposition viewed the standard Malagasy as an instrument in unifying the independent nation in construction.

The choice of LOI has pedagogical consequences and impacts on children's access to education. In the Malagasy context, different languages of instruction, French and Malagasy, are suitable for different aims: creating an elite or offering an education for all. Even among those who during the colonial period were against the use of the local language, some admitted its pedagogical advantages. During the mid-colonisation period and at independence, there were expectations that the Malagasy language would become the LOI in public schools. This was very much wanted by the Protestant. At independence, Protestants also expected that the Malagasy language would be used in exams. These attempts to implement Malagasy as the main language of schooling failed, which illustrates to what degree the choice of the LOI in the Malagasy historical context is a political issue and not one the Protestants could decide over.

## Note

1. Dahl mentions in his article, among others: Johannes Johnsen wrote a Malagasy grammar for Norwegians and Jørgen Ruud about the grammar of the Betsimisaraka dialect. Lars Dahle wrote about Madagascar and its habitants, Arne Farteinsen Valen, Lars Røstvig and Emil Birkeli studied the Sakalava culture, Lars Vig, Emil Birkeli and Jørgen Ruud studied Malagasy traditional religion and Bjørn Elle and other missionaries brought copies of the Antemoro literature written with Arabic characters to Norway and Ludvig Munthe collected information about the existence of this literature in Europe. Edvin Fagereng worked with tribe history. Lars Dahle wrote textbooks in theology, Christian Døderlein Borchgrevink wrote textbooks in physiology and pharmacology and Ove Jakob Roll Thesen in surgery.

# 9 Conclusion

This book has focused on the education provided by the Norwegian mission in Madagascar, in particular its contribution to the development of literacy, and how as an institution engaged in providing literacy education, the mission related to other institutions, especially to the colonial administration. By focusing on one actor in the Malagasy historical context, different ideologies and purposes that shaped literacy education for Malagasy pupils were analysed particularly during the two periods: mid-colonisation and independence. This book contributes to the understanding of the history of missions and their educational work. The case of the Norwegian mission in Madagascar exemplifies the relation between religion and literacy. It demonstrates the mission's purposes and the contextual features that impacted on their educational work.

The Norwegian mission was an important actor among Protestant missions in Madagascar. Protestants had a common interest in their aim of transmitting religious literacies. To help people acquire reading skills in order for them to read the Bible in their own language, was the ultimate aim seen from the perspective of the hegemonic evangelistic discourse. The arrival of the colonial power gave Malagasies an opportunity to learn to read and write without going through the missions' religious literacies. Colonial education had, however, another aim, namely to teach pupils to be loyal to France. The literacies that the colonial power brought was defined by a European perspective and was based on French Republican values. Some of these values were the same as the values brought by the missions, while others were a constant issue of dispute. The two institutions had different purposes, and therefore also important differences in their literacy policies, which is well illustrated by their choice of language as medium of instruction. In order to become French, or at least loyal to France, learning the French language was the basic criteria. In order to become Protestant Christians out of conviction, people needed to understand what Christianity meant. Only through reading the Gospel in their own language could they become conscious Christians; therefore, the local language was an important instrument in the processes of conversion.

The Norwegian mission's physical and institutional spaces for school literacy aimed at Malagasy children and youth included Sunday, bush, primary and secondary schools. School literacy practices in Sunday schools prepared children for, and even encouraged some of them to join a school. The bush- and Sunday-school disputes, at the beginning of the 1920s, as described in Chapter 4, showed that the spaces within which teaching of reading and writing took place, was important to the secular colonial power. In the mission's struggle to get around the regulations of bush and Sunday schools, the mission drew upon the alternative development discourse, and claimed to contribute to the fight against illiteracy. The director of education argued, from a French-assimilationist point of view, that learning to read in Malagasy did not necessarily lead to educational progress or to development. For him, the missions' work was strongly shaped by the evangelistic discourse with the aim to Christianise the Malagasy population. In the end, the secretary-general of the French administration found that the need to combat illiteracy was important, and therefore he implemented more flexible regulations of bush schools. From 1924, an even more liberal regulation was implemented by Governor-General Olivier's administration. Teaching reading skills through bush and Sunday schools became an important strategy for the literacy work of the Norwegian mission in Madagascar. Bush and Sunday schools provided important opportunities for pupils to engage with religious literacies.

The main reason for the mission to be involved in educational work was to spread the Lutheran faith. At the same time, their pupils had to pass official exams based on French-assimilationist literacies. Through analysing archival material and interviews, this book has shown that the mission promoted French-assimilationist, religious and contextualised literacies through their schools. Malagasy pupils experienced literacy practices, and developed skills and abilities that could be used in different aspects of their life. The former pupils at the mission school of Betafo revealed that reading and writing skills helped them get an education, a job, increase their crops, engage in society and become more independent in those activities that required literacy skills. For the few who entered the bureaucratic system, knowledge of the French language and culture was a necessity. The fact that pupils in mission schools were said to be less competent in French was a disadvantage in this regard. Many struggled to pass exams because they did not master French-assimilationist literacies well enough. A reason was that pupils in mission schools used quite a lot of time to learn Malagasy and religion.

Missionaries raised their voices when they felt that French-assimilationist literacies became too dominant in their schools, especially when it was too much at the expense of religious literacies. Missionary Büchsenschütz argued, as explained in Chapter 4, that even though their pupils had poor results due to their lack of knowledge in French, the mission would not reinforce teaching French at the expense of the mission's aims and ambitions that required religion and the Malagasy language to be taught. Missionaries were not necessarily negative towards the colonial power and they could appreciate that the French colonial power restored *order* in the Malagasy society. But, promoting French-assimilationist literacies was not part of their main purpose, and even complicated their work, but, as they operated within the colonial education system, the mission had to provide an education that allowed their pupils to pass the official exams. What differentiated mission schools from public schools was that, in mission schools, pupils were taught the Malagasy language and they learned about Malagasy culture. These alternative literacies were, however, based on the Lutheran faith and embedded in the aims of the mission (i.e. evangelisation).

The literature that the mission published is also a significant factor in explaining what kind of literacies the mission promoted. Disseminating religious and secular literature in Malagasy was an important strategy in the mission's literacy work. Through the description of the mission's printing press and the Betafo case, this study has shown that the mission, through their schools, bookstores and magazines, contributed to people's access to written materials in Malagasy by spreading literature. Even though the literature in many homes was primarily religious, it provided people with access to written material. This material was to some degree contextualised, due to the mission's focus on using the local language and local context in order for people to understand the message.

The Norwegian mission worked mainly in the Highlands, and was often also working in remote areas. Even though the potential of educational work was recognised by many of the missionaries in coastal areas, they did not have the same success as in the Highlands. Different reasons were given for this, such as the lack of educated teachers, low interest from the local population, the small number of teaching missionaries, and the fact that many of the mission's followers, also the teachers at their schools, were of Highland origin. The language used in the Bible and in church, built on the Merina dialect, was given as a main reason for the lack of results on the West Coast. Madagascar has many dialects used by different ethnic groups. Not everyone considered standard Malagasy as their own language so the question of what dialect or dialects to use in Church is politically sensitive. Missionaries working on the West Coast understood this, and some literature was written in the Sakalava dialect. The official policy of the mission was, however, in line with other Protestant missions to support and spread the standard. The missions considered this to be a factor contributing to unify the church. They were aware that language could unite and split. The failure of the Norwegian and other mission organisations, however, to develop schools in coastal areas contributed to dividing the Malagasy society, between the Highland population which had higher educational levels and people from the coastal regions, the majority of whom had lower educational achievements. The colonial power focused on this unequal distribution of schools and, on the basis of *la politique des races*, they focused their educational work in coastal regions. To have enough influence in the country, they also had to make sure, however, that public schools outnumbered mission schools in the Highlands.

The assimilation discourse was dominated by Republican values, and insisted on equality in the way that it gave people in the colonies access to French language and civilisation. People in the colonies were considered equal, but not on their own terms. They had to assimilate the French culture and language through French-assimilationist literacies. The method of teaching did not create critical thinkers, but made them adopt the colonial rulers' moral norms and disciplines. Only a small portion of the citizens got access to education, and the mastery of French language was crucial in ranking students. The colonial language was presented as a *neutral* language, in opposition to the standard Malagasy based on the Merina dialect, which would reinforce the position of this ethnic group. Nevertheless, the French language also became a powerful mechanism for social stratification. Those who managed to become assimilated, by mastering well French-assimilationist literacies, had the opportunity to become part of a new elite constructed on the terms of the colonial power. Local power structures, evident through the dominance of the Merina, played an important role in the policy of educating this elite. Colonial administrators argued that people in the coastal areas were sceptical towards the domination of Merina in the administration. In addition, colonial administrators expressed fear of the local resistance among the Merina intellectual elite. *La politique des races*, promoting regionalism to fight nationalism, was to become an important instrument to ensure the representation of different ethnic groups in this new political elite (Esoavelomandroso 1977). After independence, the link between this elite and the former colonial power, in addition to the division between different ethnic and socio-economic groups, continued to shape the political landscape.

Since the educational system of the colonial administration was based on the need for bureaucrats, very few gained access. For the mission, their main concern was to teach people general basic literacy skills and to introduce them to the Lutheran faith. In addition to religious studies, helpful for the education of pastors and catechists, they focused on teacher training, in order to be able to run primary schools. Even though it can be argued that a clerical elite was created through the mission's educational structure, elite construction in general was not the main aim. Their aim was educating the masses. Another important difference between the policies of the colonial power and the missions was that the aim of mission work was to develop a self-reliant and independent national church, whereas the literacy work of the colonial power was intended to reinforce people's dependency on the *civilised* culture. The colonial administration was at times very critical of the missions. The missions' educational structure represented something different, as their pupils were not educated for the purpose of serving the colonial power. They were educated to serve the missions, to whom the local language and self-reliance for the purpose of church building were important.

The main argument of this book is that the Protestant missions' literacy work contributed to the development of an education for Malagasy people that provided and alternative to the education of the colonial administration. The most important issue in this regard is the mission's choice of Malagasy as the LOI. Language use has social and cultural implications, as language is a bearer of culture and a mechanism of power. It had an important impact on the way Malagasy children and youth were to learn to read and write. Even in reports written for the colonial power, educationalists argued that children learn best in a language they understand. Access to a rich education is lost through the dominant use of a foreign language. Through their focus on spreading the gospel in a language that people understood, missionaries and their converts contributed to preserve, construct and develop the standard Malagasy language. Even though this written language became very much influenced by the missions' motivations, this engagement provided the Malagasy society with a written local language and an education system that was different from the French-assimilationist education policies. The promotion of an alternative to the dominant colonial French-assimilationist literacies showed the Malagasy population that literacy could be done in different ways. You could acquire reading and writing skills without using the French language.

At the time of independence in 1960, the new Malagasy nation had several options for how to build the postcolonial educational system. Teaching in French was part of the French-assimilationist policy, with the purpose to train a certain number of collaborators needed in the colonial project. It is therefore relevant to ask why French is still used as the LOI in Madagascar today, when the articulated aim is, "Education for all!" The majority of the population does not use French in their everyday lives. Every effort to contextualise the Malagasy educational system by using Malagasy as the LOI in primary schools has failed. In 2008, there was an effort by the government under the power of Marc Ravalomanana introduce Malagasy as the LOI for the first 5 years in an educational reform. However, in January 2009, Madagascar experienced a political crisis, and the political opposition led by the deported mayor of the capital, Andry Rajoelina, overthrew the regime. During his first days in power, Rajoelina made it clear that French language should continue to be an important LOI in Malagasy schools. This bears a resemblance to the incident about 80 years earlier, when Governor-General Cayla reversed the former Governor-General Olivier's reform to use Malagasy as the LOI at primary level. Many of the arguments that are used today are similar to those presented during the colonial period. This shows how the past still bears on educational debates today and how relevant it is to take a long view and look historically at the question of education in Madagascar.

# References

Amdahl, Einar. 1929. "Fra reisen: VI Vestmadagaskar." *NMt* 85 (28):221.

Anderson, Kate T. 2013. "Contrasting Systemic Functional Linguistic and Situated Literacies. Approaches to Multimodality in Literacy and Writing Studies." *Written Communication* XX (X):1–24.

Apelseth, Arne. 2004. "Den låge danninga. Skriftmeistring, diskursintegrering og tekstlege deltakingsformer 1760–1840." Ph.D. thesis in Humanities, University of Bergen.

Bakar, Abdourahim Saïd. 1988. "Small Island Systems: A Case Study of the Comoro Islands." *Comparative Education* 24 (2):181–191.

Barton, David. 2007. *Literacy: An Introduction to the Ecology of Written Language.* Malden: Blackwell Publishing.

Barton, David, and Mary Hamilton. 2000. "Literacy practices." In *Situated Literacies: Reading and Writing in Context*, edited by David Barton, Mary Hamilton and Roz Ivanic, 7–15. London: Routledge.

Barton, David, and Mary Hamilton. 1998. *Local Literacies: Reading and Writing in One Community.* London: Routledge.

Bastian, Georges. 1955. *Madagascar: Les hommes: Le pays: La mise en valeur, Editions Ny Ravinala.* Besancon: Imprimerie Jacques et Demontrond.

Baynham, Mike. 2008. "Elite or powerful literacies? Constructions of literacy in the novels of Charles Dickens and Mrs. Gaskell." In *Literacies, Global and Local*, edited by Mastin Prinsloo and Mike Baynham, 173–192. Amsterdam: John Benjamins Publishing Company.

Berge, Kjell Lars. 2006. "Perspektiv på skriftkultur." In *Utfordringar for skriveopplæring og skriveforskning i dag*, edited by Synnøve Matre, 57–76. Trondheim: Tapir akademisk forlag.

Bied-Charreton. 1968. "Le Canton de Betafo et le village d'Anjazafotsy." *Extraits des Bulletin de Madagascar* Nos 265 et 266–267.

Birkeli, Emil. 1942. "Banebryteren misjonær John Engh 4.desbr. 1867–4.desbr. 1942. Et 75-års minne." *NMt* 97 (49):3–4.

Birkeli, Emil. 1935. *Misjonshistorie I: Kristendommens utbredelse.* Oslo: Oscar Andersens Boktrykkeri.

Birkeli, Fridtjov, ed. 1954. *Misjonsskipet i den fjerde nattevakt? NMS årbok 1951–1954.* Stavanger: NMS forlag.

Birkeli, Fridtjov. 1949. "Det norske misjonsselskaps historie: Madagaskar innland." In *Det norske misjonsselskaps historie i hundre år: Bind IV: Det norske misjonsselskaps historie: Madagaskar innland, Vest-Madagaskar, Øst-Madagaskar*, edited by Fridtjov Birkeli, Emil Birkeli, Gabriel Nakkestad and Hans Bjåstad. Stavanger: Det Norske misjonsselskap, Dreyer.

Bjertnes, Fredrik. 1927. "Seksti aar med evangeliets lægedom: Sekstiaarsjubilæum i Betafo, Madagaskar." *NMt* 82 (48).

Bjertnes, Fredrik. 1923a. "II: Madagaskars Indland, Bara og Østkysten." In *NMS årbok 1923*, 62–68. Stavanger: NMS trykkeri.

Bjertnes, Fredrik. 1923b. "Madagaskars Indland, Østkyst og Bara." In *NMS årbok 1922*, 12–29. Stavanger: NMS trykkeri.

Bjertnes, Fredrik. 1921. "3: Madagaskars Indland med Østkyst og Bara." In *NMS årbok 1921*, 77–98. Stavanger: NMS boktrykkeri.

Bjertnes, Fredrik. 1920. "2: Madagaskars Indland, Bara og Østkysten." In *NMS årbok 1920*, 48–68. Stavanger: NMS boktrykkeri.

Bloch, Maurice E. F. 1998. *How We Think They Think: Anthropological Approaches to Cognition, Memory, and Literacy*. Boulder, CO: Westview Press.

Bøe, Isak. 1969b. "Madagaskar: Jubileum, brytninger og friskt initiativ." In *Sendt av Gud: NMS årbok 1966–1969*, edited by Gudmund Gjelsten, 55–60. Stavanger: Nomi forlag.

Carle, R. 1958. "La langue malgache et l'enseignement." *Territoire de Madagascar*. Services Académiques.

Carle, Rene. 1952a. *Eto Madagasikara nosy malalantsika*. Paris: Classiques Hachette.

Carle, Rene. 1952b. *Joies et Traveaux de l'île hereux: Cours élémentaire*. Paris: Classiques Hachette.

Chafer, Tony. 2007. "Education and Political Socialisation of a National-Colonial Political Elite in French West Africa, 1936–47." *The Journal of Imperial and Commonwealth History* 35 (3):437–458.

Chapus, Georges-Sully. 1930. "La Méthode de Gallieni en matière d'Enseignement." *Bulletin Economique de Madagascar* (1):265–281.

Charton, Albert. 1949. "French Tropical and Equatorial Africa." *The Yearbook of Education* :366–379.

Clignet, Remi. 1970. "Inadequacies of the Notion of Assimilation in African Education." *The Journal of Modern African Studies* 8 (3):425–444.

Cole, Michael, and Sylvia Scribner. 1981. *The Psychology of Literacy*. Cambridge: Harvard University Press.

Colonie de Madagascar et Dépendances. 1928. "L'enseignement à Madagascar." *Bulletin Économique: Publié par les soins du Gouvernement Général* 25:65–78.

Dahl, Otto Christian. 1984. *Norske misjonærers innsats i vitenskapelig arbeid*. Oslo: Universitetsforlaget.

Dahl, Otto Christian. 1968. *Contes malgaches en dialecte sakalava: Textes, traduction, grammaire et lexique*. Oslo: Universitetsforlaget.

Dahl, Otto Christian. 1957. "En tur over Vest-Madagaskar." In *Guds kirke bygges: NMS årbok 1954–1957*, edited by Sigvart Riiser, 58–63. Stavanger: NMS forlag.

Dahl, Øyvind. 2011. "Linguistic policy challenges in Madagascar." In *North-South Contributions to African Languages*, edited by Christina Thornell and Karsten Legère, 51–80. Cologne: Rüdiger Köppe.

Dahle, Lars. 1877. *Specimens of Malagasy Folk-lore.* Antananarivo, Paris: Kingdon.

Danbolt, Erling. 1948. *Det norske misjonsselskaps misjonærer 1842–1948.* Stavanger: NMS.

Danbolt, Erling. 1947. *Misjonstankens gjennombrudd i Norge: Bind I: Misjonsappellens tid 1800–1830.* Oslo: J.M. Bech trykkeri.

Danbolt, Lars Johan. 1929. "Den litterære innsats." *NMt* 84 (19):148.

Daughton, James Patrick. 2006. *An Empire Divided: Religion, Republicanism, and the Making of French Colonialism, 1880–1914.* Oxford: Oxford University Press.

Dina, Jeanne. 2006. "Le malgache, langue écrite depuis l'époque précoloniale." (Paper presented at the international conference *Languages and Education in Africa*, Oslo, Norway, 19–22 June).

Drønen, Tomas Sundnes. 2009. *Communication and Conversion in Northern Cameroon: The Dii People and Norwegian Missionaries, 1934–1960.* Leiden: Brill.

Dunaway, David K. 1992. "Method and Theory in the Oral Biography." *Oral History* 20 (2):40–44.

Edland, Sigmund. 2006. "Evangelists or Envoys? The Role of British Missionaries at Turning Points in Malagasy Political History, 1820–1840: Documentary and Analysis." Ph.D. thesis, School of Mission and Theology. Stavanger: Misjonshøgskolens forlag.

Edland, Sigmund, and Kjetil Aano. 1992. "Madagaskar." In *I tro og tjeneste: Det norske misjonsselskap 1842–1992 I*, edited by Torstein Jørgensen, 348–457. Stavanger: Misjonshøgskolen.

Eggen, Egil. 1969. "Misjonsbefalingen i dag." In *Sendt av Gud: NMS årbok 1966–1969*, edited by Gudmund Gjelsten, 20–27. Stavanger: Nomi forlag.

Esoavelomandroso, Faranirina V. 1977. " 'Politique des races' et enseignement colonial (jusqu'en 1940)." *Omaly sy anio (Hier et aujourd'hui): Revue d'études historiques* (5–6):245–256.

Esoavelomandroso, Faranirina V. 1976. "Langue, culture et colonisation à Madagascar: malgache et français dans l'enseignement officiel (1916–1940)." *Omaly sy anio (Hier et aujourd'hui): Revue d'études historiques* (3–4):105–165.

Esoavelomandroso, Manassé. 1989–1990. "L'effondrement de l'autorité royale dans la région de Betafo à la fin du XIXème siècle (1885–1895)." *Omaly sy anio (Hier et aujourd'hui): Revue d'études historiques* (29–32):307–317.

Etherington, Norman. 2005a. "Education and medicine." In *Missions and Empire*, edited by Norman Etherington, 261–284. Oxford: Oxford University Press.

Etherington, Norman. 2005b. "Introduction." In *Missions and Empire*, edited by Norman Etherington. Oxford: Oxford University Press.

FAEM. 1968. "IV Séminaire national de la FAEM: Résultats des travaux: Malgachisation et démocratisation de l'enseignement à Madagascar". Antsirabe 31.mars-6.avril.

Fagereng, Edvin Kristian Herbert, and Marline Rakotomamonjy. 1963. *Ny tantaran'ny Firenena Malagasy: Cours Moyen.* Edited by Edisiona Saholy. Tananarive: Trano Printy Loterana.

Fagereng, Kristine. 1949a. "Koto og Boto." *Kom og Se* (16 og 17).

Fagereng, Kristine. 1949b. "Naike fra Fitsiteke." *Kom og Se* (13).

Farine, Avigdor. 1969. "Society and Education: The Content of Education in the French African School." *Comparative Education* 5 (1):51–66.

Frazier, E. Franklin. 1956. "Education and the African Élite." *Transactions -3rd World Congress of Sociology* 8 (5):90–96.

Gadamer, Hans-Georg. 1989. *Truth and Method.* New York: Continuum.

Galdi, G. P., and Rochefort. 1960a. "Notes sur l'Historique de l'Enseignement à Madagascar." *Bulletin de Madagascar* 10 (171):651–665.

Galdi, G. P., and Rochefort. 1960b. "Notes sur l'Historique de l'Enseignement à Madagascar." *Bulletin de Madagascar* 10 (175):1075–1091.

Gardner, Graham. 2001. "Unreliable Memories and Other Contingencies: Problems with Biographical Knowledge." *Qualitative Research* 1 (2):185–204.

Gee, James Paul. 2008. *Social Linguistics and Literacies: Ideology in Discourses.* London: Routledge.

Goguel, Anne-Marie. 2006. *Aux origines du mai malgache: Désir d'école et compétition sociale 1951–1972.* Paris: Éditions Karthala.

Goody, Jack. 1986. *The Logic of Writing and the Organization of Society, Studies in Literacy, Family, Culture and the State.* London: Cambridge University Press.

Goody, Jack, and Ian Watt. 1963. "The Consequences of Literacy." *Comparative Studies in Society and History* 5 (3):304–345.

Gouvernement général de Madagascar et dépendances, Direction de l'enseignement. 1931. *L'enseignement à Madagascar en 1931.*

Gow, Bonar A. 1979. *Madagascar and the Protestant Impact: The Work of the British Missions, 1818–95.* London: Longman.

Graff, Harvey J. 1987. *The Legacies of Literacy: Continuities and Contradictions in Western Culture and Society.* Bloomington: Indiana University Press.

Graff, Harvey J. 1979. *The Literacy Myth: Literacy and Social Structure in the Nineteenth-Century City.* New York: Academic Press.

Graff, Harvey J., and John Duffy. 2008. "Literacy myths." In *Literacy*, edited by Brian V. Street and Nancy H. Hornberger, 41–51. New York: Springer.

Gueunier, Noël Jacques. 2004. "Recherches sur les manuels scolaires anciens à Madagascar." Ny Protestanta miatrika ny Ankehitriny eto anivon'ny Firenena, Antananarivo, 28–30 June.

Gullestad, Marianne. 2007. *Picturing Pity: Pitfalls and Pleasures in Cross-cultural Communication—Image and Word in a North Cameroon Mission.* Oxford: Berghahn Books.

Habberstad, Klara. 1965. "Det Norske Misjonsselskaps skolearbeid på Madagaskar." In *Idet dere lærer dem: Det Norske Misjonsselskaps skolearbeid på Madagascar*, edited by Ingolf Edward Hodne and Klara Habberstad, 37–60. Stavanger: Nomi Forlag.

Harries, Patrick. 2001. "Missionaries, Marxists and Magic: Power and the Politics of Literacy in South-East Africa." *Journal of Southern African Studies* 27 (3):405–427.

Haus, Alfhild. 1951. "På visitas." *Kom og Se* (9):6–7, 10.

Haut Commissariat de la République française à Madagascar et Dépendances. 1950. "L'enseignement à Madagascar." *Bulletin de Madagascar* (15): 17–27.

Heath, Shirley Brice, and Brian V. Street. 2008. *Ethnography: Approaches to Language and Literacy Research.* New York: Teacher College Press.

Hodne, Ingolf Edward. 1997. *Missionary Enterprise in African Education: The Co-operating Lutheran Missions in Natal, South Africa,1912–1955*. Stavanger: Misjonshøgskolens forlag.

Hübsch, Bruno. 2008. *L'église catholique à Madagascar: esquisse d'une histoire du xxème siècle*. Antananarivo, Paris: Foi et Justice.

Hübsch, Bruno. 1993. "Difficultés des missions catholiques à Madagascar." In *Histoire oecuménique Madagascar et le Christianisme*, edited by Bruno Hübsch, 241–256. Antananarivo, Paris: Editions Ambozontany, Editions-Diffusion Karthala.

Johansson, Egil. 2007. "The history of literacy in Sweden." In *Literacy and Historical Development: A Reader*, edited by Harvey J. Graff, 238–271. Carbondale: Southern Illinois University Press.

Jørgensen, Torstein. 1990. *Contact and Conflict: Norwegian Missionaries, the Zulu Kingdom, and the Gospel: 1850–1873*. Oslo: Solum Forlag.

Jørgensen, Torstein. 1992. "De første 100 år." In *I tro og tjeneste: Det norske misjonsselskap 1842–1992 I*, edited by Torstein Jørgensen, 11–145. Stavanger: Misjonshøgskolen.

Kallaway, Peter, and Rebecca Swartz (eds.). 2016. *Empire and Education in Afria: The Shaping of a Comparative Perspective*. New York: Peter Lang.

Kallekleiv, Berit. 1970. "Til Kom og Se." *Kom og Se: Julenummer* (12–15).

Kelly, Gail P. 1986. "Learning to Be Marginal: Schooling in Interwar French West Africa." *Journal of Asian and African Studies* 21 (3–4):171–184.

Kiwanuka, M. Semakula. 1970. "Colonial Policies and Administrations in Africa: The Myths of the Contrasts." *African Historical Studies* 3 (2):295–315.

Koerner, Francis. 1999. *Histoire de l'enseignement privé et officiel à Madagascar (1820–1995): Les implications religieuses et politique dans la formation d'un peuple*. Paris: L'Harmattan.

Kopreitan, Ole August. 1927a. "International missionskonferens." *NMt* 82 (3):21.

Kopreitan, Ole August. 1927b. "International missionskonferens i Tananarive, Madagaskar." *NMt* 82 (4):31–32.

Kral, Inge Birgita. 2007. "Writing Words—Right Way! Literacy and Social Practice in the Ngaanyatjarra World." Ph.D. thesis, Australian National University.

Langhelle, Svein Ivar. 2006. "Frå religiøst fellesskap til personlege val." In *Vestlandets Historie: Kultur*, edited by Knut Helle, Ottar Grepstad, Arnvid Lillehammer and Anna Elisa Tryti, 107–145. Bergen: Vigmostad og Bjørke AS.

Levinsen, Hanna. 1926. "Lille Kolo: Brev fra Madagaskar." *Missionsselskaps Barneblad* 31 (23):180–181.

Lewis, Martin Deming. 1962. "One Hundred Million Frenchmen: The 'Assimilation' Theory in French Colonial Policy." *Comparative Studies in Society and History* 4 (2):129–153.

Lieblich, Amia, Tamar B. Zilber, and Rivka Tuval-Mashiach. 2008. "Narrating Human Actions: The Subjective Experience of Agency, Structure, Communion, and Serendipity." *Qualitative Inquiry* 14 (4):613–631.

Lieblich, Amia, Tamar B. Zilber, and Rivka Tuval-Mashiach. 1998. *Narrative Research: Reading, Analysis, and Interpretation*. Edited by Leonard Bickman and Debra J. Rog. Thousand Oaks: Sage Publications.

Løtveit, Marta. 1961. "Les kva gasserjenta Ravaonoro fortel: Ho er nå elev på bibelskulen i Alakamisy." *Kom og Se* (3):10.

Makoni, Sinfree, and Alastair Pennycook. 2006. "Disinventing and reconstituting languages." In *Disinventing and Reconstituting Languages*, edited by Sinfree Makoni and Alastair Pennycook. New York: Multilingual Matters.

Malinowski, Bronislaw. 1943. "The Pan-African Problem of Culture Contact." *American Journal of Sociology* 48 (6):649–665.

Martin, James Robert, and Ruth Wodak. 2003. *Re/reading the Past: Critical and Functional Perspectives on Time and Value*. Amsterdam: John Benjamins Publications.

Meling, Gunnar Andreas. 1954. "Koto." *Kom og Se* (2).

Meling, Gunnar Andreas, and Maria Kjøllesdal, eds. 1977. *Guds høstfolk: Det norske misjonsselskaps misjonærer: 1842–1977*. Stavanger: Det Norske Misjonsselskap.

Meling, Lars Gabrielsen. 1928. "Madagaskars innland, Bara og Østkyst." In *NMS årbok 1928*, 23–39. Stavanger: NMS.

Mumford, W. Bryant. 1935. "Comparative Studies of Native Education in Various Dependencies." *The Yearbook of Education* :810–850.

Nakkestad, Gabriel, Christian Razanadraibe, Laurel O. Johnson, and Rajosefa Rakotovao. 1967. *Voly Maitson'Andriamanitra: Tantaran'ny Fiangonana Loterana Malagasy 1867–1967*. Antananarivo, Paris: Trano Printy Loterana.

Nielsen, John A. 1957a. "Det haster med kongens ærend." In *Guds kirke bygges: NMS årbok 1954–1957*, edited by Sigvart Riiser, 38–50. Stavanger: NMS forlag.

Nielsen, John A. 1957b. "Madagaskar i et tidsskifte: Rapport fra fellesarbeidet." In *Guds kirke bygges: NMS årbok 1954–1957*, edited by Sigvart Riiser, 68–78. Stavanger: NMS forlag.

NMS. 1922. *Programmes et emplois du temps à l'usage des écoles primaires et des garderies*. Tananarive: Imprimerie de la Mission Norvégienne.

No author. 1958. "Enseignement: Le problème de la langue." *Bulletin de Madagascar* 8 (143):337–339.

No author. 1951. "Koto." *Kom og se* (5–6):8–9.

No author. 1929. "Gutten som vilde gå på skole." *Misjonsselskapets barneblad* 34 (10):75–76.

Nome, John. 1943. *Det Norske misjonsselskaps historie i norsk kirkeliv: fra stiftelsestiden til Schreuders brudd, Det Norske misjonsselskaps historie i hundre år*. Stavanger: Dreyer.

Olivier, Marcel. 1931. *Six ans de politique sociale à Madagascar*. Paris: Bernard Grasset.

Papen, Uta. 2017. "Hymns, Prayers and Bible Stories: The Role of Religious Literacy Practices in Children's Literacy Learning." *Ethnography and Education* :1–16. Doi: 10.1080/17457823.2016.1277773

Papen, Uta. 2016. *Literacy and Education: Policy, Practice and Public Opinion*. New York: Routledge.

Papen, Uta. 2005. *Adult Literacy as Social Practice: More Than Skills*. London: Routledge.

Peterson, Derek R. 2004. *Creative Writing: Translation, Bookkeeping, and the Work of Imagination in Colonial Kenya*. Portsmouth: Heinemann.

Porter, Andrew. 2002. "Church History, History of Christianity, Religious History: Some Reflections on British Missionary Enterprise Since the Late Eighteenth Century." *Church History* 71 (3):555–584.

Prah, Kwesi Kwaa. 2009. "Winning souls through the written word." In *The Role of Missionaries in the Development of African Langauges*, edited by Kwesi Kwaa Prah, 1–33. Cape Town: The Center for Advanced Studies of African Society (CASAS).

Predelli, Line Nyhagen. 2003. *Issues of Gender, Race, and Class, in the Norwegian Missionary Society in Nineteenth-Century Norway and Madagascar*. Lewiston: Edwin Mellen Press.

Radaody-Ralarosy, P. 1951–1952. "De la nouvelle orientation de l'enseignement général indigène à Madagascar." *Bulletin de l'Academie malgache* XXX:143–150.

Raison-Jourde, Françoise. 1991. *Bible et pouvoir à Madagascar au XIXe siècle: Invention d'une identité chrétienne et construction de l'État (1780–1880)*. Paris: Karthala.

Rajaobelina, Prosper. 1973. *Tantelin-jaza vaovao: Boky famankian-teny Cours Préparatoire 2ème année: Cous Élémentaire 1ère année*. Edited by Edisiona Salohy. Antananarivo, Paris: Trano Printy Loterana.

Rajaobelina, Prosper. 1968. *Tsingory: Boky famakian-teny Cous Preperatoire 1ère et 2ème annee*, Edisiona Salohy. Antananarivo, Paris: Trano Printy Loterana.

Rajaobelina, Prosper. 1966. *Lala sy Noro: Boky iandoha-mamaky teny*. Antananarivo, Paris: Trano Printy Fiangonana Loterana Malagasy.

Rajaobelina, Prosper. 1964. *Angano sy Arira*. Antananarivo, Paris: Trano Printy Loterana.

Rajaobelina, Prosper. 1955. *Lala sy Noro: Edisiona tsotra*. Tananarive: Imprimérie Luthérienne.

Rajaonah, Faranirina. 2002. "L'école Le Myre de Vilers." In *La nation malgache au défi de l'ethnicité*, edited by Françoise Raison-Jourde and Solofo Randrianja. Paris: Éditions Karthala.

Rajoelison, Haja, and Bruno Hübsch. 1993. "L'instauration de la liberté religieuse (1861–1868)." In *Histoire œcuménique Madagascar et le Christianisme*, edited by Bruno Hübsch, 259–276. Antananarivo, Paris: Editions Ambozontany, Editions-Diffusion Karthala.

Rakotoanosy, Monique Irène Ratrimoarivony. "Historique et nature de l'enseignement à Madagascar de 1896 à 1960." Thèse du Doctorat de IIIe Cycle, Université Paris-Sorbonne Paris IV, 1986.

Rakotomamonjy, Marline. 1964. *Fianarana tantara: Boky II: Cours Élémentaire*. Edited by Edisiona Salohy. Antananarivo, Paris: Trano Printy Loterana.

Rakotomamonjy, Marline. 1961. *Fianarana tantara: Boky I: Cours Élémentaire*. Edited by Edisiona Salohy. Tananarive: Imprimerie Luthérienne.

Ravelomanana, Mpitandrina. 1968. *Ny sekolin'ny protestanta sy ny fampianarana samy hafa nataony teto Madagasikara*. Antananarivo, Paris: Edisiona Salohy.

Reisigl, Martin, and Ruth Wodak. 2009. "The discourse-historical approach (DHA)." In *Methods of Critical Discourse Analysis*, edited by Ruth Wodak and Michael Meyer, 87–121. Los Angeles: Sage Publications.

Renel, Charles. 1922. *Principe de pédagogie indigène à l'usage des Européens: Leur application à Madagascar*. Tananarive: Imprimerie Officielle.

Republica Malgache, Ministère de l'éducation nationale. 1964. *L'èvolution de l'enseignement primaire à Madagascar*.

Rosnes, Ellen Vea. 2017. "Christianisation, Frenchification and Malgachisation: Mission Education During War and Rebellion in French Colonial Madagascar in the 1940s." *History of Education*: 46 (6). Doi: 10.1080/0046760X.2017.1368723

Rosnes, Ellen Vea. 2016. "Protestant and French colonial literacies in Madagascar at the beginning of the 20th century." In *Empire and Education in Africa: The Shaping of a Comparative Perspective*, edited by Peter Kallaway and Rebecca Swartz, 271–297. New York: Peter Lang.

Rosnes, Ellen Vea. 2013. "With a Church Comes a School: Protestant Mission Education in Madagascar." *Southern African Review of Education* 19 (2):72–91.

Rosnes, Ellen Vea, and Monique Rakotoanosy. 2016. "Contextualiser la place du français et du malgache dans le système éducatif du Madagascar: Une perspective historique." *Paedagogica Historica: International Journal of the History of Education: Special Issue: ISCHE 36* (London) (I-II).

Rugset, Dorthea. 1925. "En fortælling fra Madagaskar." *NMt* 79 (49):401.

Schaanning, Karen Dorothea. 1922. "Hvad gassiske barn læser." *Missionsselskapets Barneblad* 27 (21):162–164.

Schaanning, Karen Dorothea. 1921. "Vore skoler paa Madagaskar." *NMt* 76 (4):49–54.

Sjursen, Leif. 1960. "Som en susen i kornet sommerdag." In *Høsten er stor: NMS årbok 1957–60*, edited by Sigvart Riiser, 55–61. Stavanger: Nomi forlag.

Sjursen, Leif. 1957. "Ved midtsommertid." In *Guds kirke bygges: NMS årbok 1954–1957*, edited by Sigvart Riiser, 51–57. Stavanger: NMS forlag.

Skeie, Karina Hestad. 2013. *Building God's Kingdom: Norwegian Missionaries in Highland Madagascar 1866–1903*. Leiden: Brill.

Snekkenes, Arthur. 1960. "Den unge kirke i den nye gassiske republikk." In *Høsten er stor: NMS årbok 1957–60*, edited by Sigvart Riiser, 43–54. Stavanger: Nomi forlag.

Snekkenes, Arthur. 1954. "Vi forlater misjonsskipet, og går på besøk ombord i kirkeskipet." In *Misjonsskipet i den fjerde nattevakt? NMS årbok 1951–1954*, edited by Fridtjov Birkeli. Stavanger: Misjonsselskapets forlag.

Snekkenes, Arthur. 1951. "På lynvisitt til Madagskar innland, skogen og Bara." In *Misjonsskipet går videre: NMS årbok 1948–1951*, edited by Emil Birkeli, 98–113. Stavanger: NMS forlag.

Stanley, Brian. 2009. *The World Missionary Conference, Edinburgh 1910*. Grand Rapids: Wm. B. Eerdmans Publishing Company.

Stolee, Peter B. 1951. "Misjonen som banebryter for lesekunsten." *Norsk tidsskrift for misjon* 5 (3):129–144.

Strand, Ole. 1937. "Andreas fra Betafo: Trekk av en livshistorie." *NMt* 92 (16):5–6.

Strand, Ole. 1928. "Madagaskars Indland, Bara og Østkysten." In *NMS årbok 1927*, 35–55. Stavanger: NMS trykkeri.

Strand, Ole. 1923. "Arbeidet i Betafo og Soavina 1922." *NMt* 78 (15): 246–249.

Street, Brian V. 2009. "The future of 'social literacies'." In *The Future of Literacy Studies*, edited by Mike Baynham and Mastin Prinsloo, 21–37. New York: Palgrave Macmillan.

Street, Brian V. 1984. *Literacy in Theory and Practice*. Cambridge: Cambridge University Press.

Street, Joanna C., and Brian V. Street. 1991. "The schooling of literacy." In *Writing in the Community*, edited by David Barton and Roz Ivanic, 143–166. Newbury Park: Sage Publications.

Sæveraas, Magnus. 1951. "'Blås bodi ut då vindar'." In *Misjonsskipet går videre: NMS årbok 1948–51*, edited by Fridtjov Birkeli, 114–117. Stavanger: NMS forlag.

Tjelle, Kristin Fjelde. 2014. *Missionary Masculinity, 1870–1930: The Norwegian Missionaries in South-East Africa*. Basingstoke: Palgrave Macmillan.

Tjelle, Kristin Fjelde. 2011. "Missionary Masculinity: The Case of the Norwegian Lutheran Missionaries to the Zulus, 1870–1930." Ph.D. thesis, School of Mission and Theology.

Torbjørnsen, Thor. 1964. "Et merkeår i gassisk kirkeliv." In *NMS årbok 1964*, edited by Sigvart Riiser and Arthur Harstad, 30–39. Stavanger: Nomi Forlag.

Torbjørnsen, Thor. 1960. "Større enn tempelet." In *Høsten er stor: NMS årbok 1957–60*, edited by Sigvart Riiser, 62–66. Stavanger: Nomi forlag.

Vigen, James, and Jacques Tronchon. 1993. "Dynamism ecclécial et affrontements (1896–1913)." In *Histoire œcuménique Madagascar et le Christianisme*, edited by Bruno Hübsch, 325–348. Antananarivo, Paris: Éditions Ambozontany, Éditions-Diffusion Karthala.

White, Bob W. 1996. "Talk About School: Education and the Colonial Project in French and British Africa (1860–1960)." *Comparative Education* 32 (1):9–25.

World Missionary Conference. 1910. *Report of Commission III: Education in Relation to the Christianisation of National Life*. Edinburgh.

# Archival Material

Augagneur, Victor. 1907a. "Discour du Gouverneur Général Augagneur le 06.09.1907." ANOM_D6(4)59.

Augagneur, Victor. 1907b. "Letter dated 15.05.1907 to former colleagues." ANOM_D6(4)59.

Béréni, Ange. 1923. "Note dated 19.06.1923 to the Governor-General." ARM_F185.

Berthier, Hugues. 1924. "Letter dated 12.09.1924 to the President of IPC." FLM_TA_75G.

Bjertnes, Fredrik. 1925. "Circular no. 175 dated 10.07.1925 to the missionaries." FLM_TA_100D.

Bjertnes, Fredrik. 1923. "Circular no. 150 dated 31.08.1923 to the missionaries in the highlands." FLM_TA_100D.

Bjertnes, Fredrik. 1922. "Letter dated 22.09.1922 to the Governor-General." FLM_TA_75G.

Bjertnes, Fredrik. 1920. "Circular no. 114. dated 00.00.1920 to the missionaries in the three Lutheran missions." FLM_TA_100D.

Brunet, Auguste. 1923. "Arrêté du 20 juin 1923 modifiant les articles 14–15 et 16 du Titre IV de l'arrêté du 23 Novembre 1906."ARM_F185.

Bøe, Isak. 1969a. "Letter to the Missionaries dated 12.11.1969." FLM_TA_101B.

Colonial administration. 1960. "Monographie de Betafo." ARM_516.

Colonial administration. 1954. "Monographie de Betafo: Renseignements d'ordre politique." ARM_508.

Colonial administration. 1939. "Liste numérique et nominative des garderies par région et districts avec leur effectif d'elèves." ARM_G556.

Conseil d'enseignement protestant. 1958. "Minutes from meetings 1958–1962." FLM_TA_77F.

de Pressensé, Francis. 1907. "Letter dated 16.03.1907 to M. le Ministre et cher Collègue." ANOM_D6(4)59.

Devaux. 1920. "Letter dated 06.11.1920 to the Director of Civil Affairs." ARM_F185.

Doumergue, Gaston. 1903. "Letter dated 08.12.1903 to Governor-General Galliéni." ANOM_D6(4)53.

Fagereng, Edvin. 1958. "Letter dated 14.11.1958." FLM_TA_77F.

Fampianarana Protestanta eto Madagasikara. 1960. "Zaikaben'ny mpiton-dra sekoly tamin'19–22 Jolay 1960: Tao Faravohitra FFM Antananarivo." FLM_TA_77F.

Galliéni, Joseph. 1904. "Circular dated 13.02.1904 to Mission representatives." ANOM_D6(4)54.

Garbit, Hubert Auguste. 1923. "Letter dated 08.02.1923 to the Secretary of IPC." FLM_TA_75G.

Garbit, Hubert Auguste. 1922. "Letter dated 07.12.1922 to the Secretary of the IPC." FLM_TA_75G.

Garbit, Hubert Auguste. 1921. "Arrêté du 25. Février 1921 modifiant l'article 14 de l'arrêté du 23 novembre 1906 relatif à l'enseignement privée à Madagascar." ARM_F185.

Gouvernement général de Madagascar et dépendances. 1951. "Projet de reglementaion de l'enseignement privé." FLM_TA_78C.

Guitou. 1925. "Note sur les missions à Madagascar 1925." ANOM_D6(4)50.

IPC. 1922a. "Letter dated 13.11.1922 to the Governor-General." FLM_TA_75G.

IPC. 1922b. "Letter dated 18.12.1922 to the Governor-General (draft)." FLM_TA_75G.

IPC. 1920. "A Statement on the Necessity of a Revision of Legislation in regard to Public Worship in Madagscar. Limitations, Restrictions and Abuses under the Present Regime." FLM_TA_70A.

IPC. no date. "Draft of letter to the Governor-General." FLM_TA_70G.

ISC. 1964a. "Meeting report 11.01.1964." FLM_TA_358B.

ISC. 1964b. "Meeting report 23.03.1964." FLM_TA_358B.

ISC. 1964c. "Meeting report 25.04.1964." FLM_TA_ 358B.

ISC. 1964d. "Meeting report 30.05.1964." FLM_TA_358B.

ISC. no date. "Letter to the IPC President." FLM_TA_77F.

ISC. no date (between 1955–1963). "Toro-dalana." FLM_TA_85A.

Jacobsen, Alfhild. 1965. "Letter to the teaching missionaries dated 08.05.1965." FLM_TA_ 85C.

Jacobsen, Alfhild. 1964a. "Letter to the teaching missionaries dated 01.04.1964." FLM_TA_85C.

Jacobsen, Alfhild. 1964b. "Letter to the teaching missionaries dated 13.04.1964." FLM_TA_ 85C.

Jacobsen, Alfhild. 1964c. "Letter to the teaching missionaries dated 16.05.1964." FLM_TA_85C.

L'Administrateur en chef des Colonies. 1923. "Letter dated 27.06.1923." FLM_TA_70F.

Le Gouverneur Général de Madagascar et Dépendances. 1906. "Arrête relatif à l'enseignement privé à Madagascar dated 22.11.1906." ARM_F187.

Machard, Guy. 1923. "Letter dated 28. 10.1923 to the Superindendent of the NMS." FLM_TA_70I.

Machard, Guy. 1920. "Note dated 17.11.1920 to the Governor-General." ARM_F185.

Mondain, Gustave. 1923a. "Letter dated 12.03.1923 to the Governor-General." ARM_F185.

Mondain, Gustave. 1923b. "Letter dated 19.05.1923 to the Governor-General." ARM_F185.

Mondain, Gustave. 1923c. "Letter dated 21.04.1923 to the Governor-General." ARM_F 185.

Moretti. 1934. "Report dated 15.03.1934: Mission d'inspection 1933–1934: Concernant le rôle de la langue indigène dans l'enseignement." ANOM_3D16.

NMS. 1970. "Referat fra felleskonferansen og forretningsutvalget for Madagaskar. Forretningsutvalgets forhandlinger 1969." MHS_A-1045_D_Da_L0640_01_konf_Mad_1970_a.

NMS. 1966. "Referat fra den fjortende ordinære felleskonferanse for Madagaskar Antsirabe 6.-17.mars." MHS_A-1045_D_Da_L0636_01_konf_Mad_1966_b.

NMS. 1965a. "Instruks for Det Norske Misjonsselskaps misjonærer." MHS-A-1045/Boks 815/2.

NMS. 1965b. "Referat fra den trettende ordinære felleskonferanse for Madagaskar Antsirabe 7.-24. mars." MHS_A-1045_D_Da_L0635_01_konf_Mad_1965_a.

NMS. 1965c. "Referat fra konferansen for Øst-Madagaskar Antsirabe marsi forbindelse med felleskonferansen." MHS_A-1045_D_Da_L0635_01_konf_Mad_1965_f.

NMS. 1964a. "Letter to the Norwegian Development Aid dated 24.06.1964." FLM_TA_311A.

NMS. 1964b. "Referat fra den tolvte ordinære felleskonferanse for Madagaskar Antsirabe 1.-19. Mars." MHS_A-1045_D_Da_L0634_01_konf_Mad_1964_a.

NMS. 1963. "Referat fra den ellevte ordinære norske felleskonferanse for Madagaskar Antsirabe 3.-21. mars." MHS_A-1045_D_Da_L0633_01_konf_Mad_1963_a.

NMS. 1962. "Referat fra den tiende ordinære norske felleskonferanse for Madagaskar Antsirabe 4.- 20. mars." MHS_A-1045_D_Da_L0632_02_konf_Mad_1962_a.

NMS. 1961. "Referat fra den niende ordinære norske felleskonferanse for Madagaskar: Antsirabe 5.-21. mars." MHS_A-1045_D_Da_L0632_01_konf_Mad_1961_a.

NMS. 1960a. "Aarsmeldingene fra de norske misjonærene i fellesinstitusjonene paa Madagaskar." MHS_A-1045_D_Da_L0631_01_konf_Mad_1960_f.

NMS. 1960b. "Referat fra den åttende ordinære felleskonferanse for Madagaskar Antsirabe 6.- 22.mars." MHS_A-1045_D_Da_L0631_01_konf_Mad_1960_a.

NMS. 1959. "Referat fra den sjuende ordinære norske felleskonferanse for Madagaskar Antsirabe 1.-16. mars." MHS_A-1045_D_Da_L0630_01_konf_Mad_1959_a.

NMS. 1958. "Referat fra den femte ordinære norske felleskonferanse for Madagaskar Antsirabe 2.-23. mars." MHS_A-1045_D_Da_L0629_01_konf_Mad_1958_a.

NMS. 1957. "Referat fra den femte ordinære norske felleskonferanse for Madagaskar paa Antsirabe." MHS_A-1045_D_Da_L0628_01_konf_Mad_1957_e.

NMS. 1955. "Referat fra den tredje ordinære norske felleskonferanse på Madagaskar Antsirabe 9.- 25.mars." MHS_A-1045_D_Da_L0627_01_konf_Mad_1955_a.

NMS. 1954. "Referat fra den andre ordinære norske felleskonferanse på Madagaskar Antsirabe den 7.-25.mars." MHS_A-1045_D_Da_L0626_01_konf_Mad_1954_a.

NMS. 1953. "Referat fra den første ordinære norske felleskonferanse på Madagaskar Antsirabe 1.mars-19.mars." MHS_A-1045_D_Da_L0625_02_konf_Mad_1953_a.

NMS. 1952a. "Referat fra Felleskonferansen for Madagaskar Innlands Nordkrets og Sørkrets. 75. konferans på Antsirabe 23. mars-8. april." MHS_A-1045_D_Da_L0625_01_konf_Mad_1952_a.

NMS. 1952b. "Referat fra konferansen for Vest-Madagaskar. Antsirabe 20. februar-3. mars." MHS_A-1045_D_Da_L0625_01_konf_Mad_1952_b.

NMS. 1952c. "Referat fra Øst-Madagaskars konferanse 20. februar-5. mars." MHS_A-1045_D_Da_L0625_01_konf_Mad_1952_c.

NMS. 1950a. "Referat fra forhandlingene på 17. konferens for Øst-Madagaskar holdt på Antsirabe 14.mars-3.april." MHS_A-1045_D_Da_L0624_01_konf_ Mad_1950_a.

NMS. 1950b. "Referat fra konferansen for Madagaskars innland, skogen og Bara. 73. konferens på Antsirabe mars." MHS_A-1045_D_Da_L0624_01_konf_ Mad_1950_c.

NMS. 1948. "Referat av Madagaskar innlands konferanseforhandlinger 71. konferanse 11.-24.april på Antsirabe." MHS_A-1045_D_Da_L0623_01_konf_ Mad_1948_b.

NMS. 1945. "Konferansereferat. Madagaskar innland. Antsirabe 15.-30. april." MHS_A-1045_D_Da_L0621_09_konf_Mad_1945.

NMS. 1938. "Referat av konferensforhandlingene i Morondava 23.mai-2.juni." MHS_A-1045_D_Da_L0620_02_konf_Mad_1938_b.

NMS. 1935. "Referat av 58de konferensens forhandlinger i Fianarantsoa 10–20 mars." MHS_A-1045_D_Da_L0619_02_konf_Mad_1935_c.

NMS. 1933a. "Instruks for Det Norske Misjonsselskaps misjonærer 1933." MHS-A-1045/Boks 928/2.

NMS. 1933b. "Referat av 56de konferenses forhandlinger paa Antsirabe 12.-22. mars." MHS_A-1045_D_Da_L0618_04_konf_Mad_1933_b.

NMS. 1932. "Referat av konferensforhandlingene i Morondava 5.-16. juni." MHS_A-1045_D_Da_L0618_03_konf_Mad_1932_a.

NMS. 1930a. "Referat av 53de konferenses forhandlinger paa Antsirabe 9.-20. mars." MHS_A-1045_D_Da_L0618_01_konf_Mad_1930_a.

NMS. 1930b. "Referat av konferensforhandlingene i Morondava 8.-24. april." MHS_A-1045_D_Da_L0618_01_konf_Mad_1930_b.

NMS. 1929. "Referat av konferensforhandlingene i Tulear." MHS_A-1045_D_ Da_L0617_04_konf_Mad_1929_b.

NMS. 1928. "Referat av konferensforhandlingene i Tuléar." MHS_A-1045_D_ Da_L0617_03_konf_Mad_1928_b.

NMS. 1927. "Referat av 50de konferenses forhandlinger i Fianarantsoa 13.-24. mars." MHS_A-1045_D_Da_L0617_02_konf_Mad_1927_a.

NMS. 1926. "Referat av konferensforhandlingene i Tuléar." MHS_A-1045_D_ Da_L0617_01_konf_Mad_1926_b.

NMS. 1925. "Referat av konferensforhandlingerne i Morondava." MHS_A-1045_D_Da_L0616_06_konf_Mad_1925_b.

NMS. 1924a. "Referat av 47de konferenses forhandlinger paa Fianarantsoa 10.-22. mars." MHS_A-1045_D_Da_L0616_05_konf_Mad_1924_a.

NMS. 1924b. "Referat av konferensforhandlingerne i Tuléar." MHS_A-1045_ D_Da_L0616_05_konf_Mad_1924_c.

NMS. 1923a. "Referat av 46de konferenses forhandlinger paa Antsirabe 9.-24. mars." MHS_A-1045_D_Da_L0616_04_konf_Mad_1923_a.

NMS. 1923b. "Referat av konferensforhandlingerne i Tuléar." MHS_A-1045_ D_Da_L0616_04_konf_Mad_1923_b.

NMS. 1922. "Referat av 45de konferenses forhandlinger paa Antsirabe 10.-25. mars." MHS_A-1045_D_Da_L0616_03_konf_Mad_1922_a.

NMS. 1921. "Referat av 44de konferenses forhandlinger paa Antsirabe 11.-23. mars." MHS_A-1045_D_Da_L0616_02_konf_Mad_1921_a.

NMS. 1920. "Referat av 43de konferenses forhandlinger i Fianarantsoa." MHS_A-1045_D_Da_L0616_01_konf_Mad_1920_a.

NMS. 1908. "Referat af konferentsforhandlingerne paa Fisakana." MHS_A-1045_ Konf_ref_Mad_1908.

NMS. 1867. "Instrux for det Norske Misionsselskabs Udlendinge (Efter revisionen paa Generalforsamlingen 1867)." MHS_A1045:D:Da:Daa:L0005:15.

NMS Superintendent. 1927–1939. "Circulaires to church employees from the Superintendent NMS 01.12.1927, 11.12.1929, 10.12.1930, 02.12.1932, 02.01.1937, 02.12.1938, 02.12.1939." FLM_TA_79B.

Parrot, Abel A. 1922. "Letter dated 17.09.1922 to the NMS Superintendent." FLM_TA_75G.

Parrot, Abel A. 1921. "Circular dated 25.06.1921 to church employees." FLM_ TA_79B.

Parrot, Abel A. no date. "Note presented to the Governor-General." ANOM_ D6(4)53.

Pegourier. 1928. "Report dated 12.04.1928: Mission 1927–1928: Service de l'enseignement (Education des Indigène)." ANOM_3D12.

Rajaobelina, Prosper. 1958. "Letter dated 06.03.1958 to school Directors." FLM_TA_77F.

Rajaobelina, Prosper, and Jacques Vernier. 1952. "Propositions envoyée par le IPC à tous les Missionaires et Directeurs d'écoles." FLM_TA_78C.

Rajaona. no date. "Izay mba hahamafyorina ny olona amin'ny Fiangonantsika Loterana." FLM_TA_79E.

Ravelomanana, Hermann. 1961. "Attachment to letter dated 04.05.1961 to the General-Secretary of NMS schools." FLM_TA_77F.

Renel, Charles. 1923a. "Letter dated 21.03.1923 to the Governor-General." ARM_ F 185.

Renel, Charles. 1923b. "Letter dated 29.05.1923 to the Governor-General." ARM_ F 185.

Renel, Charles. 1921. "Letter dated 17.10.1921 to the Director of Civil Affairs." ARM_F 185.

Siegfried, Jules, Eugène Reveillau, Paul Bourely, and Marc Reville. 1907. "Letter dated 22.03.1907 to Governor-General Augagneur." ANOM_D6(4)59.

Snekkenes, Arthur. 1953. "Letter dated 25.03.1953 to colleagues." FLM_TA_ 100G.

Snekkenes, Arthur. 1950. "Letter dated 11.12.1950 to the High Commissionaire." FLM_TA_84K.

The archives of the superintendent of the mission. 1962–1971. "Correspondance between NMS and the Norwegian Development Agency." FLM_TA_311.

The archives of the superintendent of the mission. 1950–1959. "FIDES subventions." FLM_TA_87.

The Director of Education. 1943. "Letter to the Secretary General." ANOM_ D6(4)59.

Vialle, Jean. 1958. "Circulaire No. 2." FLM_TA_85C.

# Websites

MHS. 2017. "NMS: People and places", accessed 3.08.2017, www.mhs.no/arkiv/?351.

Oxford Dictionaries. 2015. "Oxford Dictionaries" Oxford University Press, accessed 1.04.2015, www.oxforddictionaries.com/definition/english/contextualize.

# Qualitative Interviews

An elder in Betafo, 14.01.2012.

Female sunday school teacher. Pers.com. 03.11.2011.
Former female missionary Anne Marie Reimers. Pers.com. 16.10.2012.
Former female missionary Astrid Gidskehaug. Pers.com. 31.05.2010.
Former female missionary Eldrid Aamland. Pers.com. 23.11.2012.
Former female missionary Elfrid Søyland. Pers.com. 09.06.2011.
Former female missionary Helena Trydal. Pers.com. 21.11.2012.
Former female missionary Helga Eikeland. Pers.com. 31.05.2010.
Former female missionary Kari Johanne Honningdal. Pers.com.
    03.09.2011.
Former female missionary Tordis Sandvik. Pers.com. 31.05.2011.
Former female pupil 1. Pers.com. 09.01.2012.
Former female pupil 5. Pers.com. 03.12.2011.
Former female pupil 6. Pers.com. 03.12.2011.
Former female teacher 1. Pers.com. 14.01.2012.
Former female teacher 5. Pers.com. 06.02.2012.
Former male missionary Anders Martin Andersen. Pers.com.
    27.09.2011.
Former male pupil 2. Pers.com. 12.01.2012.
Former male pupil 3. Pers.com. 20.12.2011.
Former male pupil 7. Pers.com. 06.10.2011.
Former male pupil 8. Pers.com. 12.01.2012.
Former male pupil 9. Pers.com. 31.01.2012.
Former male pupil 10. Pers.com. 14.01.2012.
Former male teacher 3. Pers.com. 27.01.2012.
Former male teacher 4. Pers.com. 12.12.2011.
Former pupil Daniel. Pers.com. 14.01.2012.
Former pupil George. Pers.com. 19.12.2011.
Former pupil Haja. Pers.com. 17.01.2012.
Former pupil Honorine. Pers.com. 26.01.2012.
Former pupil Jean. Pers.com. 25.01.2012.
Former pupil Naivo. Pers.com. 21.12.2011.

Former pupil Olga. Pers.com. 21.12.2011.
Former pupil Patrick. Pers.com. 10.01.2012.
Former pupil Rolland. Pers.com. 09.01.2012.
Former pupil Sarah. Pers.com. 14.01.2012.
Isabelle, Director FFL Jeno. Pers.com. 2012 and e-mail 2014.
Père Odon. Pers. com. 10.01.2012.
Principal Assistant KLB. Pers.com. 31.01.2012.

# Index

Note: Page numbers in *italics* indicate figures and those in **bold** indicate tables.

Printed in the United States
by Baker & Taylor Publisher Services